IMAGES
*of America*

# CORINTH

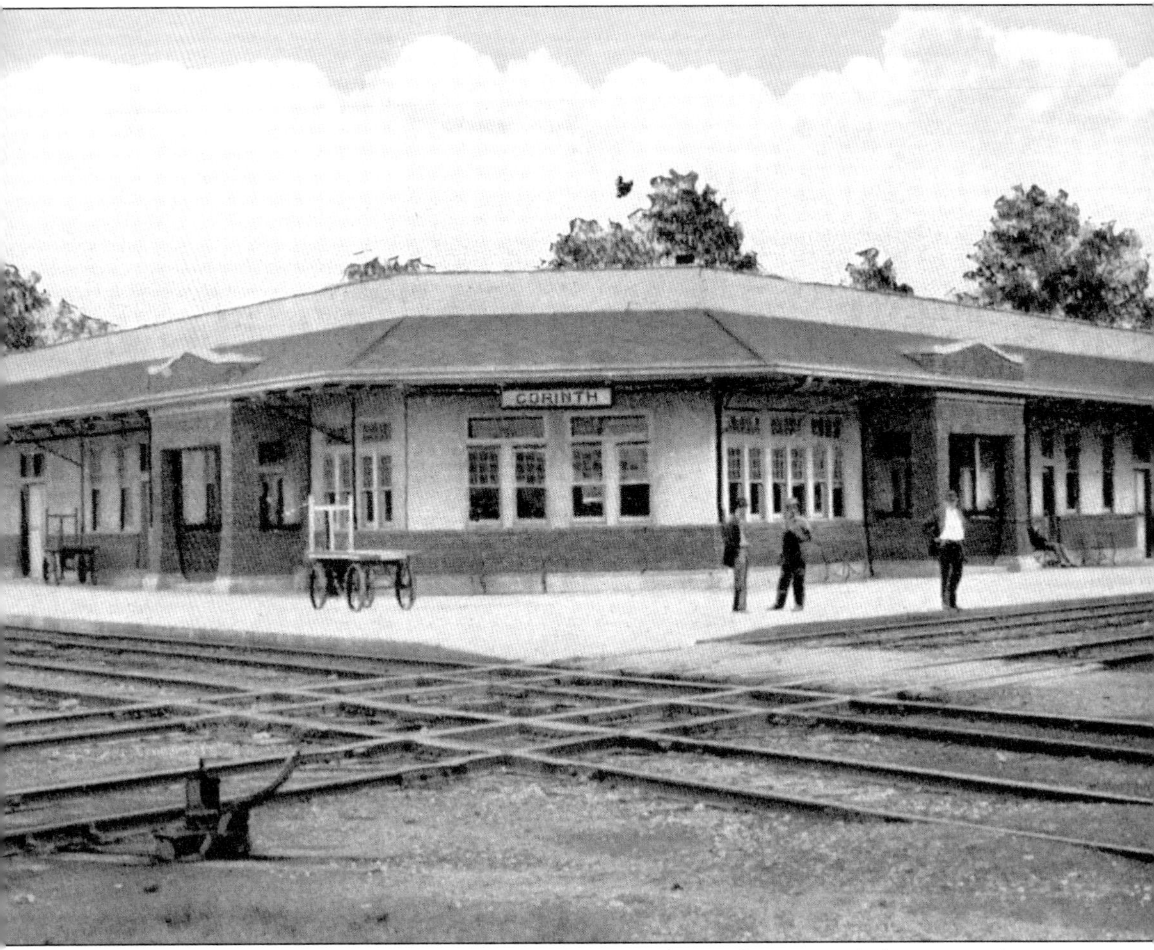


Corinth, Mississippi, was born a rail town and grew up during the most turbulent era in American history. The strategic rail lines that gave the town life made it a hotly contested prize fiercely fought for by both Union and Confederate forces throughout the Civil War. As front-row spectators to history, Corinthians witnessed the costly battles of Shiloh and Corinth, the largest siege in the western hemisphere, and countless untold stories of life lived in the shadow of war. In time, the rails once again brought hope and commerce as new chapters were added to Corinth's story. Even today, with the golden age of rail long since passed, no resident or visitor can long escape the mournful call of lonesome whistles or the rhythmic sounds of the passing cars as nameless trains carry their cargo across America.

**On the Cover:** The same rail lines that held such vital importance in 1862 play host to a more peaceful meeting here at the juncture of the Memphis & Charleston and the Mobile & Ohio rail lines in 1916. Pictured between a pair of switch engines in the Corinth rail yard is each engine's five-member crew along with other railway personnel. Engine No. 534 is seen facing north on the Mobile & Ohio track where it meets the southern engine of the Memphis & Charleston, which is facing west.

IMAGES
*of America*

# CORINTH

Jesse Ables and LuAnne Parrish

ARCADIA
PUBLISHING

ISBN 978-0-7385-9124-7

Published by Arcadia Publishing
Charleston, South Carolina

Printed in the United States of America

Library of Congress Control Number: 2011937050

For all general information, please contact Arcadia Publishing:
Telephone 843-853-2070
Fax 843-853-0044
E-mail sales@arcadiapublishing.com
For customer service and orders:
Toll-Free 1-888-313-2665

Visit us on the Internet at www.arcadiapublishing.com

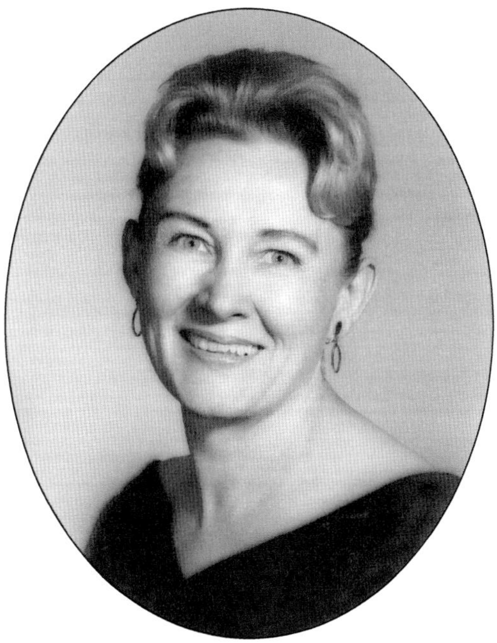

*It is only fitting that this offering be dedicated to my beloved mother, Nelda Boatman Parrish, the first female realtor in Corinth and Alcorn County, the first appointed female justice of the peace, and in 1994 a member of the original freshmen class of inductees into the Mississippi Association of Realtors' Hall of Fame—and always Corinth, Mississippi's, number-one booster!*

# Contents

# ACKNOWLEDGMENTS

The authors give their heartfelt thanks to the staff members of the Corinth Crossroads Museum for their invaluable help and support in allowing us the unfettered use of their iconic images of Corinth through the years. Unless otherwise noted, all images appear courtesy of the Corinth Crossroads Museum. We must also express our great appreciation to our fellow Corinthians, too numerous to mention, for sharing their photographs and memories with us.

Dr. William Jackson was so generous with his postcard collection that we will never be able to thank him enough. Our special thanks goes to Lou Perry for sharing her knowledge and family photographs of early Corinth. Thanks also to the wonderful Stephanie Sandy, whose immaculate research, along with her interest in and dedication to her adopted hometown, has been a remarkable gift to all Corinthians—we are eternally grateful.

Nothing in this offering will be original or new, but rather, we stand on the shoulders of giants who paved the way by researching, recording, and generously sharing their knowledge with anyone who cared to learn. We will be forever in the debt of local historians Margaret Greene Rogers, Hugh Horton, and Robert U. Jones, for all three were amateurs in the sense that they did not often receive monetary remuneration for sharing their extensive knowledge of Corinth, but rather did so freely so others might know how special our hometown truly was and is.

As a child growing up in Corinth, I was fortunate to be born into a family of extraordinary storytellers. I heard tales of "west" Corinth on a daily basis, so my great appreciation goes to my maternal grandmother, Luna, for her wonderful family tales of Corinth, and my mother, Nelda, who helped to shape the history of Corinth in her own right. A native Corinthian, she was born in 1921, literally in the shadow of Colonel Rogers's obelisk at Battery Robinett. In the early 1960s, she began her career as a realtor, which allowed her to indulge her lifelong passion of sharing the wonders and benefits of living in Corinth, Mississippi, with anyone interested in purchasing a piece of what she considered to be "the closest thing to heaven you could have on earth."

In addition to her role as an outstanding realtor, she was a nonpareil wife, mother, daughter, sister, and friend to all who had the privilege and pleasure of knowing her.

# INTRODUCTION

Ask any realtor, investor, or land speculator what the three most important characteristics for a piece of property are, and the answer will always be location, location, and location.

So it was with Corinth, Mississippi, from the moment of its inception as Cross City in 1854. Surveyors Houston Mitchell and Hamilton Mask laid off and divided into streets and lots the acreage that had been acquired from William Lasley, who had deeded right-of-way to the intersection of the newly laid tracts of the Memphis & Charleston Railway, running east and west, with the Mobile & Ohio line, running north and south. As the only major rail crossing in what was then the western part of the United States, the small town was to occupy a place of great strategic importance. This was especially true during the coming war between the states, but it continued unabated into the 20th century and beyond.

The town's immediate proximity to the Mississippi and Tennessee state line, which was only a scant four miles from the center of the town, contributed to Corinth being at various times from the 1940s through the 1960s the "marriage capital" of the entire country as a result of Mississippi's lack of residency or blood test requirements for marriage. In the 1950s and 1960s, Corinth was also known as "Little Chicago" because of the town's excess of prostitution, gambling, bootlegging, and criminal activity that occurred on a daily basis at cheap dives that infested the state line only a stone's throw away. Murder, mayhem, and vice of every kind resided side by side with a city as moral and upright as the fictional Mayberry inhabited by Opie, Andy, and Aunt Bea of television lore. The war between legendary lawman Buford Pusser of *Walking Tall* fame and the denizens of the state-line mob has been well documented in various books, newspaper articles, songs, and movies, as well as in countless stories added to the local lore by many of the residents of the area who watched the drama unfold in their own backyard. Names well known to Corinthians, such as Carl "Towhead" White and Louise and Jack Hathcock and their underlings, victims, and adversaries, became a part of the fabric of daily life in Corinth.

The town had the dichotomy of a wide-open, lawless state-line crime syndicate existing cheek by jowl with a community that produced many notable citizens. World-famous aviator Roscoe Turner was a winner of both the Bendix Trophy Race and the Thompson Trophy Race in the 1930s, when air races were second only to baseball games in fan attendance. Industrialist W.P. Adams, entrepreneur Abe Rubel, businessman Benjamin Franklin Liddon, artist Russell Keaton (originator of the 1940s "Flyin' Jenny" comic strip), noted author Thomas Hal Phillips (novelist and screenwriter of *Nashville*), and many other people of varying degrees of renown were from Corinth.

No Corinthian, native or transplant, rich or poor, black or white, is more than a stone's throw from the railroad, which spawned the city and figured so prominently in the everyday life of its citizenry. The same rails that played such an important a role throughout Corinth's history also contributed to the city's ability to rebound from repeated burnings at the hands of both Union and Confederate occupation forces, as well as the loss of two entire city blocks to fire in 1924. Consistently ranked around 25th in population among Mississippi's 82 counties every decade by the US census, Corinth and Alcorn County traditionally rank in the top five in the state for industrialization and has been considered the leading manufacturing center in northeast Mississippi. Add this to the average Corinthian's enormous capacity for enjoying parades, festivals, and gatherings of any type—large or small—and one of the city's mottos from the 1970s still applies today: "Corinth . . . WhatAPlaceToLive."

# *One*

# Genesis and the Coming of War

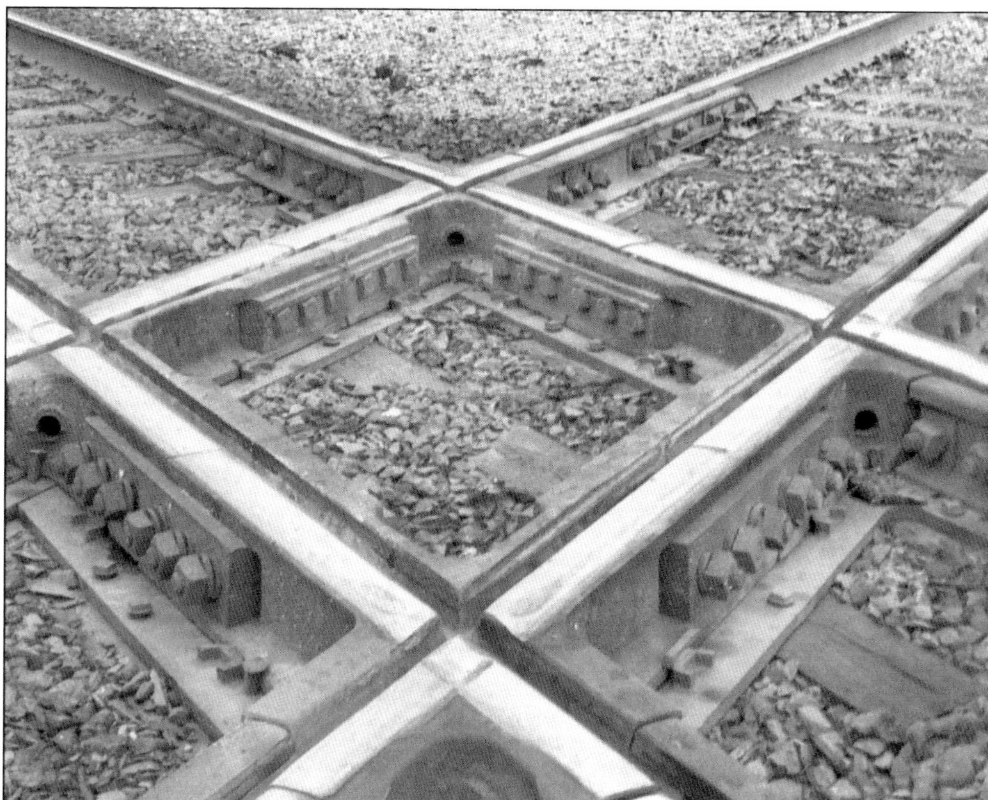

A crossroads is defined as "an intersection of two or more roads" or "a point at which a crucial decision must be made that will have far-reaching consequences." For over 150 years, Corinth has been such a place. Great deeds and events have taken place here, acts both heroic and otherwise have occurred here, and great men and women have been born and died here. Corinth has always remained a community at the crossroads.

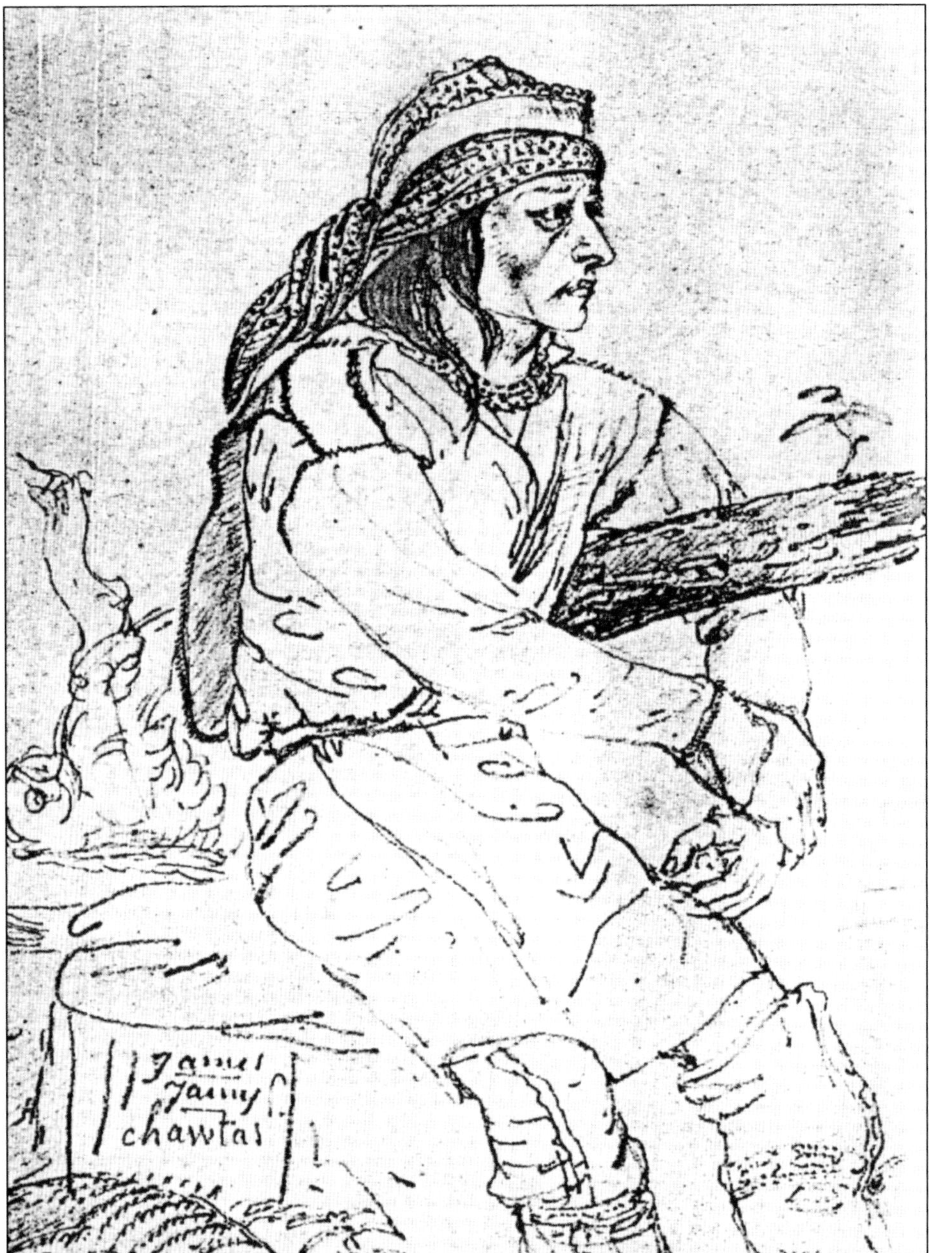


An artist's conjectural sketch of a Chickasaw brave illustrates what advancing settlers would have likely encountered as they moved westward. In 1817, Mississippi became the 20th state to join the Union. One of the foremost Chickasaw leaders of that time was Chief Tuscumbia, who moved back to Corinth, his home territory, from northwest Alabama and the area that would later bear his name. He spent his remaining days farming land about 10 miles south of present-day Corinth until his death in 1834. His widow sold the property to their neighbor, Ruffin Coleman, for $820 in 1836, when she and her family joined other members of their tribe on the Trail of Tears to Indian Territory. In 1838, the property was again sold to Hezekiah B. Mitchell for $2,000. (Courtesy of Lou Perry.)

Patriarch of one of northeast Mississippi's earliest families, Hezekiah B. Mitchell bought and settled on land that was once the ancestral home of Chickasaw chief Tuscumbia in 1838. As the first white settler in the area, he established a trading post for Indians at the first settlement, Danville. Two of his sons, Houston and Eli, were instrumental in the founding and development of Corinth. (Courtesy of Lou Perry.)

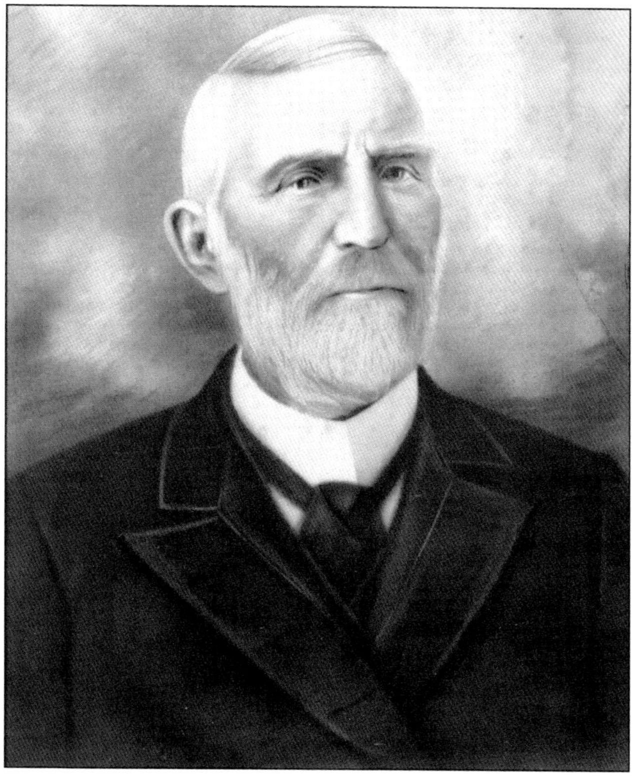

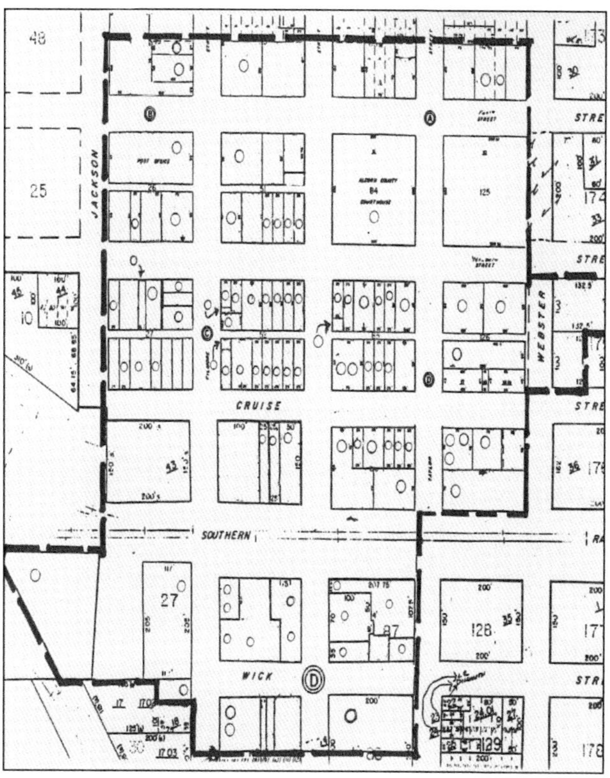


In the late 1840s, the Memphis & Charleston and the Mobile & Ohio Railroad companies were organized and quickly made plans to survey and lay rail lines. Surveyors Houston Mitchell and Hamilton Mask determined in 1854 that the two lines would cross at right angles on land owned by William Lasley, who had deeded the right-of-way to the rail lines. Later that year, Lasley sold his remaining property to Mitchell and Mask. They immediately began to lay off the land into streets, blocks, and lots, much like the plan illustrates. This became known as the Mitchell and Mask Survey. Houston Mitchell and Hamilton Mask are generally recognized as the founders of Corinth. They also gifted the settlement with a full city block in the center of town, which would become the site of the courthouse.

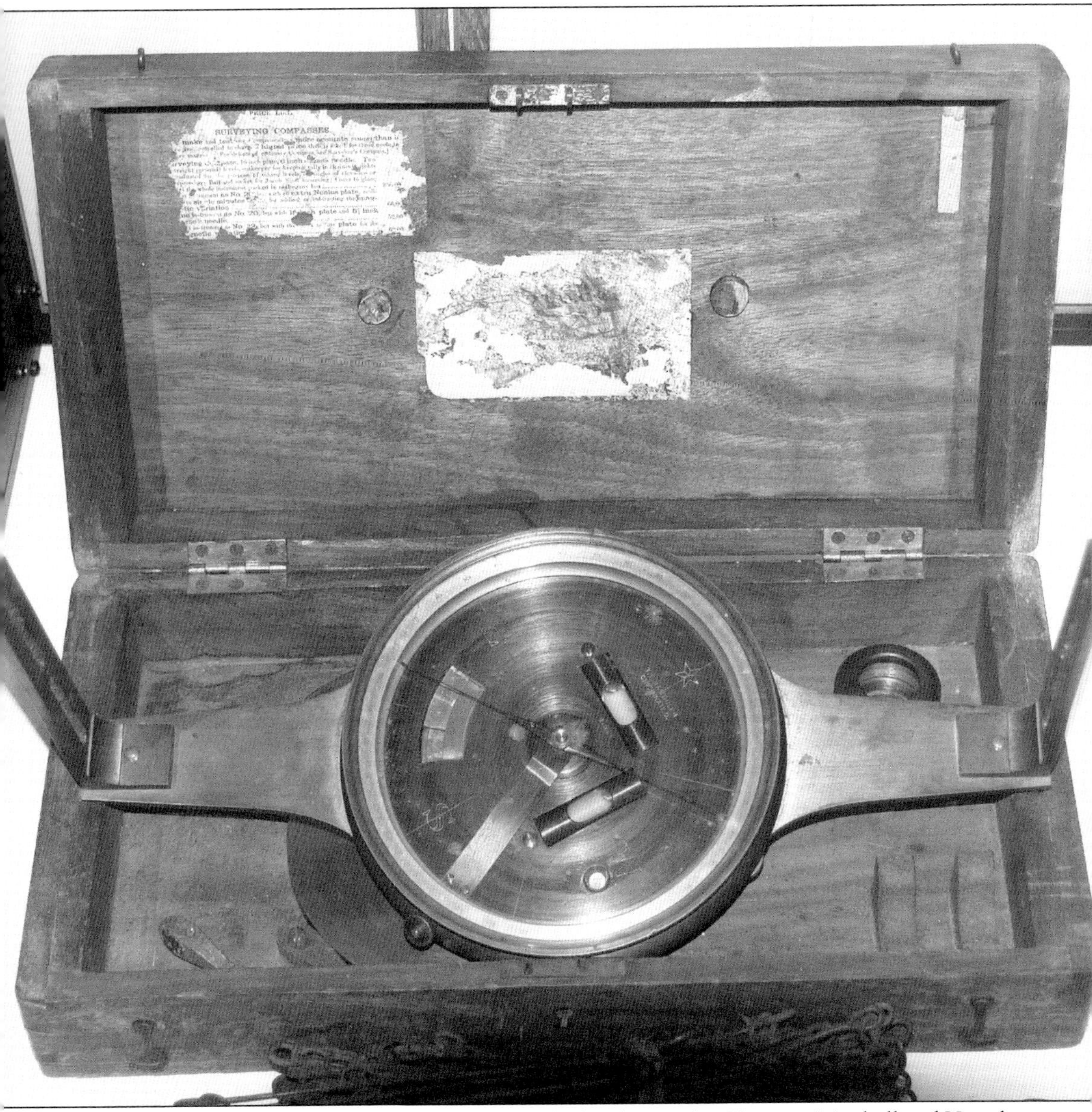


Pictured are the actual survey instruments used by brothers-in-law Houston Mitchell and Hamilton Mask to lay out the Mitchell and Mask Survey of Cross City—later named Corinth—into streets, blocks, and lots after the rail line crossing was determined. The instruments are on loan by the Mitchell family as a permanent display at the Corinth Crossroads Museum.

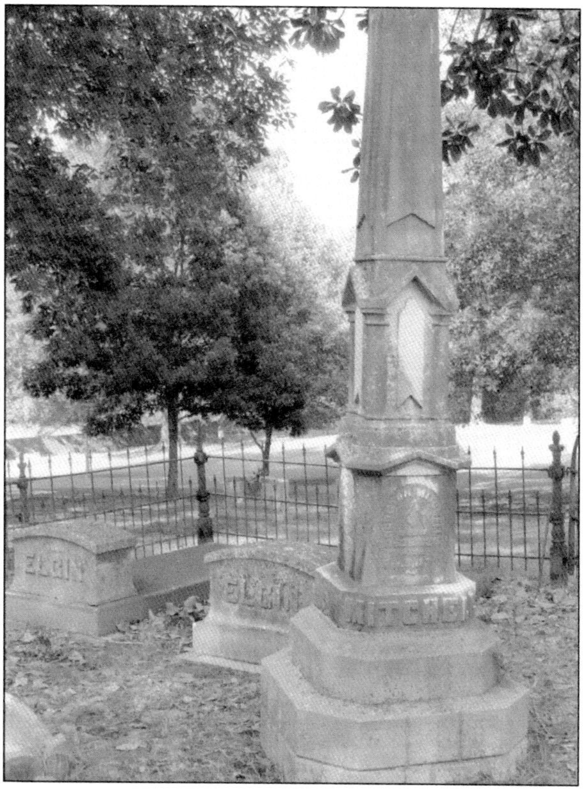


The Mitchell family plot is located in the City Cemetery, the oldest graveyard in Corinth, with its first burial being in 1842. Other first families buried here include members of the Adams, Borroum, Clausel, Cox, Curlee, Dalton, Elgin, Ellis, Howell, Hutson, Hyneman, Jobe, Johns, Kilpatrick, Ledbetter, Liddon, McCullar, Miller, New, Overton, Perry, Phillips, Reynolds, Siegrist, Simmons, Tschudi, Waits, and Young families, among others. (Courtesy of Lou Perry.)

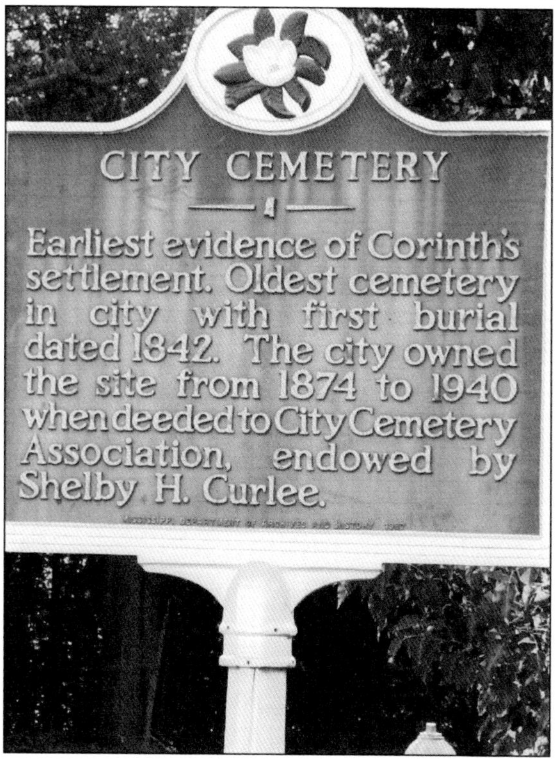

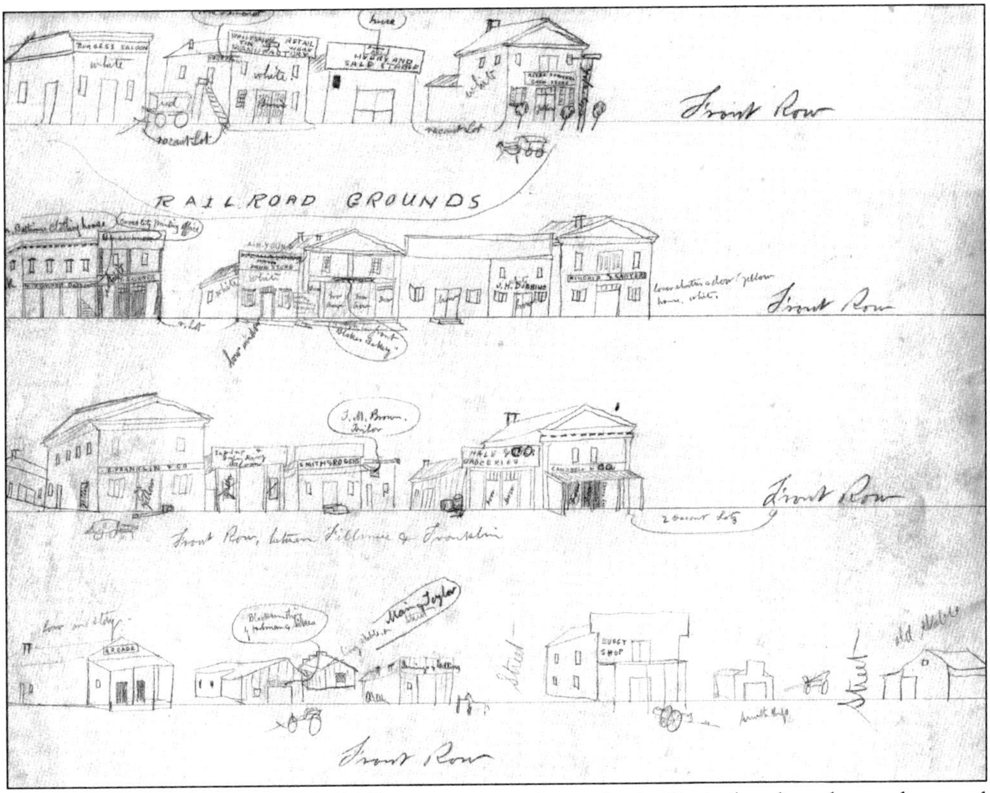


In 1860, visiting engineer M.A. Miller spent several months in Corinth, where he made pencil sketches of businesses and residential streets along with several homes around the city that still stand today. After the city was made a seat of justice in 1859, a combination courthouse and city hall was erected, as seen in the Miller sketch below. (Courtesy of Todd Sanders.)

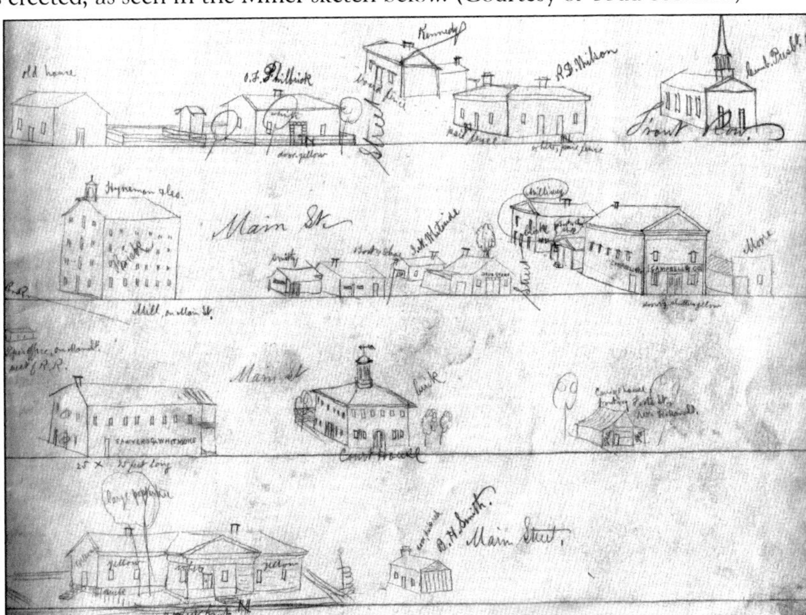

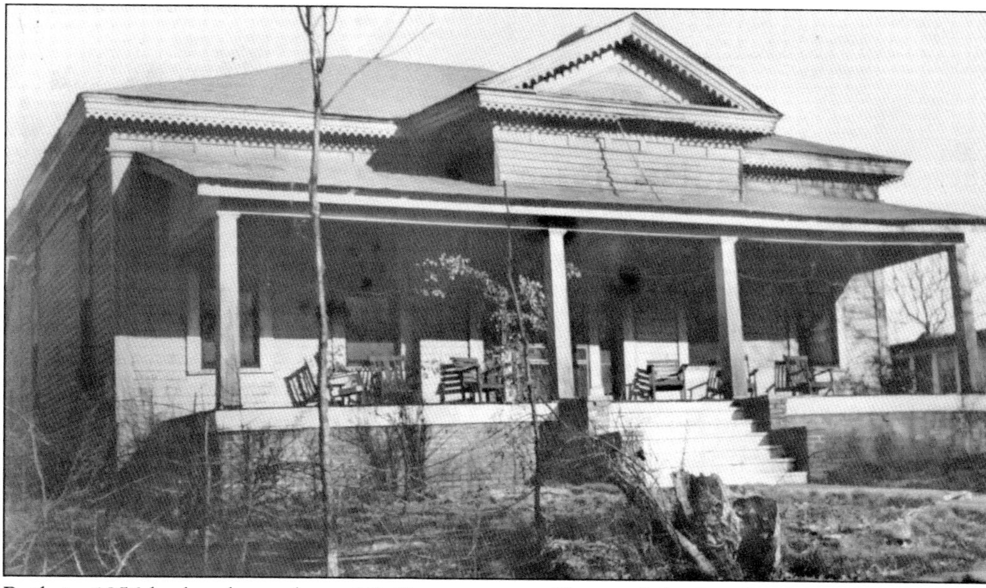

Built in 1856 by local merchant I.P. Young as a wedding gift for his daughter, the name Fish Pond House is derived from an architectural detail on the roof of a tin container used to catch rainwater. It served as headquarters for generals P.G.T. Beauregard and J.C. Breckinridge in the spring of 1862. It has been fully and lovingly restored by its current owners, John and Carole Spencer, who acquired the home in 1967.

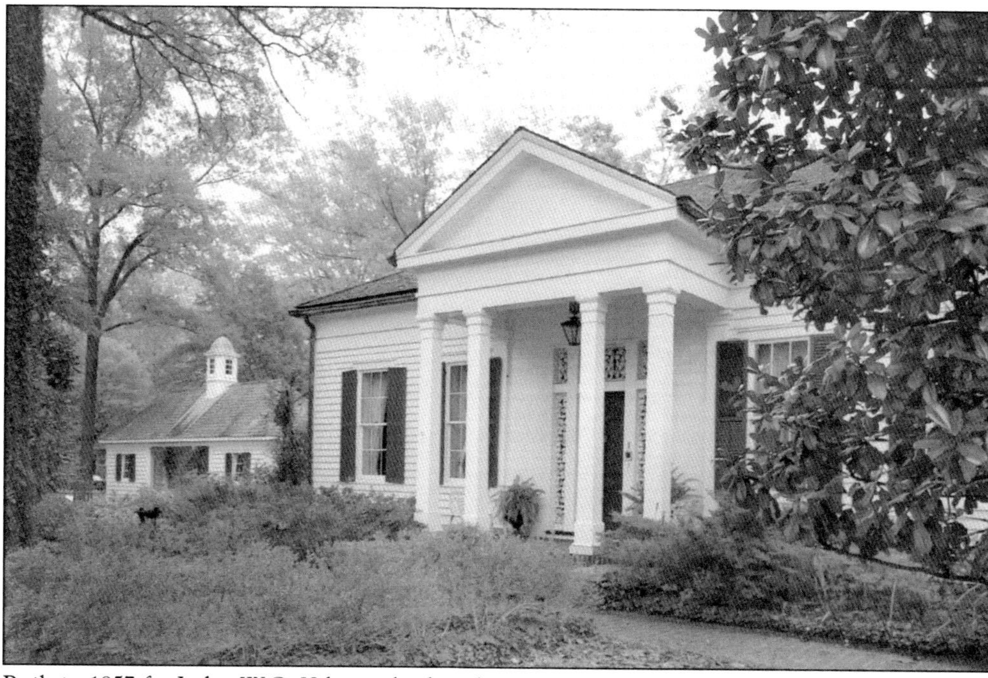

Built in 1857 for Judge W.G. Kilpatrick, this classic Greek Revival home played host to generals from both sides during the war. Bought in 1866 by Sarah Martin, "Oak Home" has been occupied continuously by her descendants ever since. The current occupants are Rosemary and H.L. "Sandy" Williams, who have preserved the feeling of its 19th-century roots while adding 21st-century comforts and conveniences.

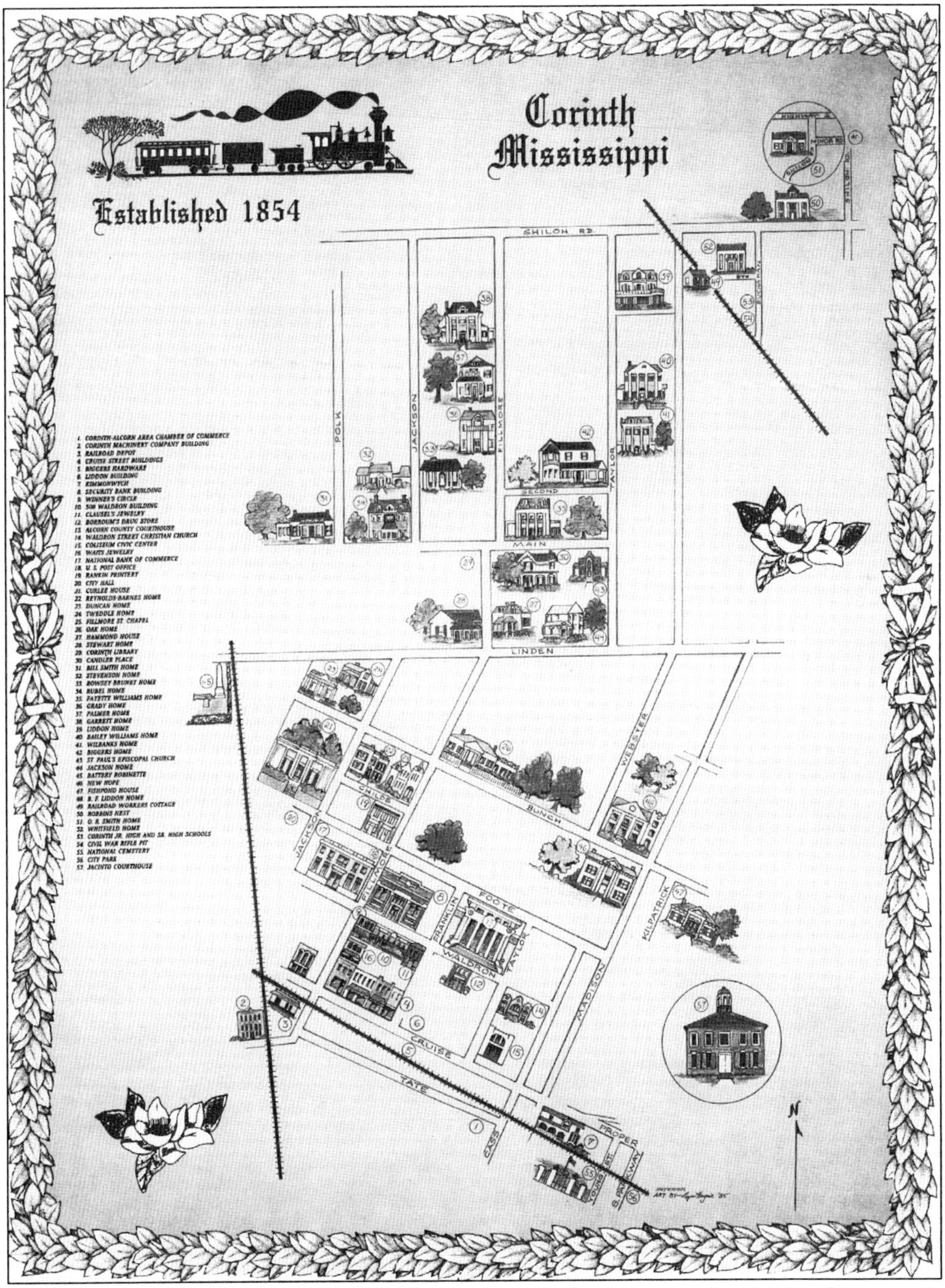


Created in 1985 by artist Lynn Boatman Haynie, this map for the city's self-guided walking tour is a modern-day rendering of Corinth as it was in its earliest days, showing the city as early citizens would have seen it. The map features homes, businesses, and churches that are still in use today. (Courtesy of Lynn Boatman Haynie.)

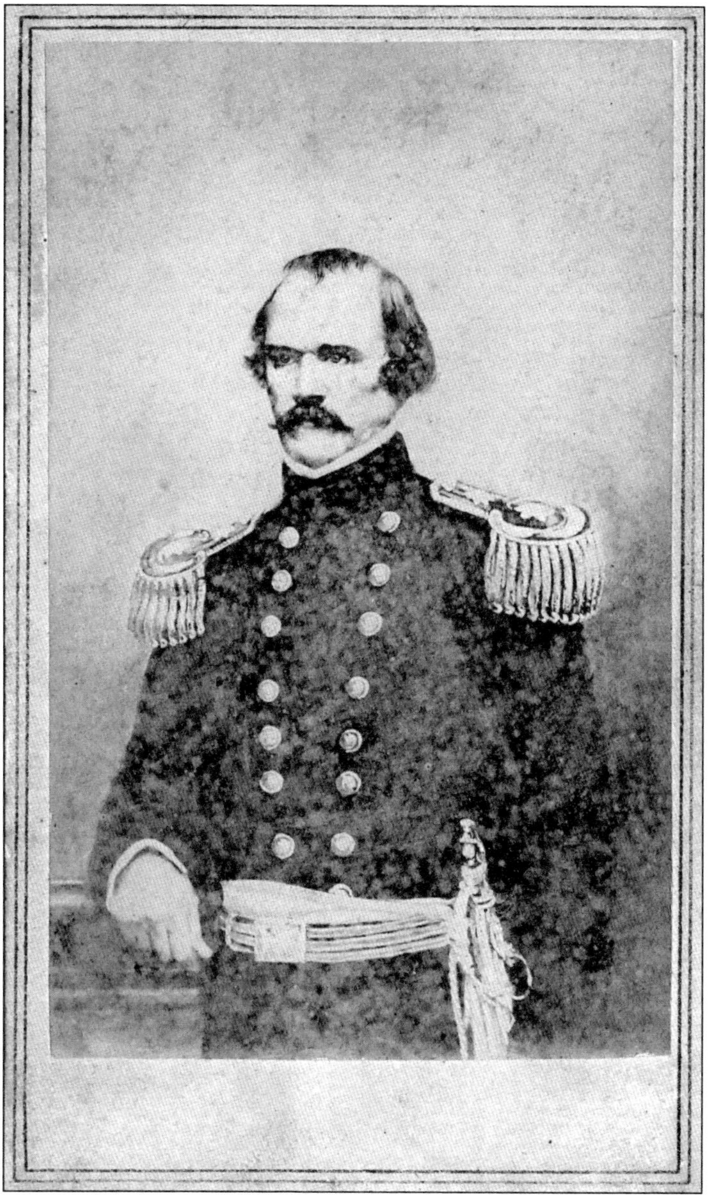

Considered to be one of the most brilliant strategic minds of his generation, West Point graduate Albert Sidney Johnston was appointed full general by his dear friend and Confederate president, Jefferson Davis. Johnston was given command of the Western Department, where he raised the Mississippi army to defend lines in the West. In the process of organizing his forces in Corinth, word reached him of the Union advance. In spite of opposition, most notably from General P.G.T. Beauregard, General Johnston determined to take the fight to the enemy, declaring, "I would fight them if they were a million!" He launched a massive surprise attack early on the morning of April 6, 1862, and after an entire day of fierce fighting, succeeded in pushing the Union forces all the way back to the banks of the Tennessee River. In the process, he was mortally wounded, and command passed to Beauregard, who withdrew to Corinth the next day. Considered by President Davis and many historians to be a turning point in the conflict, Albert Sidney Johnston was the highest-ranking casualty of the war on either side.

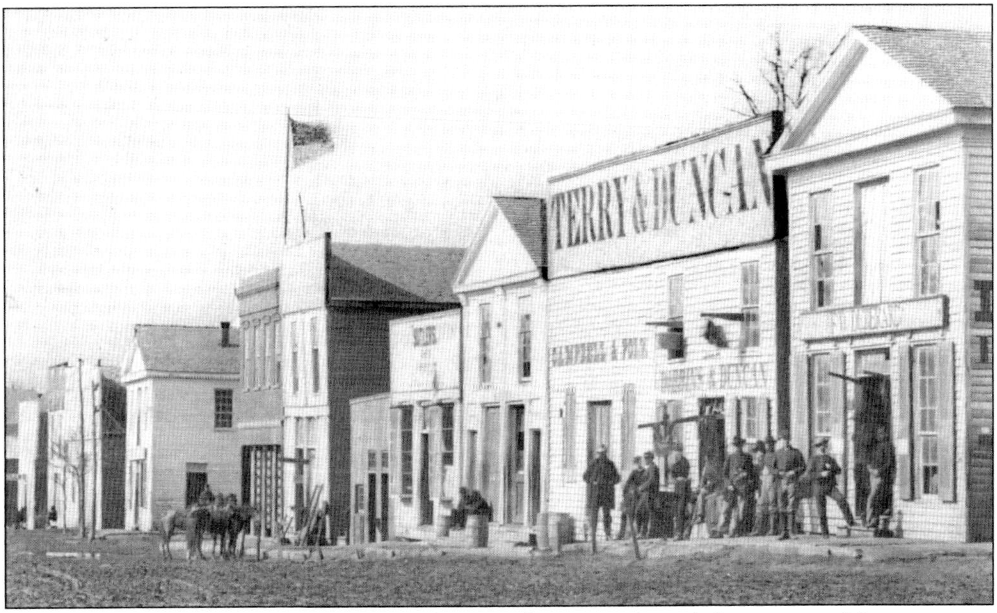


A group of soldiers is seen on Front Street (present-day Cruise Street) during one of three separate occupations by Union and Confederate troops as control of Corinth was repeatedly fought for and exchanged. Over the course of the conflict, 14 generals, both Union and Confederate, had their headquarters in Corinth.

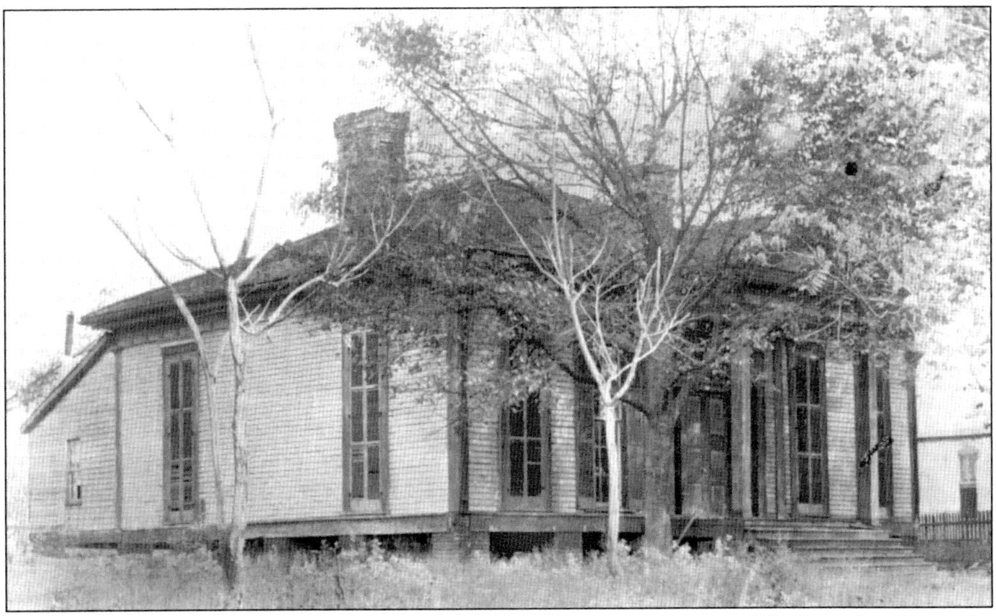

Pictured is the site of General Beauregard's headquarters prior to his masterful retreat from Corinth. Faced with overwhelming superiority of forces, he concocted an elaborate hoax evacuating the sick and wounded, along with his heavy artillery and tons of vital supplies, to Tupelo. His troops gave the impression of massive reinforcements arriving by cheering wildly, as buglers and drummers played. "Quaker" guns were set up along the earthworks, as campfires were kept burning while the troops quietly slipped away. (Courtesy of Dr. William Jackson.)

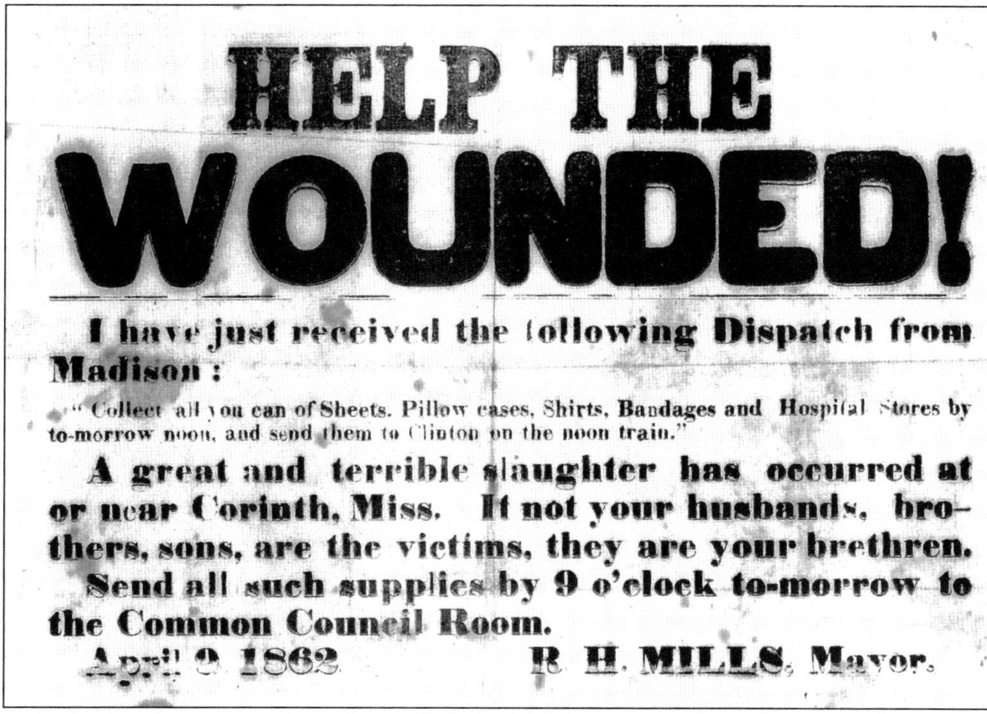
# HELP THE WOUNDED!

**I have just received the following Dispatch from Madison:**

"Collect all you can of Sheets, Pillow cases, Shirts, Bandages and Hospital Stores by to-morrow noon, and send them to Clinton on the noon train."

**A great and terrible slaughter has occurred at or near Corinth, Miss. If not your husbands, brothers, sons, are the victims, they are your brethren.**

**Send all such supplies by 9 o'clock to-morrow to the Common Council Room.**

**April 9 1862 R. H. MILLS, Mayor.**

Immediately after the carnage at Shiloh, Confederate forces fell back to Corinth, flooding the city with overwhelming casualties from both sides and prompting the desperate plea pictured here. Women from all over the South flocked to the aid of local women, who were inundated by the steady stream of wounded and dying men.

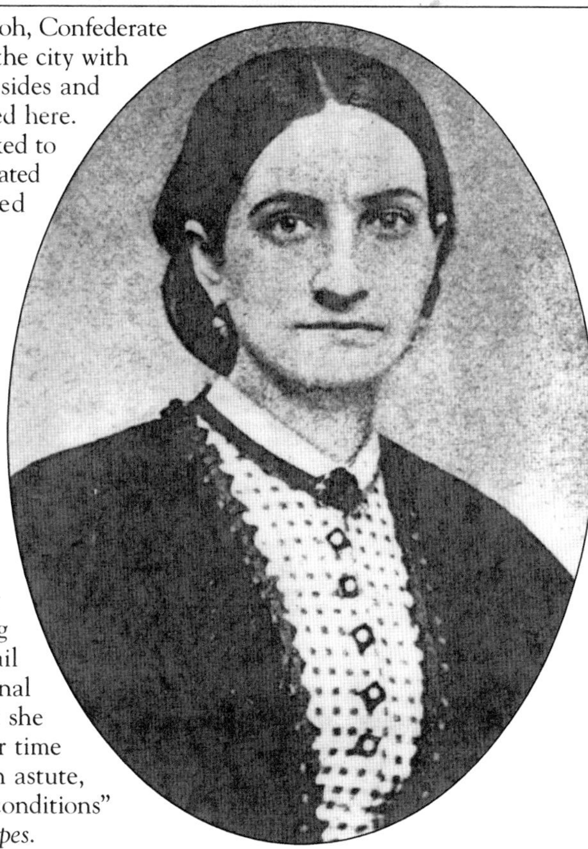

Among the first to answer the call for nurses at Corinth was Kate Cumming of Mobile, Alabama, who arrived by rail even as the battle still raged. Her journal offers a firsthand account of all that she witnessed and experienced during her time in Corinth and has been termed "an astute, authoritative account of events and conditions" in *Heroines of Dixie: Spring of High Hopes*.

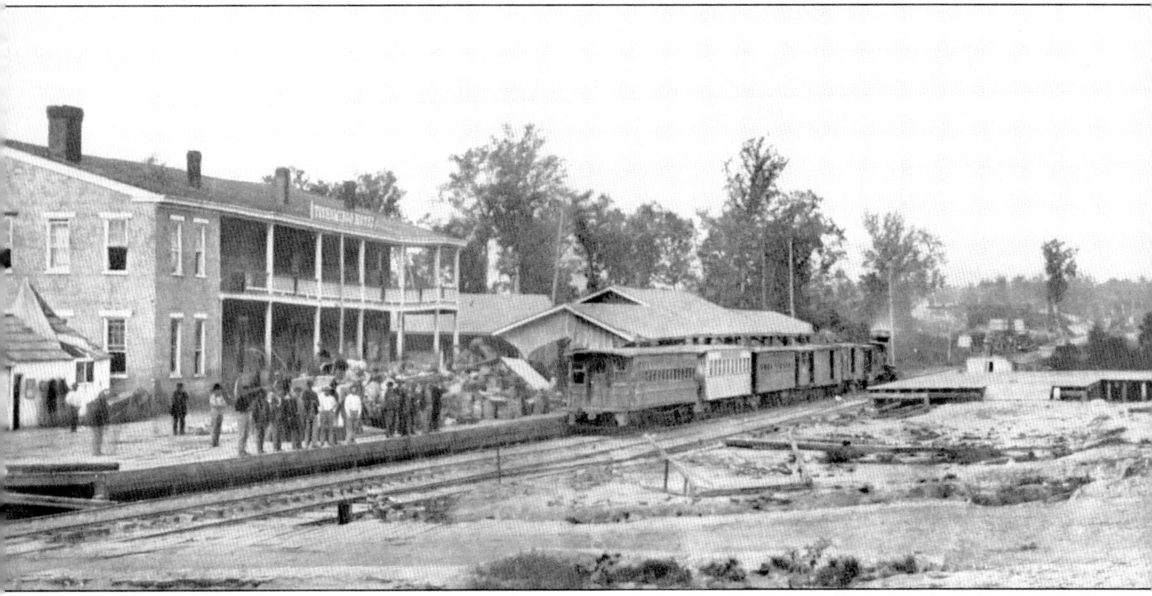

The Tishomingo Hotel, located right across from the rail intersection, overflowed with sick, wounded, and dying soldiers from both sides after the Battle of Shiloh. Every other hotel, boardinghouse, public building, and private residence in the city was being used for the same purpose. The hotel was where Kate Cumming was assigned to nurse, and her journal speaks starkly that "men are lying all over the [hotel], on their blankets, just as they were brought from the battle-field. . . . The foul air from this mass of human beings at first made me giddy and sick, but I soon got over it."

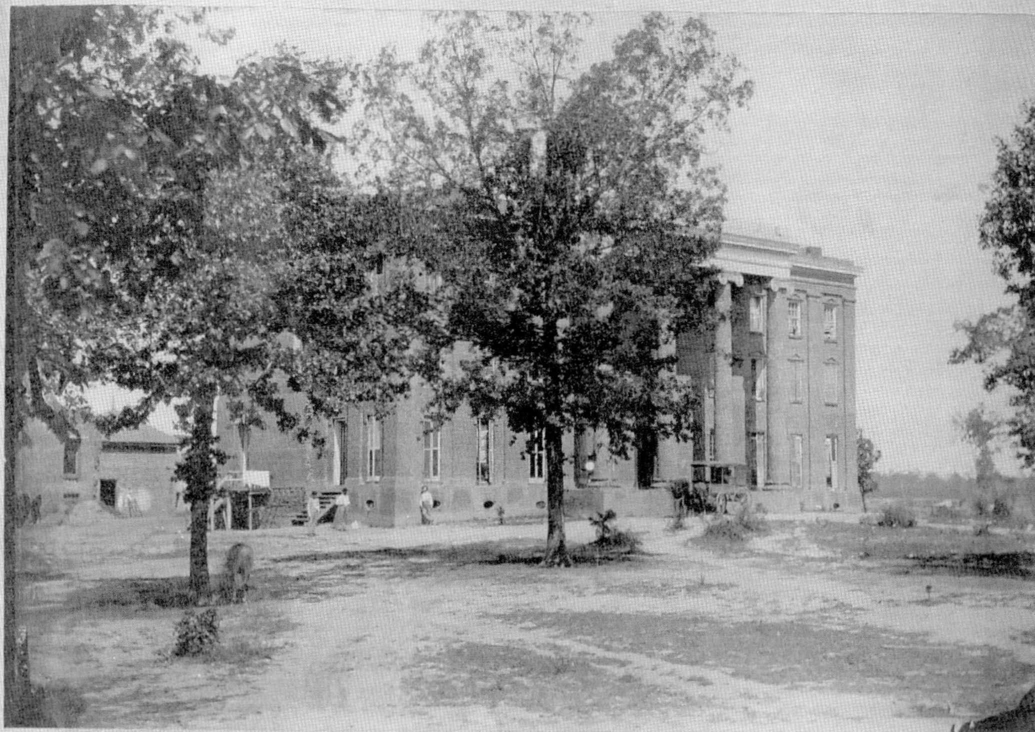

The only known existing image of Corona College is seen here. In 1857, Rev. L.B. Gaston and his wife founded the school, which was one of the first institutions of higher learning for women in the South. Built on five acres of land deeded to them by Houston and Martha (Whitmore) Mitchell, the school was intended for "the founding and establishment of a Seminary of Education and Literature of a high order." The school was originally known as the Gaston Institute before the name was changed to Corona College. Prior to the outbreak of war, young girls from across the South were offered a three-year collegiate course and postgraduate work. Both Union and Confederate occupying forces used the school as a hospital to care for the sick and wounded casualties from both sides after the Battle of Shiloh and the subsequent Battle of Corinth, which took place six months later. Nurses Ella King Newsome and Kate Cumming attended the wounded for the Confederate army, while Mary Ann "Mother" Bickerdyke assumed command under the Union army occupation. In January 1864, along with all buildings and works of a public nature, Corona College was burned to the ground by retreating Federal forces.

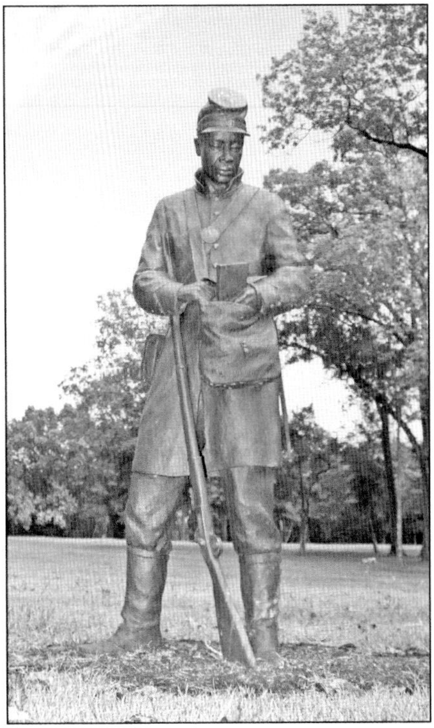

When Corinth fell to Federal forces in 1862, it immediately became a destination for slaves seeking freedom. Since the early-war precedent of designating runaways as contrabands of war, countless slaves fled to the closest Union lines and were soon put to work as laundresses and laborers on fortifications, earthworks, and repairing the rails. In Corinth, over 6,000 men, women, and children escaped to the protection of Union lines. A model camp for "contraband" was established by Gen. Grenville M. Dodge to house the refugees.

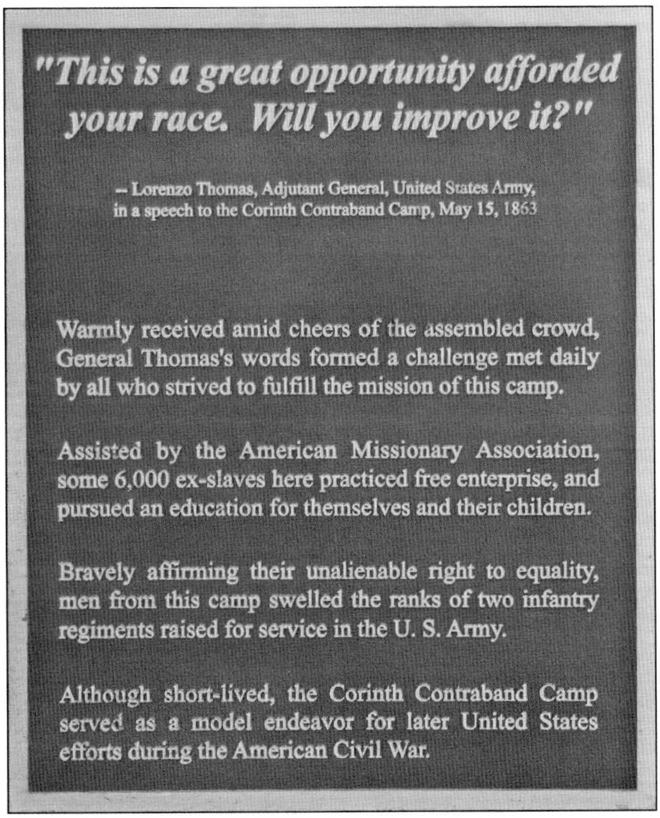

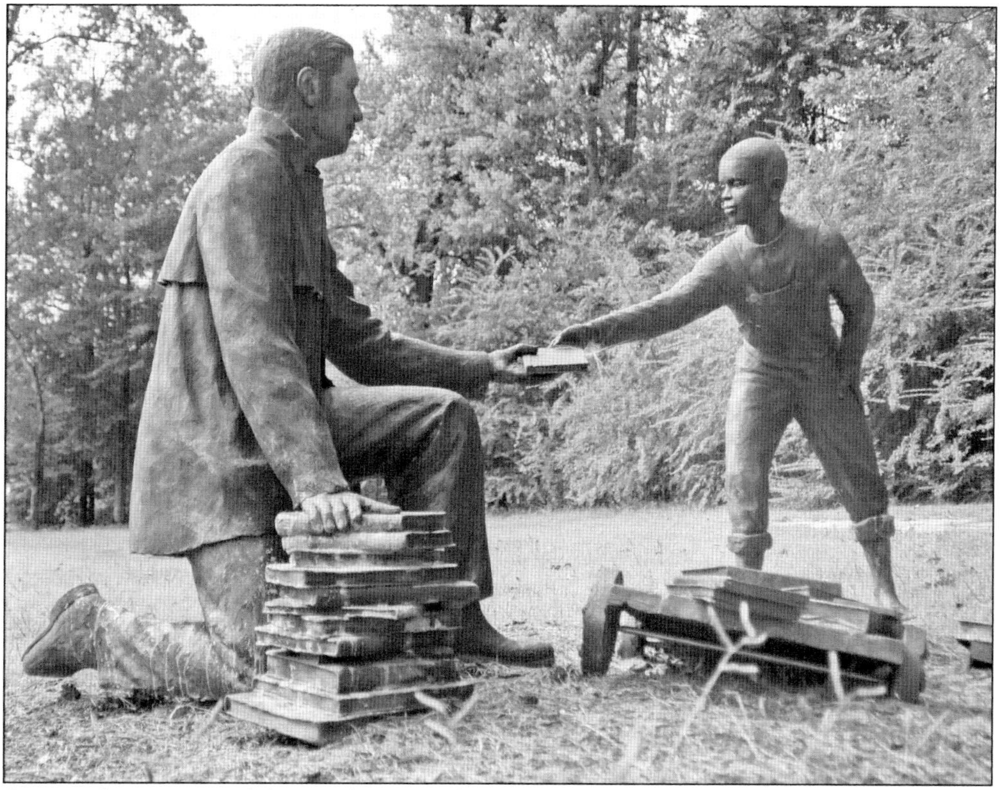

Over its short two-year lifespan, the Corinth Contraband Camp was a model endeavor featuring homes, a church, a school, and a hospital. The inhabitants of the camp undertook farming and cultivation for the first time as freedmen and freedwomen and showed a profit of between $4,000 and $5,000. Over 1,000 children and adults learned to read and write while at the encampment. (Courtesy of the National Park Service.)

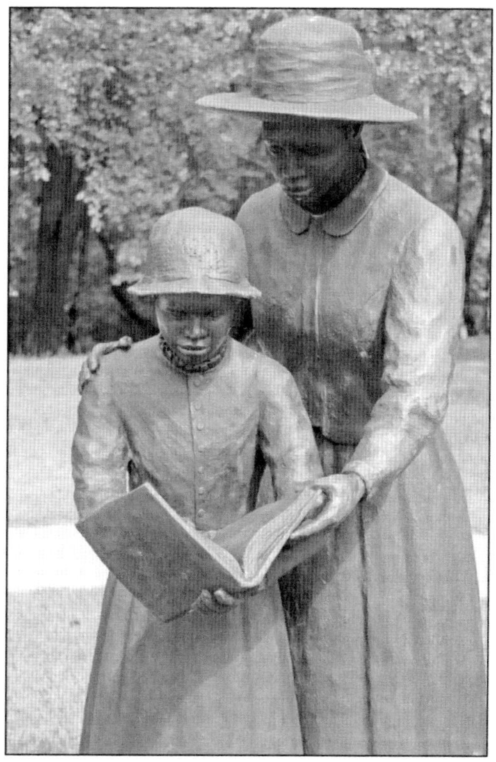

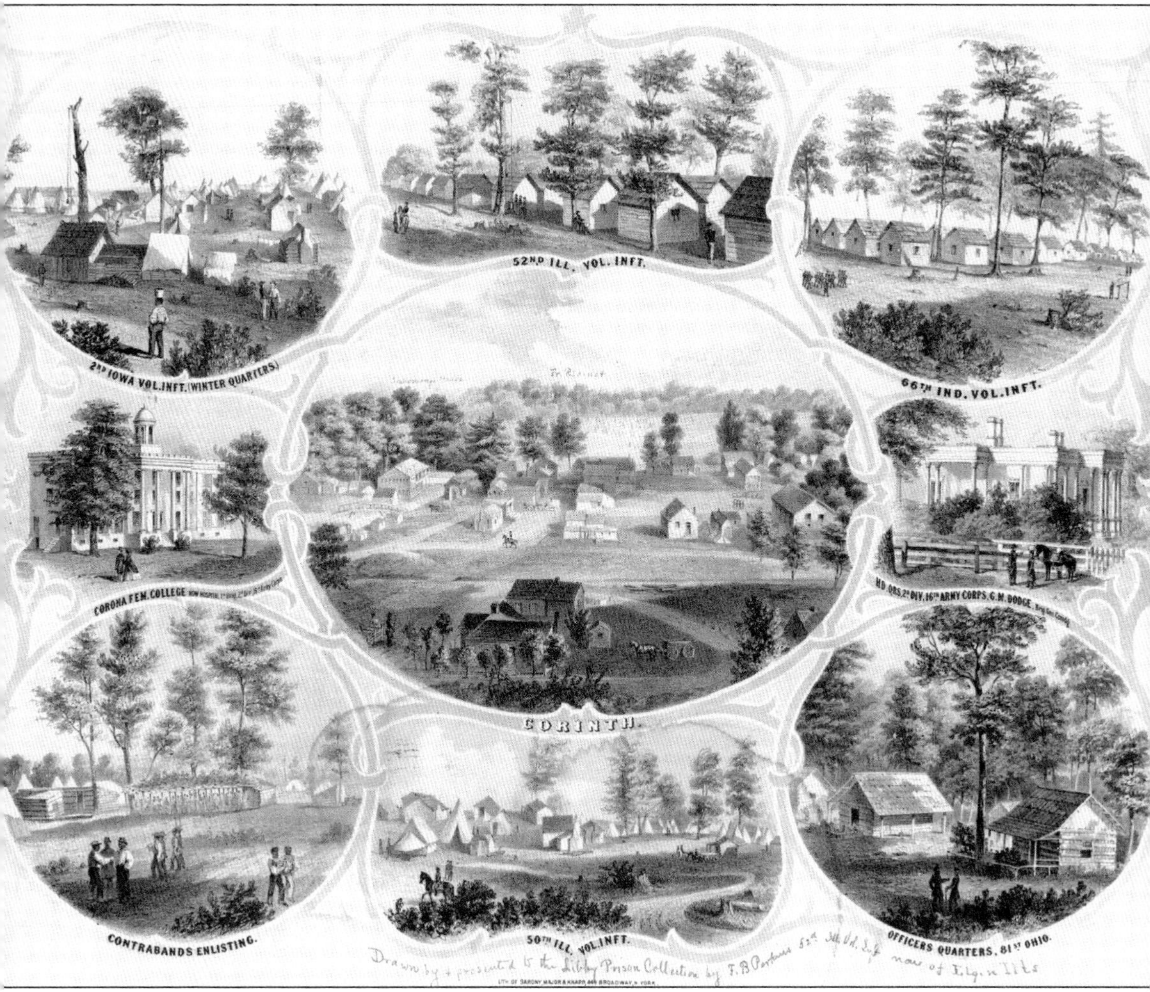


This 1862 sketch of various scenes from Union-occupied Corinth includes (clockwise from middle left) Corona Female College; the 2nd Iowa Volunteer Infantry (winter quarters); the 52nd Illinois Infantry; the 66th Indiana Volunteer Infantry; the headquarters of 2nd Division 16th Army Corps of Gen. G.M. Dodge, brigadier general commanding; officers' quarters of the 81st Ohio; the 50th Illinois Volunteer Infantry; and a rare depiction of "contrabands" enlisting. F.B. Perkins, the man who drew the sketch, served with the 52nd Illinois Volunteer Infantry. It later became a widely distributed lithograph.

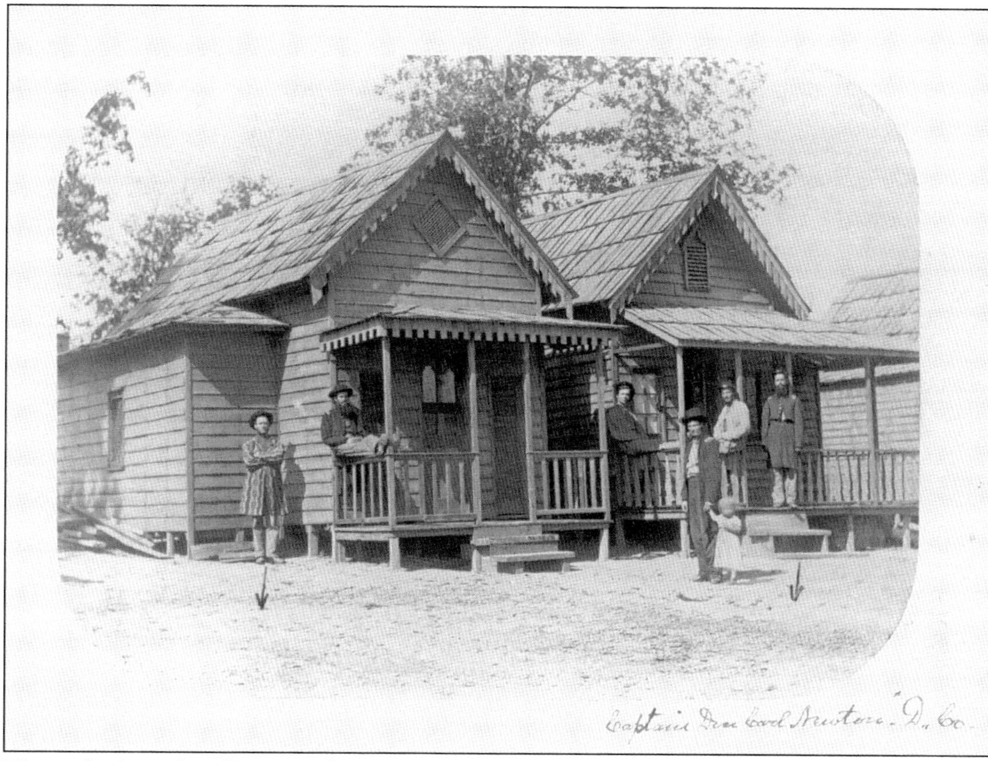

These photographs of Union officers' quarters at Corinth more than likely would have been built either in part or entirely by the labor of newly freed slaves from the nearby Contraband Camp. Based on the widespread practice of families visiting troops at their winter quarters, and from the presence of the small girl holding the hand of the officer in the lower right foreground, it might be inferred (but not proven) that these cabins are serving as winter quarters and that the soldiers might be receiving welcome visits from family members.

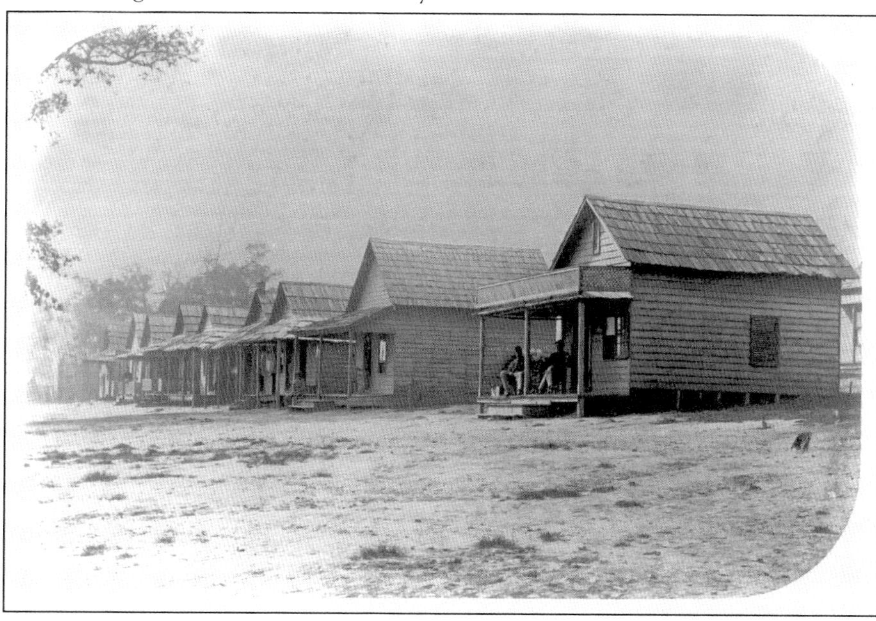

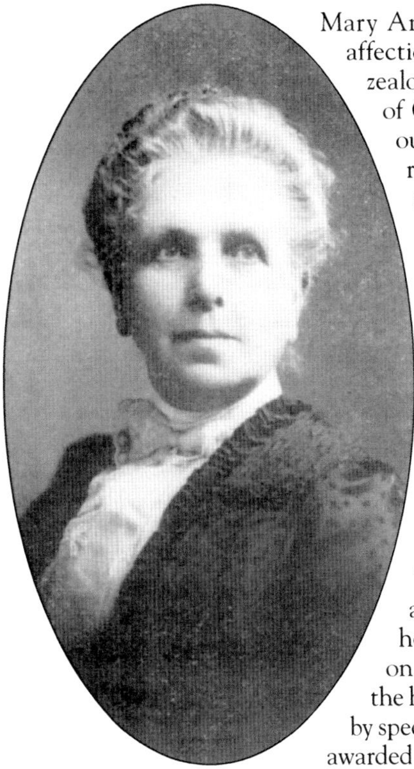

Mary Ann "Mother" Bickerdyke, as she was universally and affectionately known by her "boys," the enlisted men she so zealously tended, became chief of nursing under the sanction of Gen. U.S. Grant. Known by the officer corps for her outspoken and often insubordinate disregard for the army red tape and military procedures, she was not above riding roughshod over anyone, regardless of rank or station in life, who sought to interfere with her self-appointed duties. When asked once by a surgeon upon whose authority she acted, she replied, "On the authority of the Lord God Almighty, have you anything that outranks that?" No doubt General Sherman gave credence to her claim; because of her reply, the surgeon in question complained, and upon learning said nurse was "Mother" Bickerdyke, Sherman is famously reported to have responded, "Oh, well, in that case I can't help you. She ranks me. You'll have to see President Lincoln." She became a particular favorite of Sherman's for her service to his men and was said to have been the only female allowed in his camp. Throughout the war, she followed his troops, rendering aid and comfort despite any effort to oppose or forestall her. She set up over 300 hospitals and aided the wounded on 19 battlefields. At the conclusion of the war, she rode at the head of the XV Corps in the Grand Review in Washington by special invitation of General Sherman, and in 1886 Congress awarded her a special pension of $25 a month.

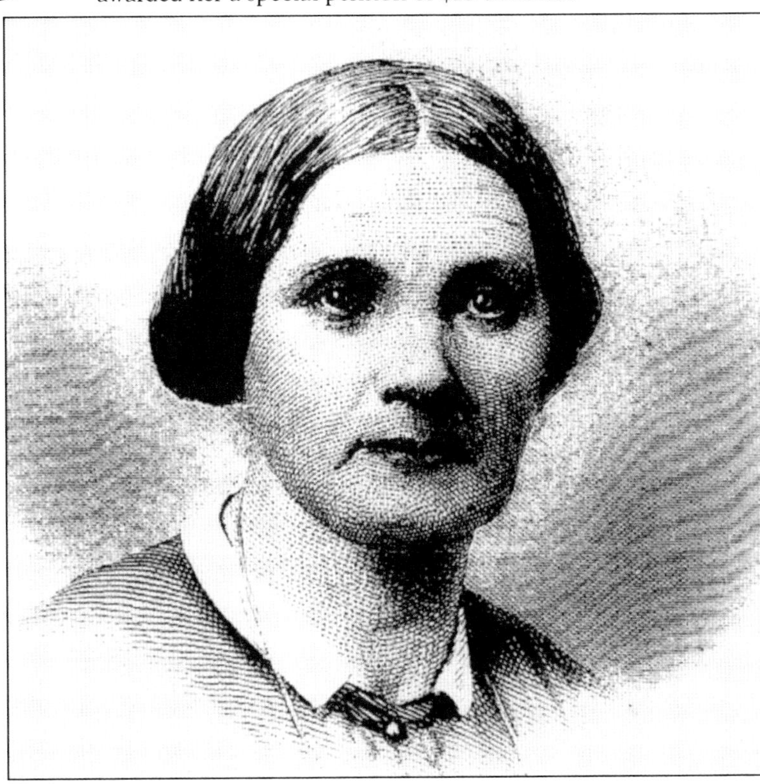

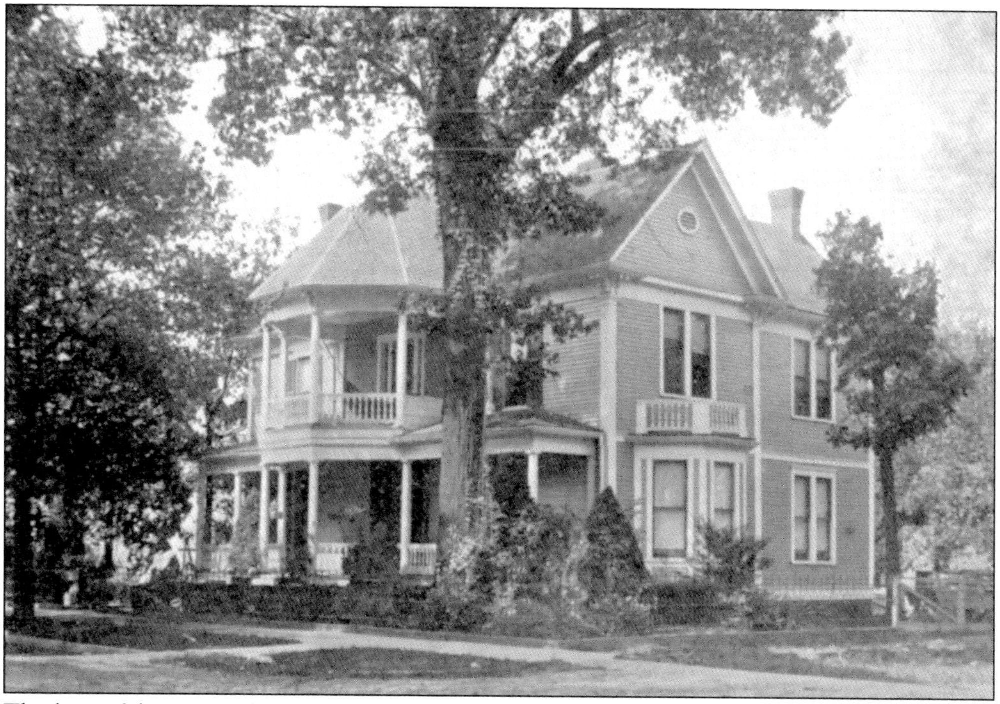

This beautiful Victorian home was located on the corner of Foote and Polk Streets and was occupied by the Elgin family. During the Federal occupation of Corinth, it served as the headquarters of Gen. U.S. Grant. It was torn down in the 1950s, and the lot became the present-day site of Corinth City Hall. (Courtesy of Dr. William Jackson.)

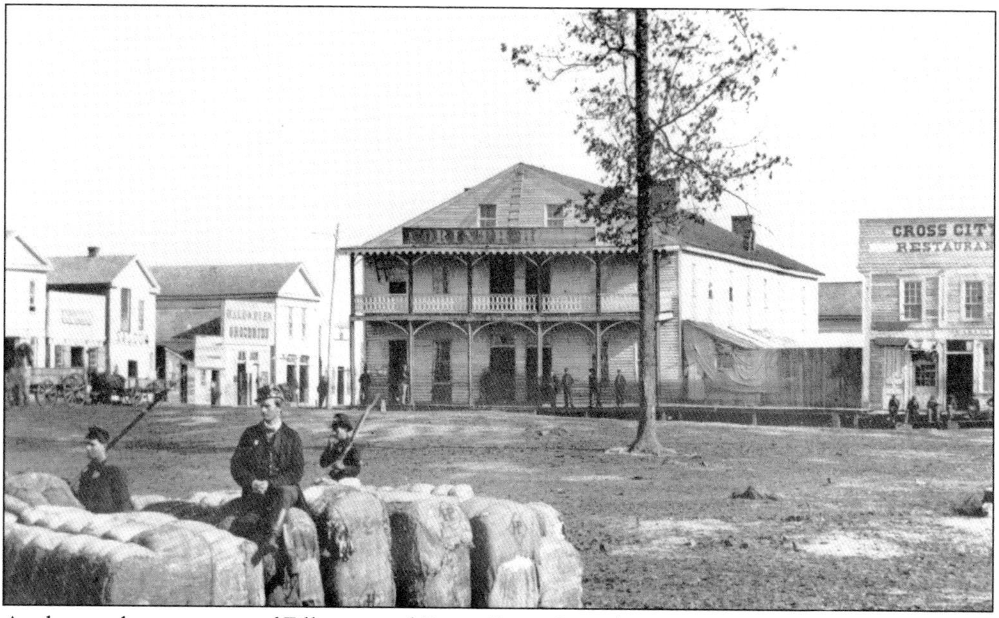

At the southeast corner of Fillmore and Front (later Cruise) Streets, Union troops guard cotton bales in front of the Corinth House and the Cross City Restaurant during the Federal occupation of Corinth prior to the Battle of Corinth in the fall of 1862. Before the Federal occupation, the Corinth House was operated by W.B. Pannell as a social center for CSA officers.

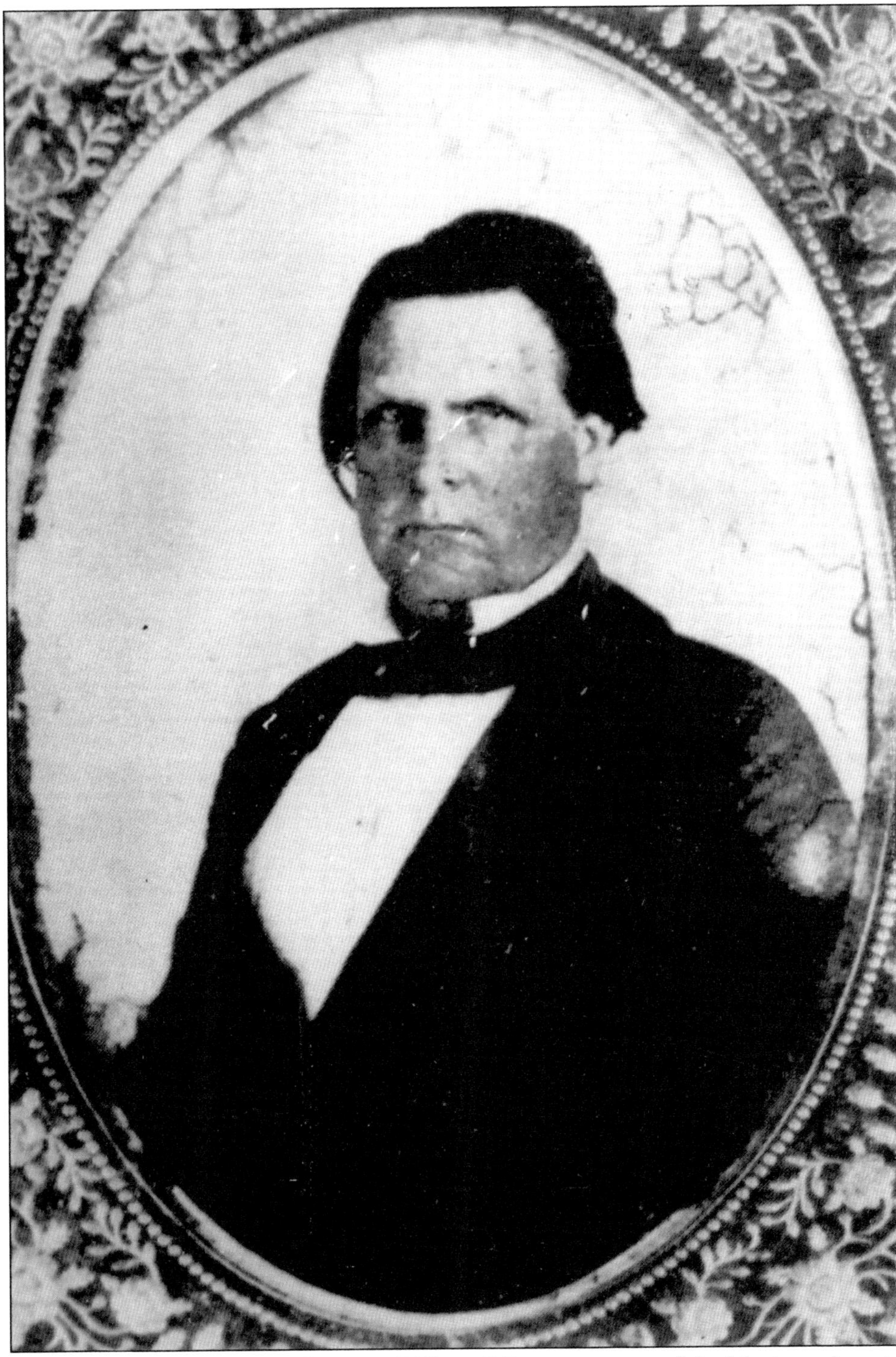

This is an early daguerreotype of a young William P. Rogers, veteran of the Mexican–American War and close friend and comrade of Pres. Jefferson Davis. During the Civil War, he served as a colonel in the Second Texas Infantry and died a hero's death on the second day of the Battle of Corinth.

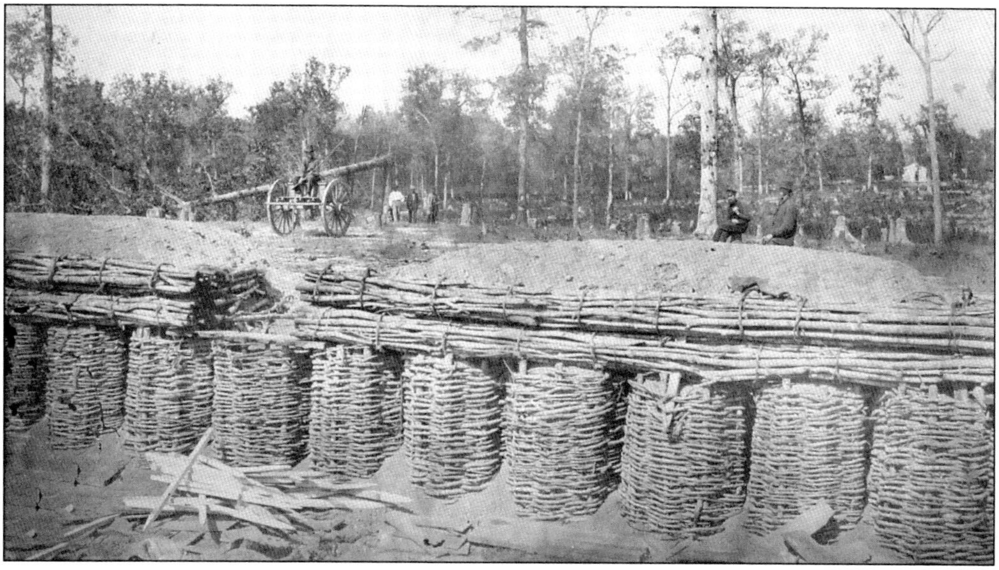

This photograph of Battery Powell, which is one of the 16 discontinuous sites ringing the city, shows the dirt-filled woven baskets, known as gabions, that comprised the ramparts with the troops pictured above awaiting the coming attack. Heavily fortified by both Union and Confederate occupying forces during the conflict, Corinth boasts some of the most pristine earthworks and fortifications still existing today.

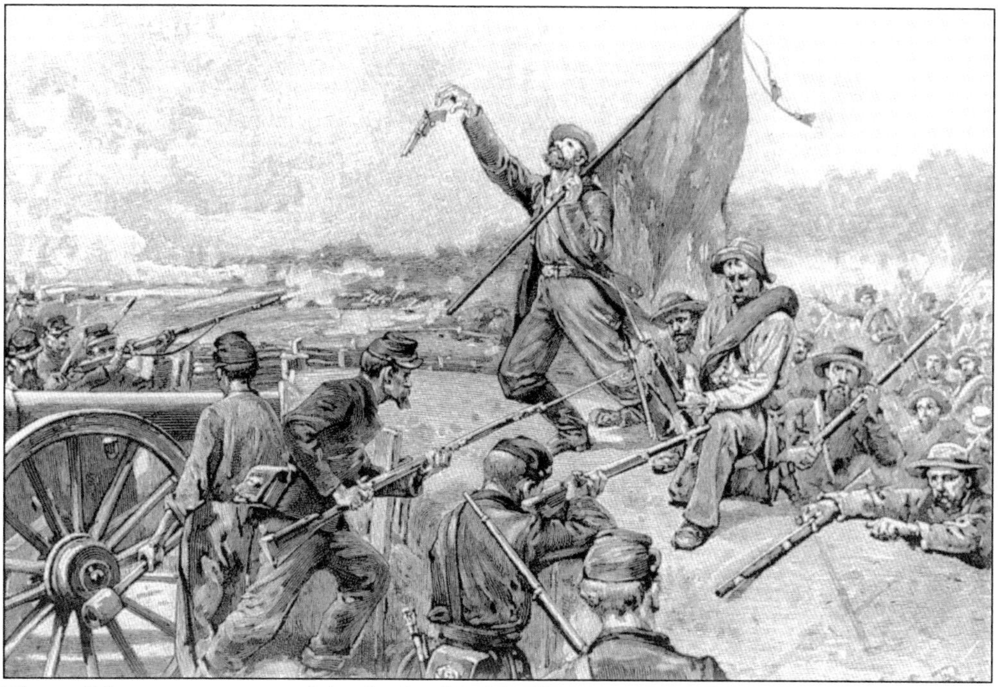

This well-known engraving of the death of Col. William P. Rogers of the Second Texas Infantry depicts him leading his troops in the third charge against Battery Robinett after having his "beautiful black horse" shot out from under him. Several accounts state that while leading his men on the third assault, he seized the regimental flag from a fallen color-bearer and climbed to the apex of the parapet to lift the flag in triumph, only to be felled by a barrage of fire.

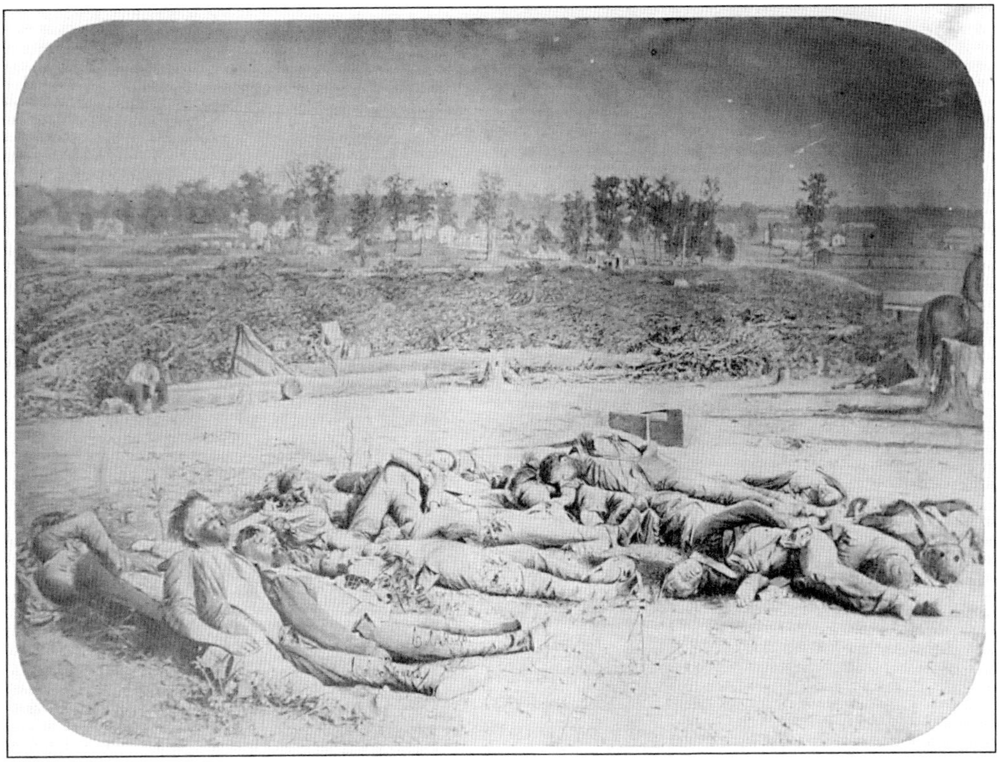

Above, Confederate dead lay gathered at the foot of the parapet at Battery Robinett, with the body of Colonel William P. Rogers on the far left, while below lies a lone unknown soldier. These are the only known images of soldiers killed in battle in the western theater, which were taken on October 4 or October 5 by one of the local photography studios.

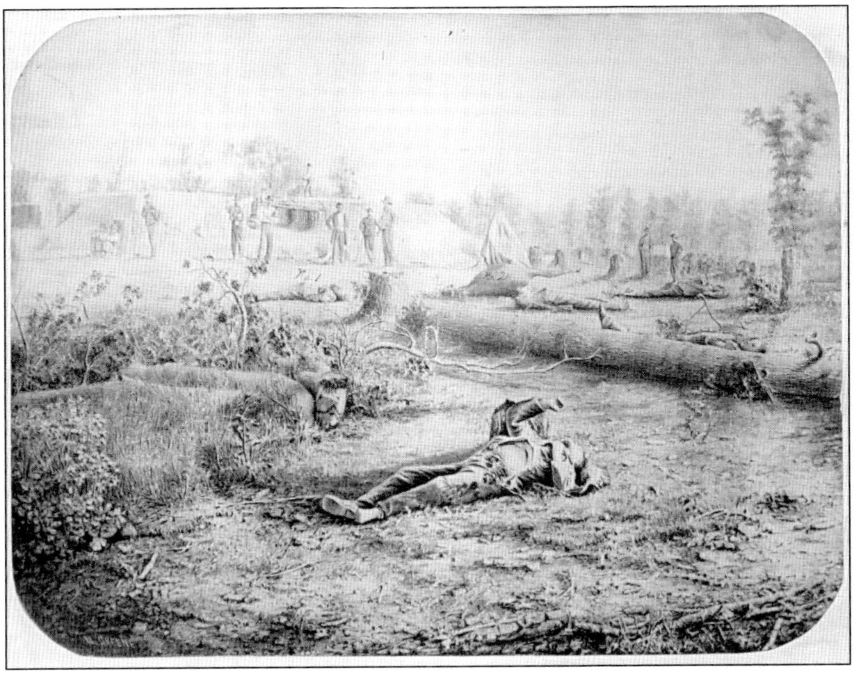

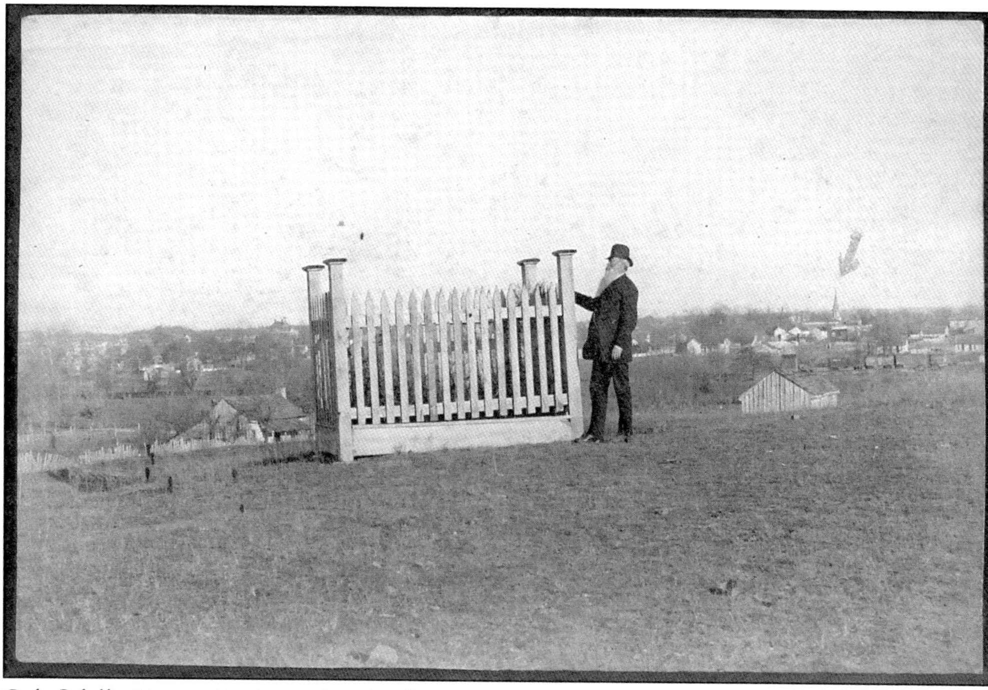

Col. Odelle Henson is pictured paying his respects at the grave of Colonel Rogers with the city of Corinth spread out in the background. Although notorious for denying Confederates a burial with military honors, in a tribute to his personal bravery, General Rosecrans ordered that Colonel Rogers be buried where he fell, attended with full military honors. He said, "He was one of the bravest men that ever led a charge. Bury him with military honors and mark his grave, so his friends can claim him. The time will come when there will be a monument here to commemorate his bravery." General Rosecrans's prediction proved to be remarkably prescient. In 1912, the United Daughters of the Confederacy, along with Rogers's descendants, met to dedicate a white marble obelisk atop a hill overlooking the battlefield to mark his gravesite.

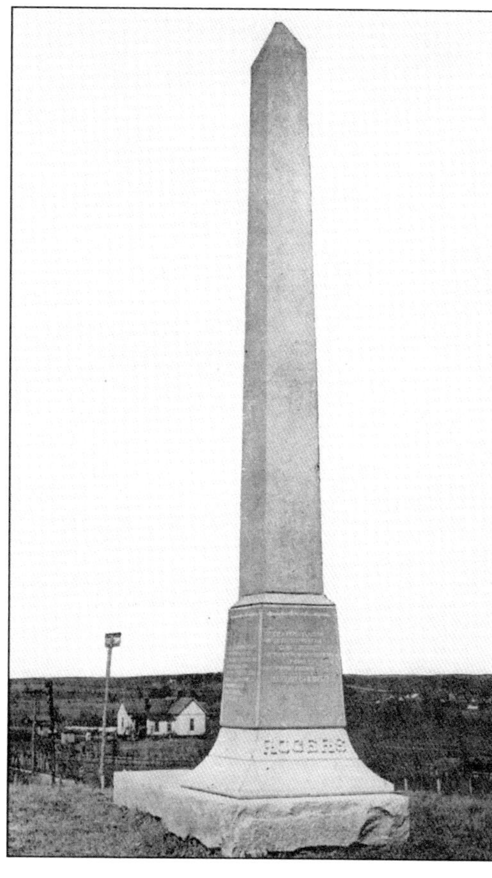

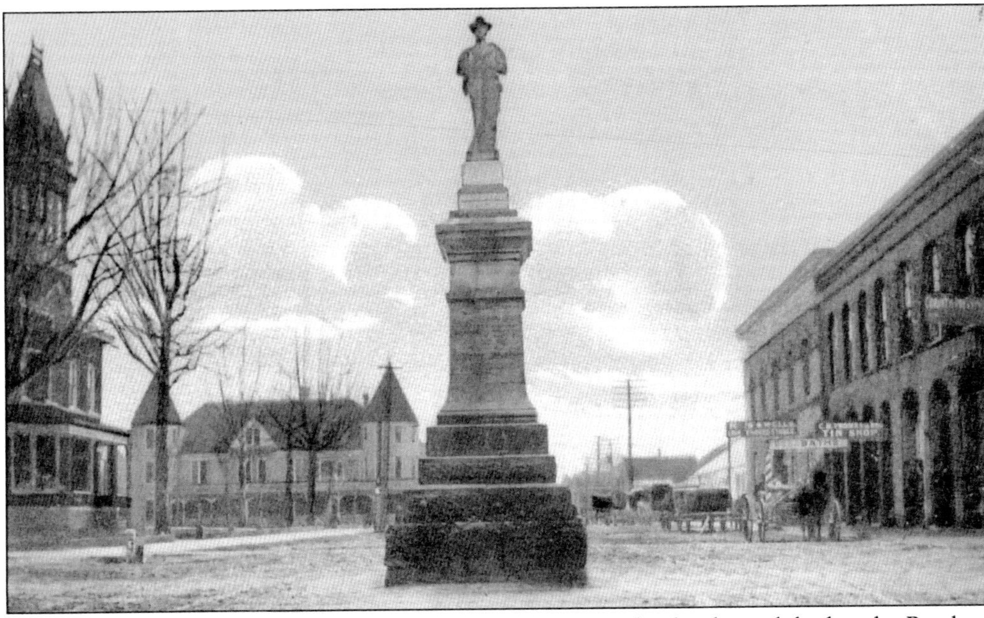

The monument that honors Col. W.P. Rogers and the men who fought and died at the Battle of Corinth was dedicated in 1906. It stood at the intersection of Franklin and Waldron Streets until 1919, when it was moved to the nearby corner of the Alcorn County Courthouse square. The inscription, dedicated to the memory of Colonel Rogers, states, "As long as courage, manliness and patriotism exist, the name of Rogers will be honored among men. He fell in the front of the battle in the center of the enemy's stronghold."

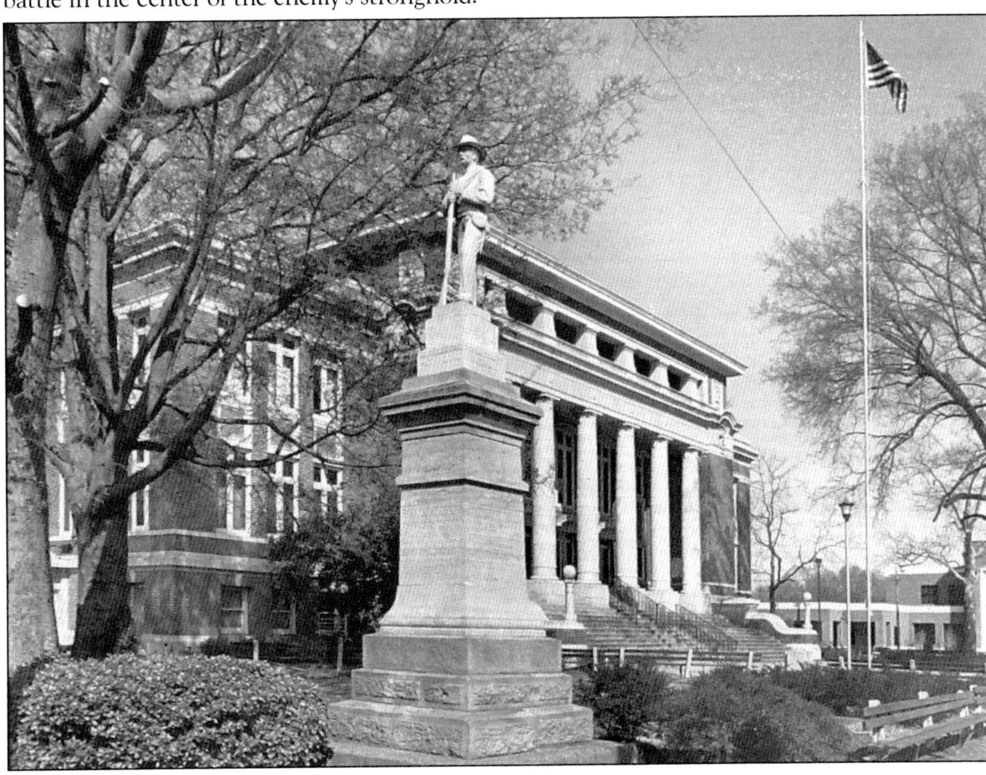

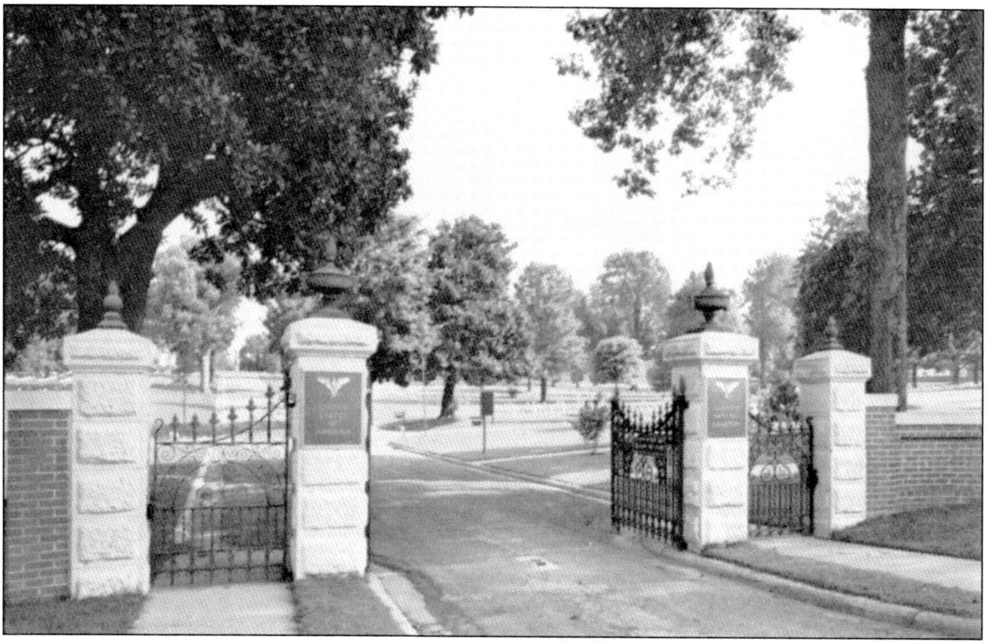

Located in the heart of Corinth, the Corinth National Cemetery was established as a central burial site for the 2,300 Union casualties of the Battle of Corinth and from other clashes around the city. The dead represented 273 Union regiments from 15 states. There are three Confederate soldiers interred in the Corinth National Cemetery: two known and one unknown. In addition, the National Cemetery contains the final resting place for servicemen from each branch of the services and from every subsequent conflict. (Courtesy of the US Department of Veterans' Affairs.)

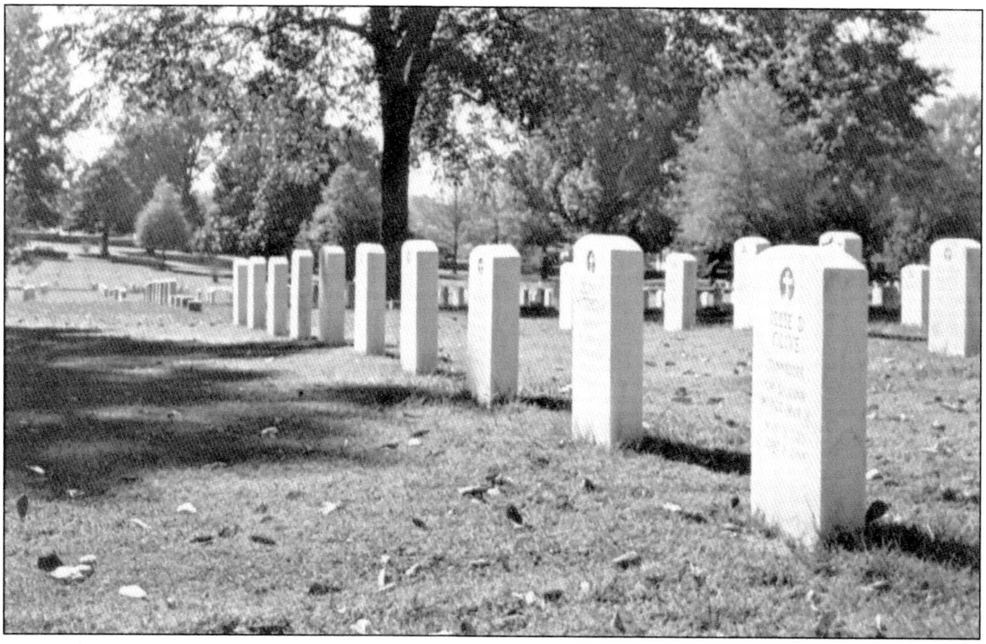

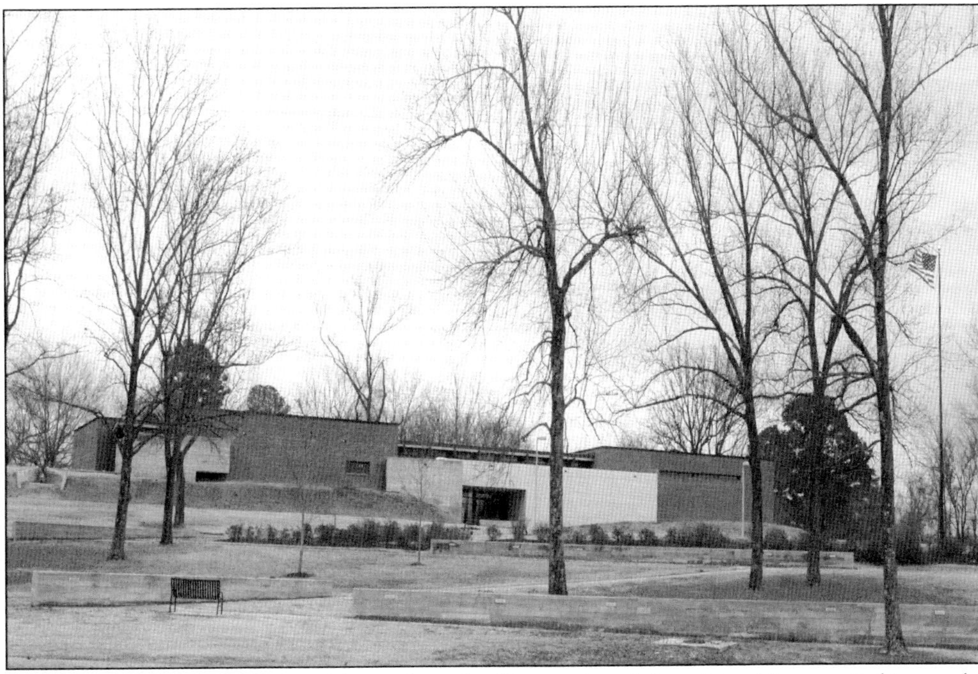

Dedicated on July 24, 2004, and located on the 20-acre site of the original Battery Robinett, the Corinth Civil War Interpretive Center is one of the 16 discontinuous sites that comprise the Siege and Battle of Corinth National Historic Landmark, which is operated as a unit of Shiloh National Military Park. Throughout the site, cast bronze pieces by the Lugar Foundry of Eads, Tennessee, symbolize the detritus of war and lead up the walkway to the exhibit hall that features life-size human figures of bronze. In the fountain courtyard, visitors will arrive at the *Stream of American History 1770–1870*, the culmination of a unique, never-to-be-forgotten experience.

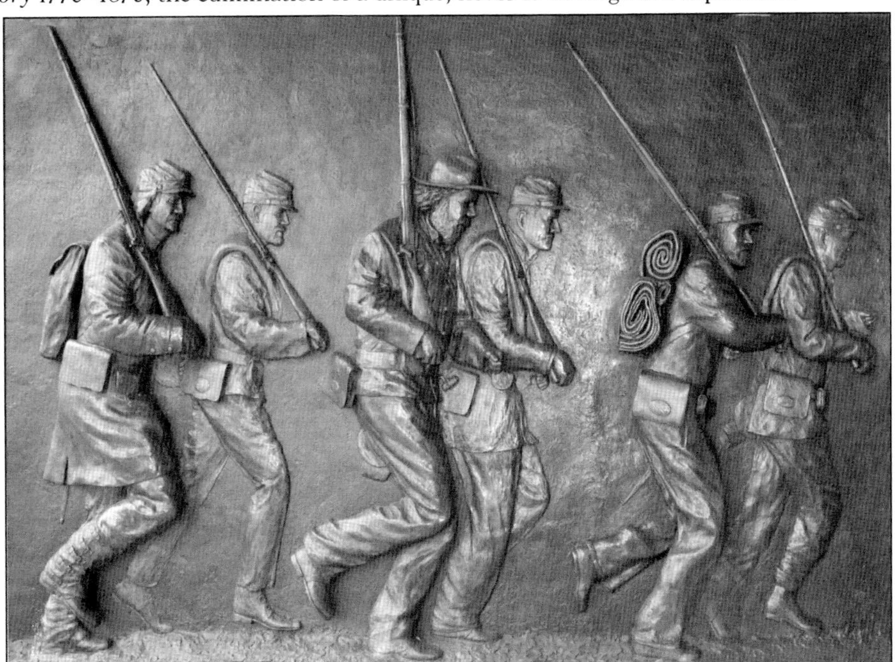

# *Two*

# A Center of Commerce, Industry, and Culture

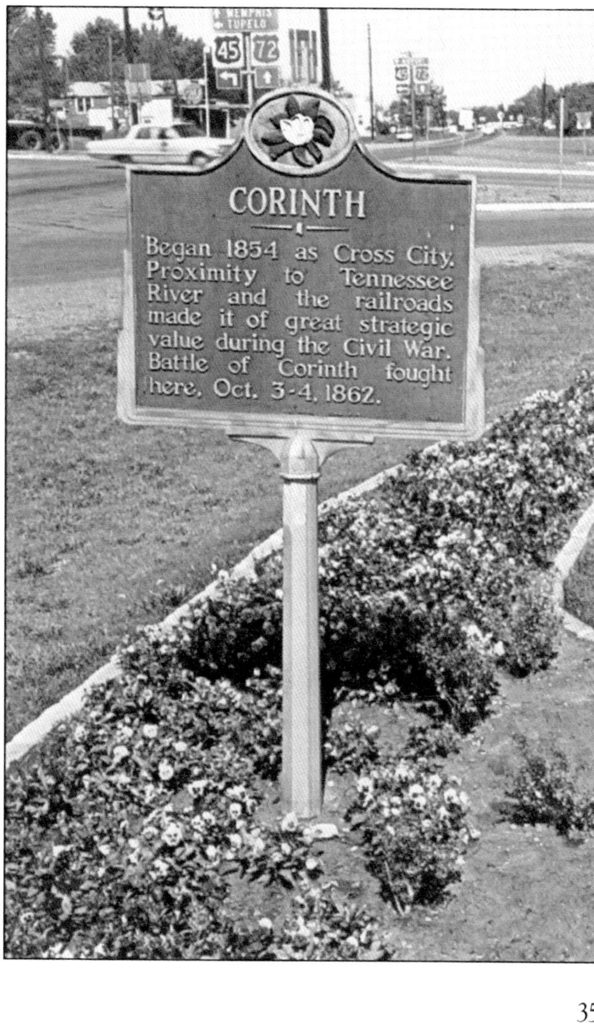


"It's not everyone that can get to Corinth," wrote the famous Latin poet Horace in regard to another world-renowned city at the crossroads, though the one to which he was referring was in Greece. In keeping with the mid-Victorian fad, the original name of Cross City was changed soon after the city's founding to the more classical Corinth after another city known as a center of commerce, industry, and culture.

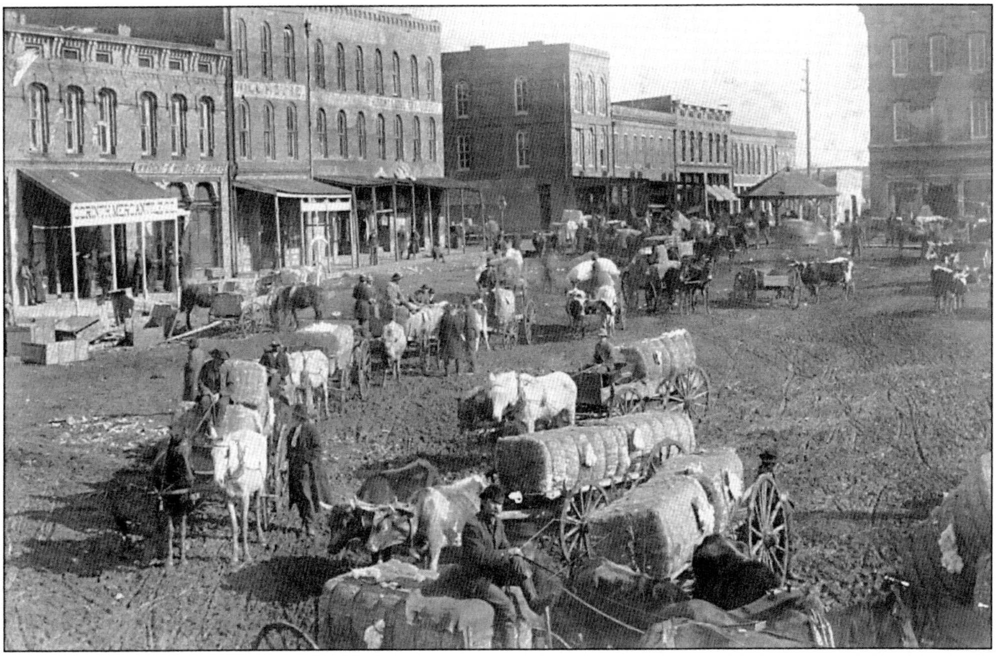

The same rails that had brought death, destruction, and near ruin to the city also became its salvation at the end of the Civil War. The constant sound of train whistles as they arrived and departed daily heralded the return of commerce and an economy that was able to make a much more rapid recovery than the rest of the state. By the turn of the century, hundreds of cotton bales were seen stretching west from Rubel's Department Store over an entire city block down to the corner of Cruise and Jackson Streets. They were awaiting inspection by local cotton graders, seen standing atop the bales and loading them onto the nearby rails for shipment to mills throughout the nation. (Courtesy of Dr. William Jackson.)

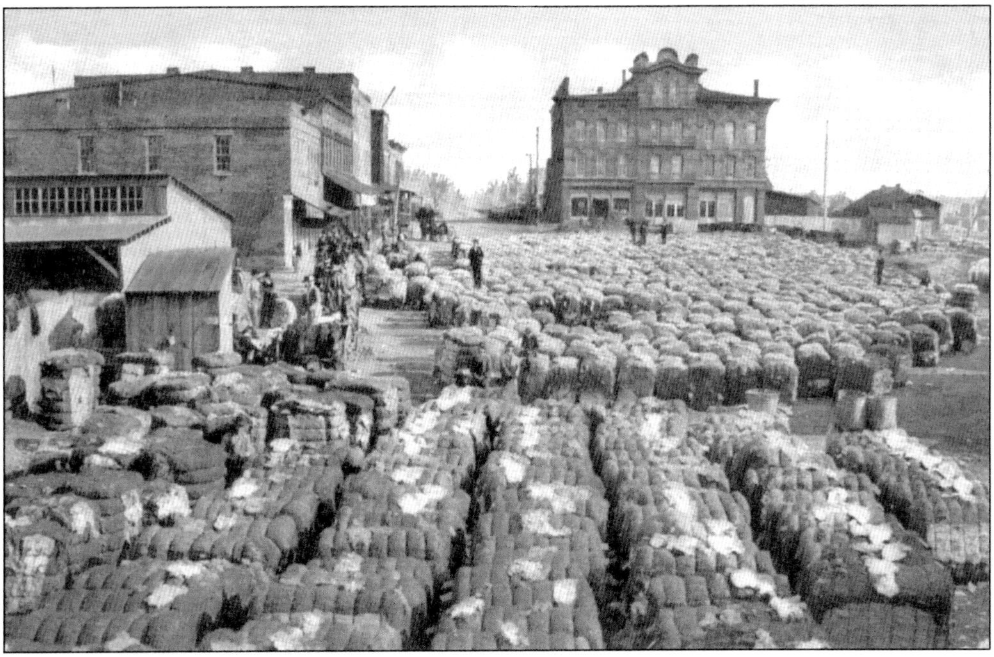

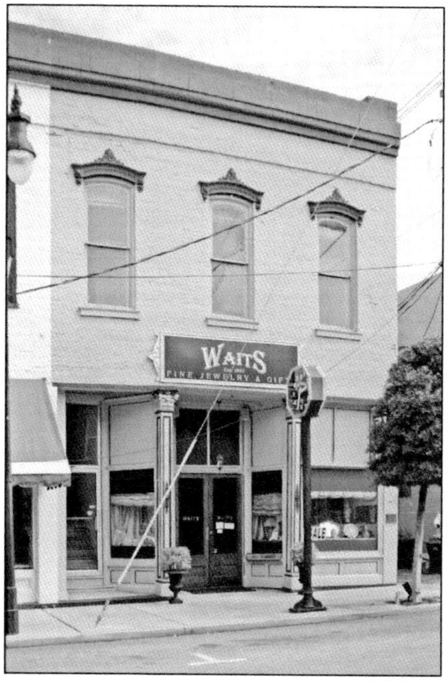


Wait's Jewelry Store, the oldest business in the city, originally opened in 1865 by James Waits, a Confederate soldier stationed in Corinth during the war who returned to open a watch shop. James's son E.F. Waits operated the store until his death in 1938, when his widow, Eugenia, assumed the day-to-day operation. She was legendary among Corinth brides for her uncanny ability to remember the china pattern of any bride who had ever registered with her, no matter how long ago it may have been. She worked 76 years at Waits, from 1926 until her retirement in 2002. In a story recounted by Eugenia Waits to Wanza Gray, Mr. E.F. Waits was a prolific inventor and invetcrate tinkerer who built a bamboo airplane in 1910 on the top floor of the adjacent building and was temporarily stumped as to how to get it downstairs. According to Eugenia's recollection, he succeeded by removing the wings and reassembling it outside. The flight of the *Demoiselle* flying contraption was featured in an April 1911 article in *Popular Mechanics*. She also recalled the many times Mr. Waits's great friend, famed aviator Roscoe Turner, would stop in for a visit while in town and bring his pet lion, Gilmore, with him. Instructed to lie down, Gilmore would comply and regally recline while shoppers would gingerly come and go.

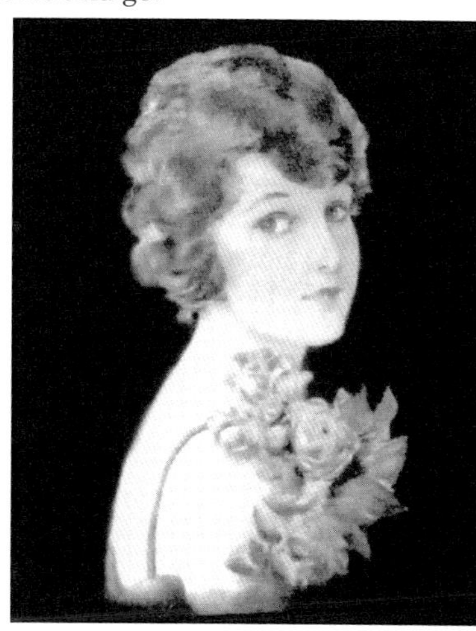

This portrait, painted by E.F. Waits of his bride, Eugenia, was part of a window display when she died in 2005. In May 2006, Waits Fine Jewelry and Gifts was bought by Rosemary and H.L. "Sandy" Williams, who have lovingly restored and preserved the store just as it might have appeared to patrons over 100 years ago. (Courtesy of Wanza J. Gray.)

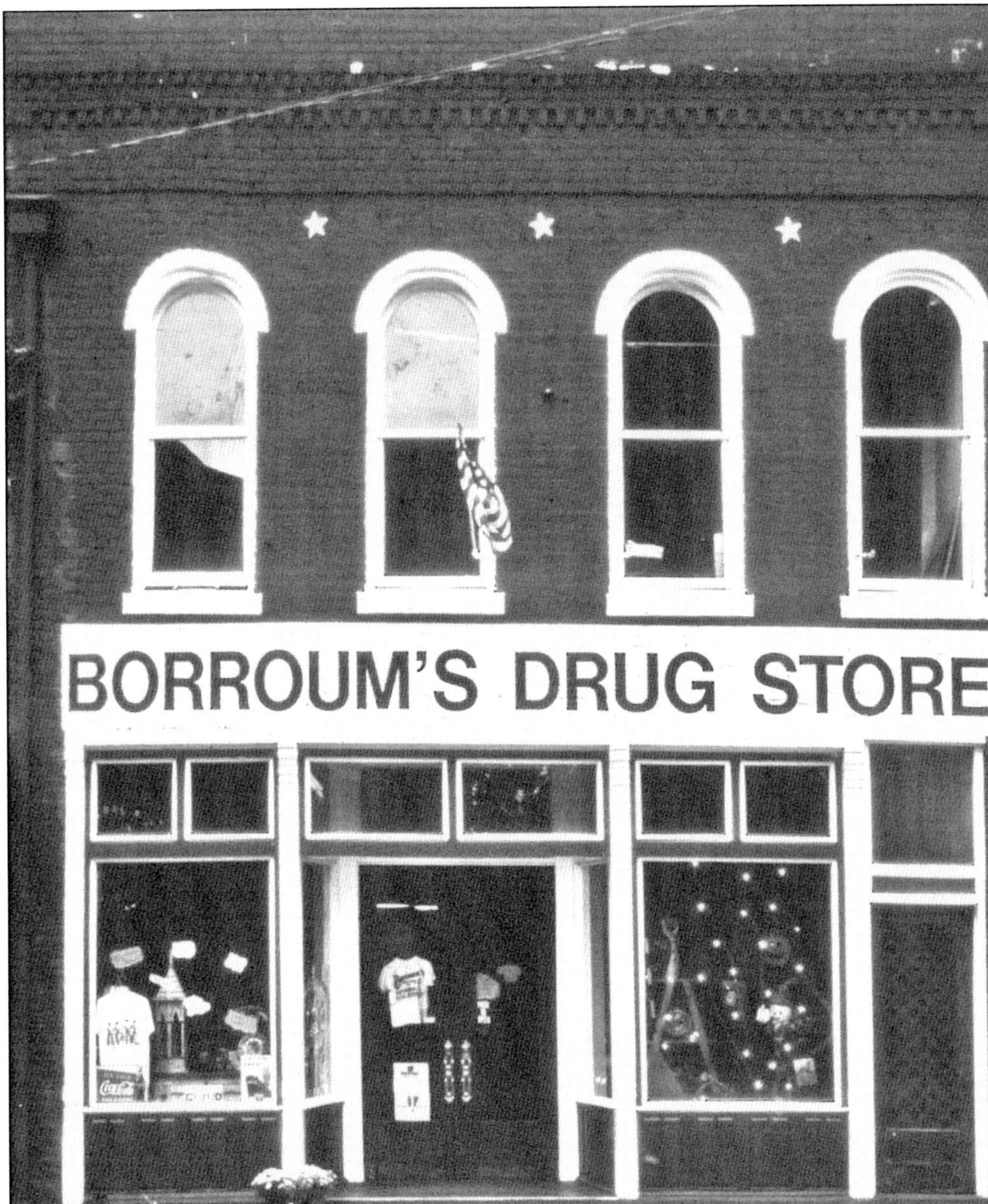


Originally from Oxford, Mississippi, Dr. Andrew Jackson Borroum stopped in Corinth on his way home from the war and decided to stay. He founded Borroum's Drug Store in 1869 directly across from the courthouse. It is the oldest continually running drugstore in Mississippi and has seen four generations of the family serve as its pharmacist.

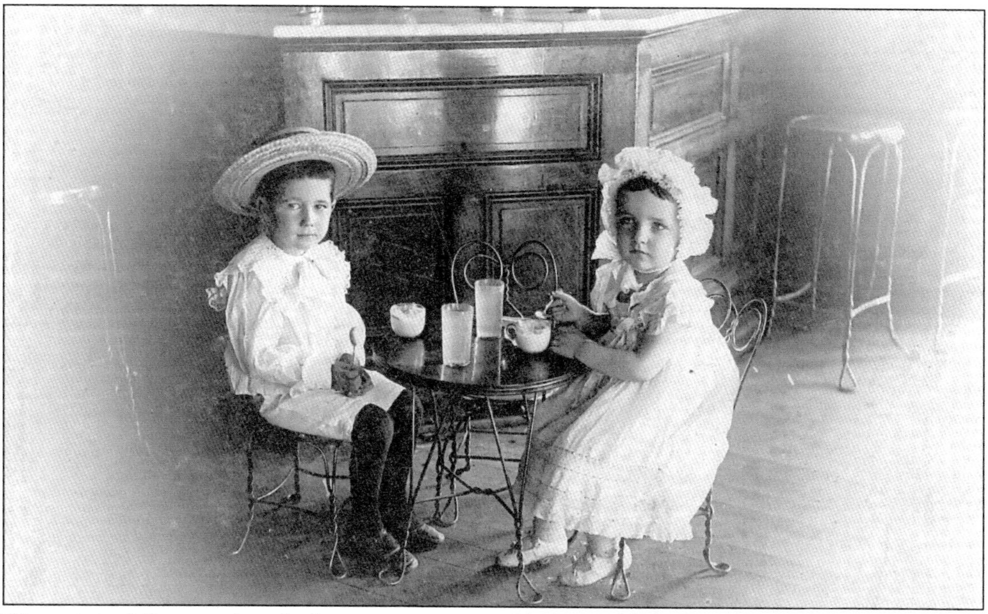

The original Borroum's soda fountain was most likely established in the 1880s and boasted a zinc-lined icebox under the counter and a beautiful marble countertop. A tasty cherry Coke or root beer could be purchased for a nickel and a glorious ice cream sundae for just a dime. Here, two unidentified children enjoy a treat in front of what appears to be the original soda fountain. Larger versions of the miniature table and chairs can still be found in the store. (Courtesy of Camille Mitchell.)

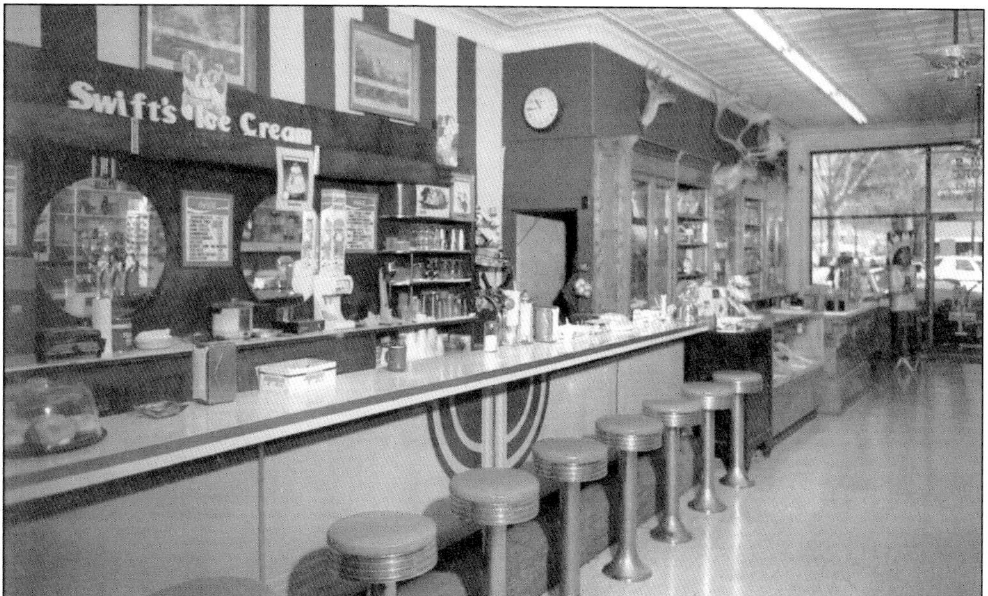


According to most historical accounts, the "Golden Age of Soda Fountains" was from the 1830s until their complete collapse in the 1970s. Despite this, Borroum's continues to operate a soda fountain. Customers can also enjoy the free in-store museum, comprised of one of the largest antique handgun and Native American artifact collections in the tri-state area, assembled by Col. J.L. Borroum, who was an avid lifelong collector. (Courtesy of Camille Mitchell.)

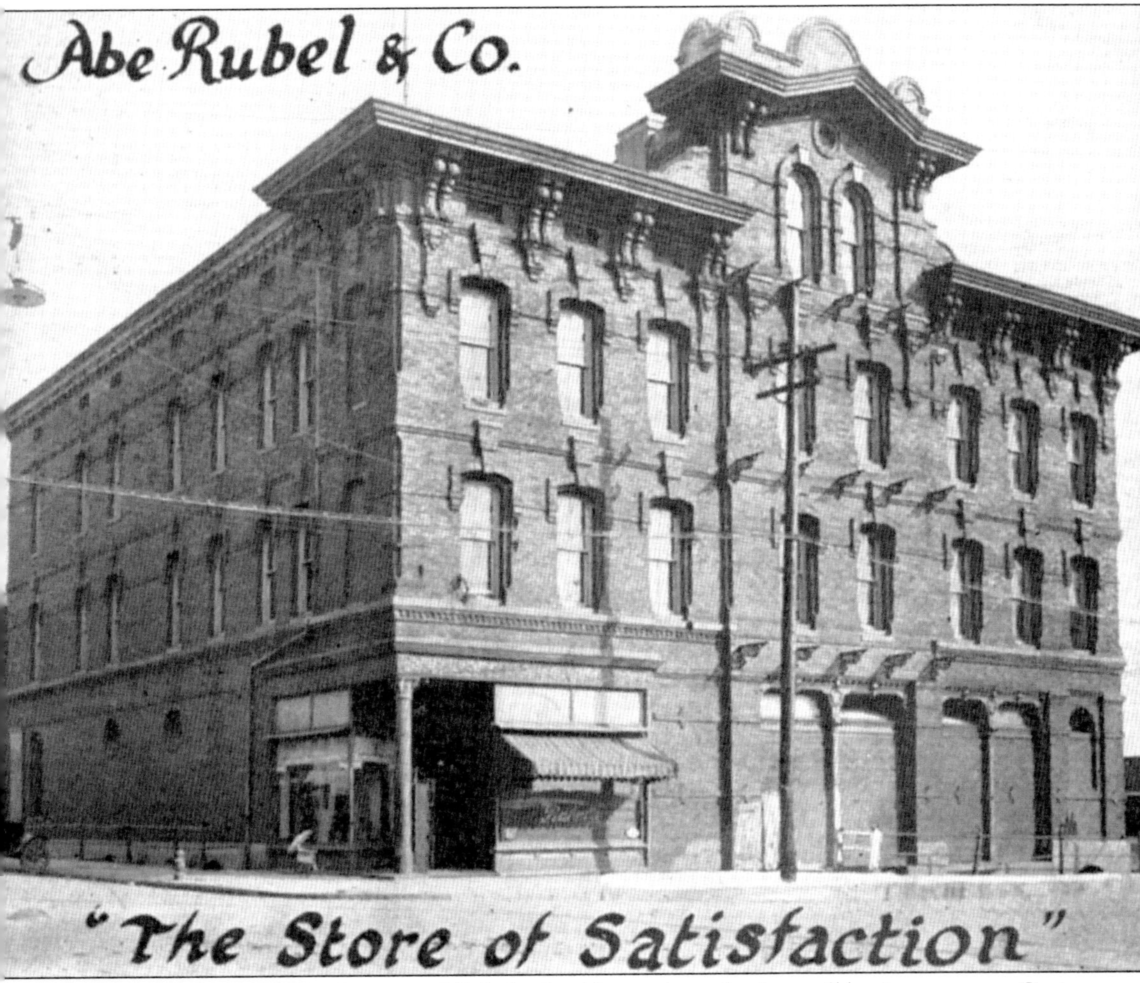


Prior to the Civil War, Emmanuel Rubel, a Jewish merchant, had a small business on west Cruise Street. Around 1875, it is believed that local architect Martin Siegrest was in charge of erecting the three-story brick building, which housed E. Rubel and Company on the ground floor. The top two floors were designed as a hotel, but only the three retail stores on the ground floor prospered under Emmanuel Rubel and his partner, Leopold Seckels. (Courtesy of Dr. William Jackson.)

Rubel's Department Store was later purchased by Emmanuel Rubel's nephew Abe, who was joined by his two eldest sons, Adolph and Simon, in running the store until its closing in 1957. According to an unpublished memoir by native Corinthian Nelda Parrish, "The motto on the double glass front door was 'Satisfaction Guaranteed.' As you entered the store, a rotund Dave Sharp greeted you with a big smile! Mind you, this was before Wal-Mart, but Abe Rubel knew how important a greeter was! The memories of shopping at Rubel's will always be a joy."

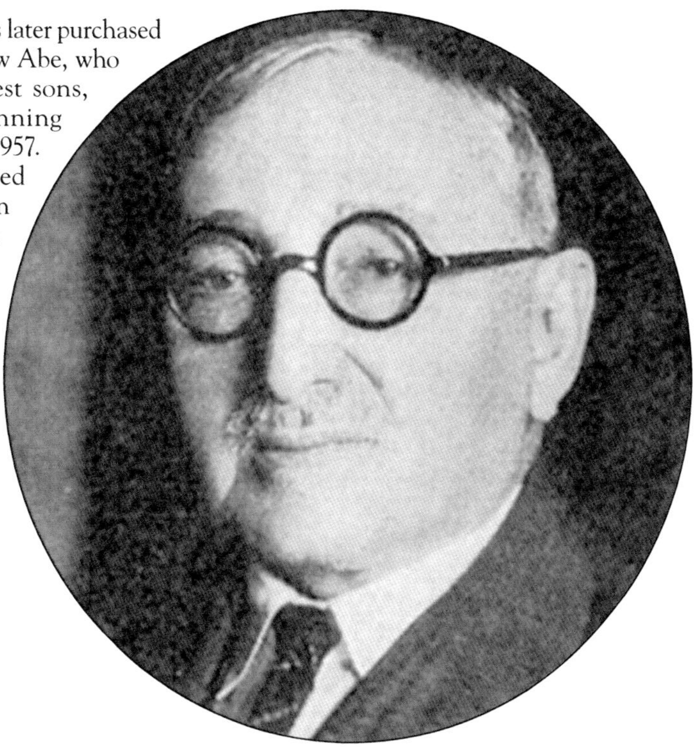

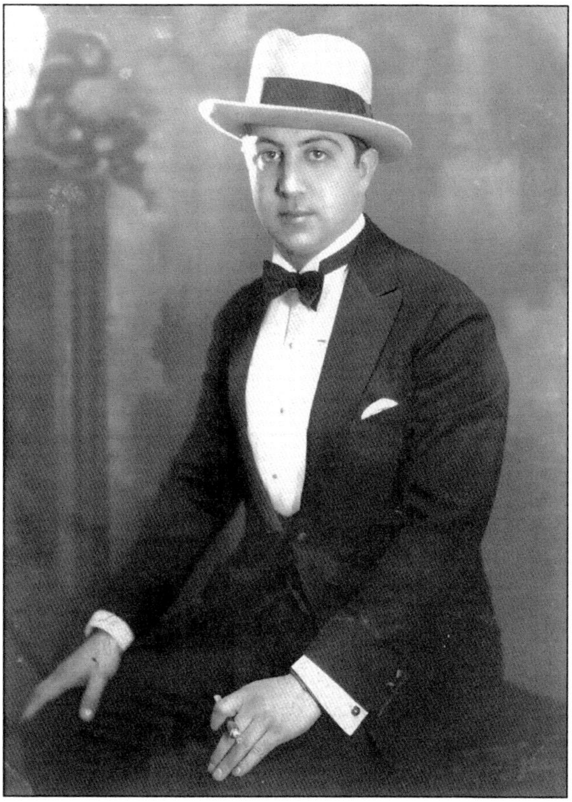

Continuing with the quote from an unpublished memoir by Nelda Parrish, "The bargain basement was for the thrifty shoppers, the main floor had piece goods, ladies clothes, shoes, and accessories, and a men's department where everything was first class merchandise coming from markets that showed their wares in New York City. Mr. Simon Rubel [pictured] went twice a year on buying trips for the upcoming season." (Courtesy of LuAnne Parrish-Simon.)

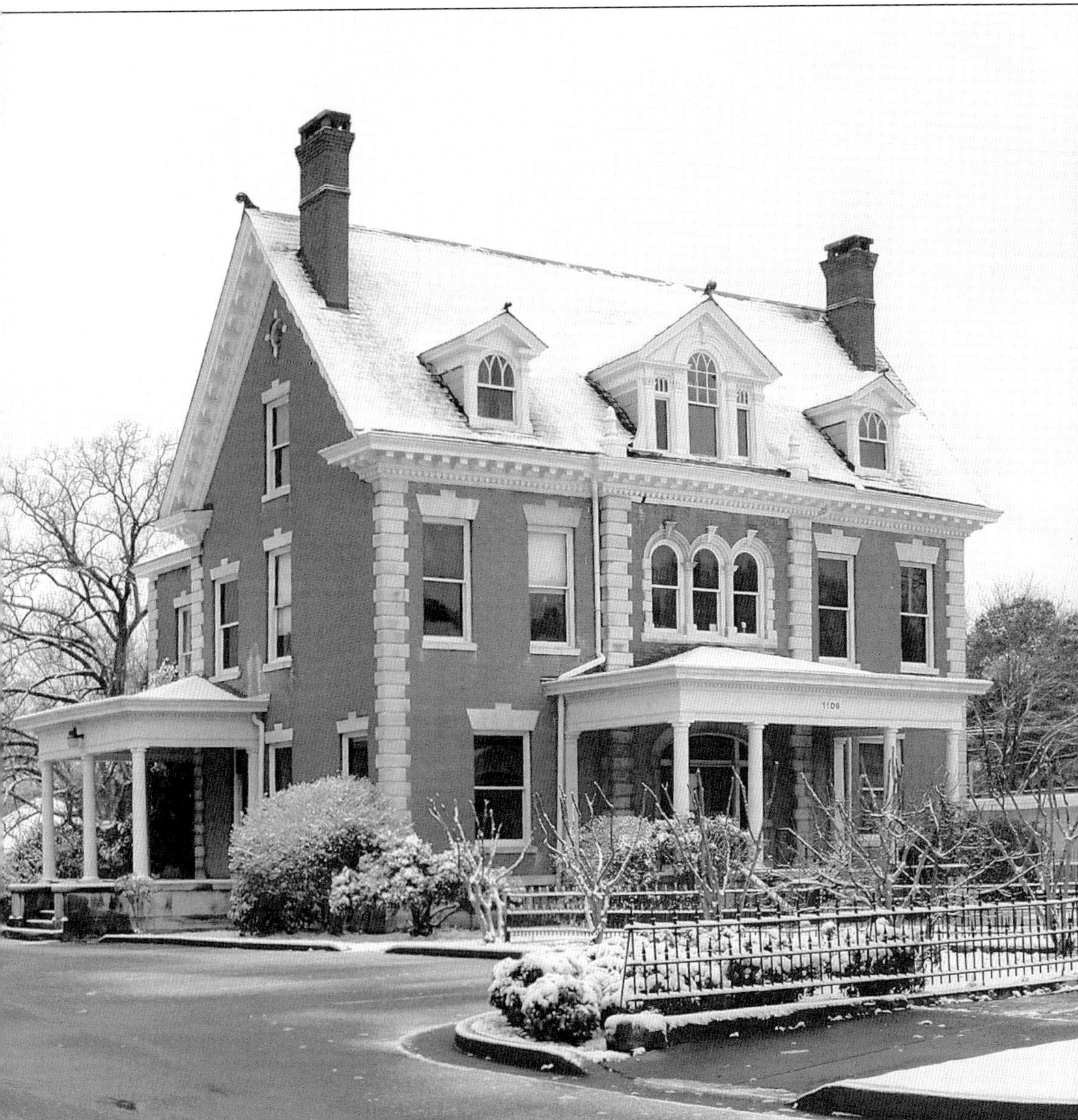

This imposing brick and stone home located on the corner of Main and Jackson Streets was built in 1904 for the Abe Rubel family and is considered to be one of the finest examples of Colonial Revival architecture in Mississippi. The home is comprised of 16 rooms, an attic, cellar, and halls. The redbrick accents the house's beauty and stone trim. The dormers on the third floor each have triple-arched windows, with the center Palladian window serving to emphasize the details of the other two. Three arched, stone-trimmed windows are located above the portico, while beautiful beveled glass sidelights and transoms flank the substantial leaded glass front door. This photograph shows the snow-covered Rubel house as it appears today; the home is currently owned by the First Baptist Church.

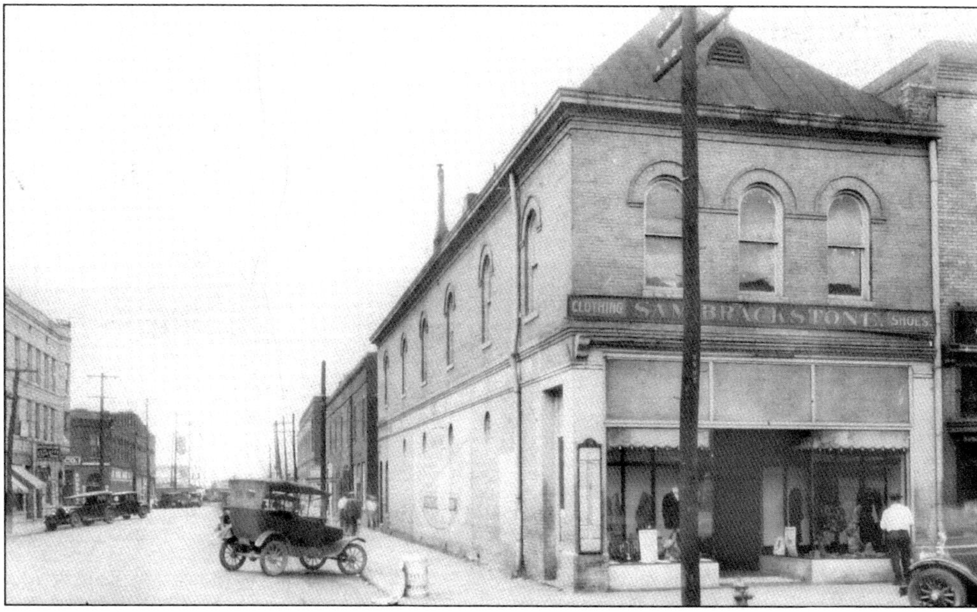


In 1898, Abe Rubel lost the distinction of sole Jewish merchant in Corinth when Samuel Brackstone emigrated from Russia and settled in the city. His department store, pictured here in the 1920s, is the present-day home of Clausel's Jewelry. One of Samuel's sons, LeRoy B. Brackstone, became a physician of some note in the Corinth and Alcorn County area and continued to practice general medicine until his death in 1985 at the age of 76.

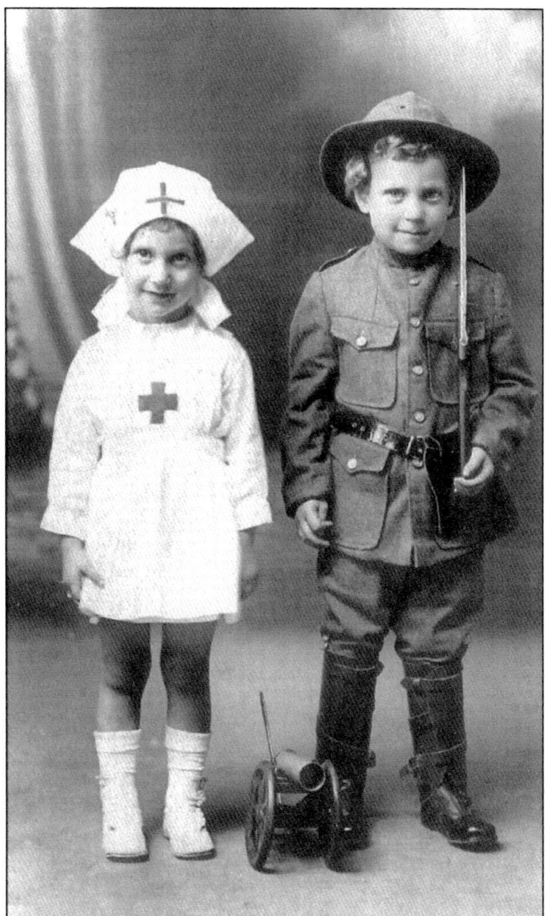

In 1918, during the early days of America's involvement in World War I, patriotic fervor was at its peak. Two of merchant Samuel Brakstone's children, Gloria and Fernand, are pictured in their World War I costumes. Fernand, with toy cannon at his feet and rifle shouldered at the ready, is dressed as a doughboy and waiting to answer his country's call to arms, while his sister Gloria, dressed as a Red Cross nurse, stands ready to render aid and comfort should the need arise.

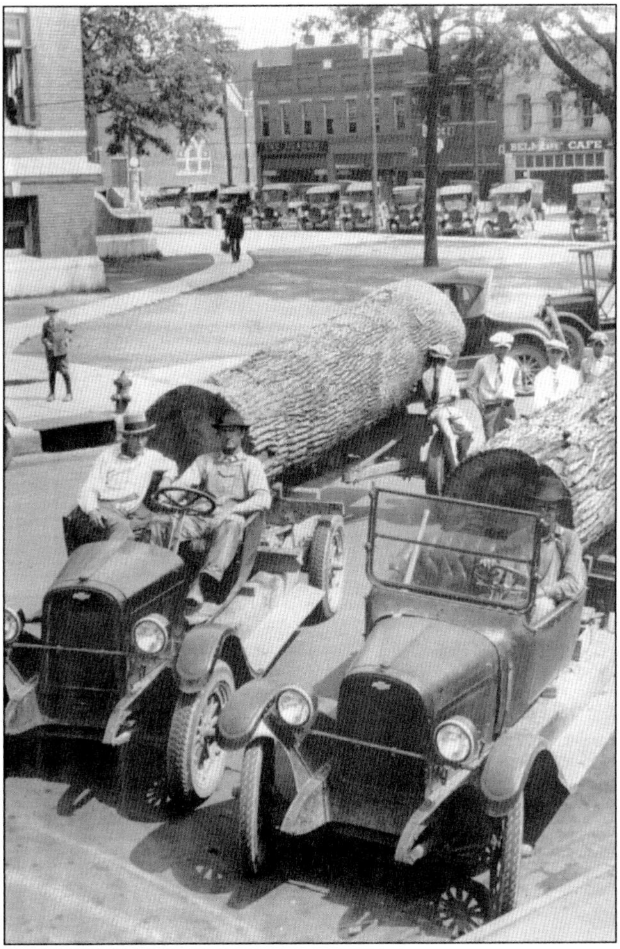

Logging was an important source of income for the local economy after the war. Sawmills, planing mills, and lumber companies provided building materials. Cabinet shops and furniture factories helped to furnish homes near and far, while more specialty products included barrels, cross arms for light and telegraph poles, and even caskets. By 1917, Corinth was the largest two-by-four market in the world and second in the South for the manufacturing of wood products.

Farmers within a 50-mile radius who relied on cotton as their cash crop brought their harvest directly to the buyers, whose offices were in the upper floors of buildings on Cruise and Waldron Streets. A total of 80 percent of the cotton bought came directly from the farmers, while the remaining 20 percent came from one of 14 gins located throughout the county and across the state. (Courtesy of Dr. William Jackson.)

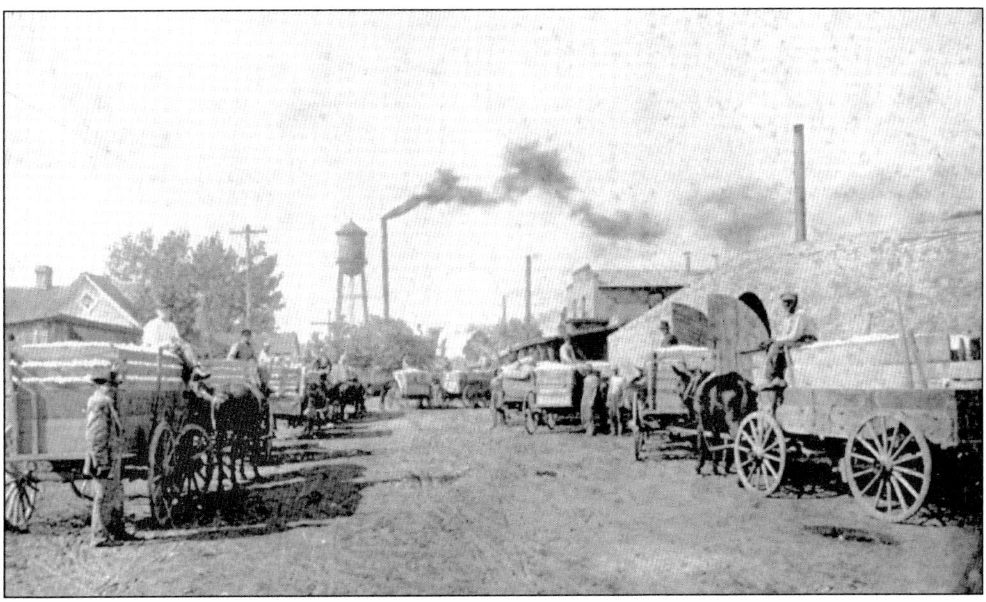

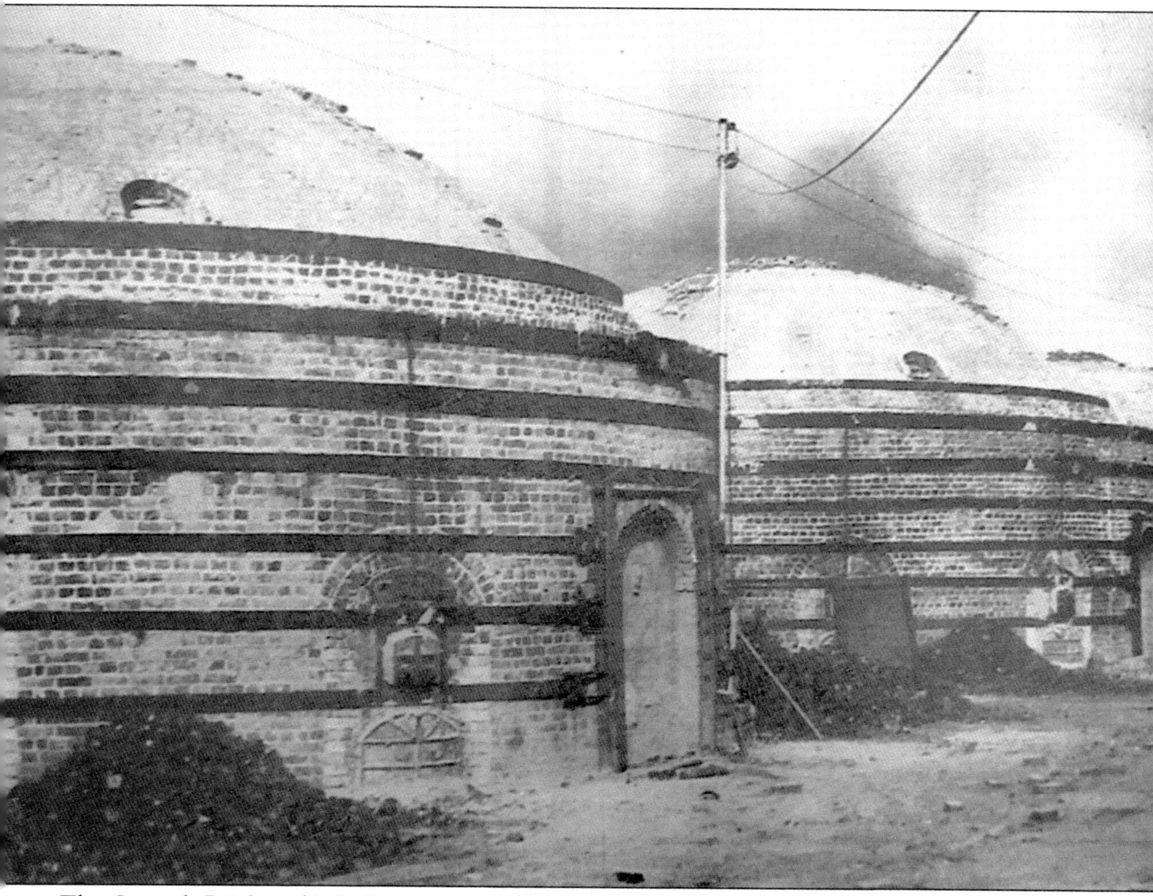

The Corinth Brick and Tile Company was located in west Corinth, where approximately two million bricks a month were manufactured using local clay, local wood, and coal for firing. As the only company of its kind within a 300-mile radius, the company enjoyed a sterling reputation for superior quality. The company's bricks were shipped to Oxford for use in the construction of buildings at the university, as well as throughout the neighboring states for more than 75 years. At its peak production, 12 kilns were in constant operation, and more than 100 people were employed.

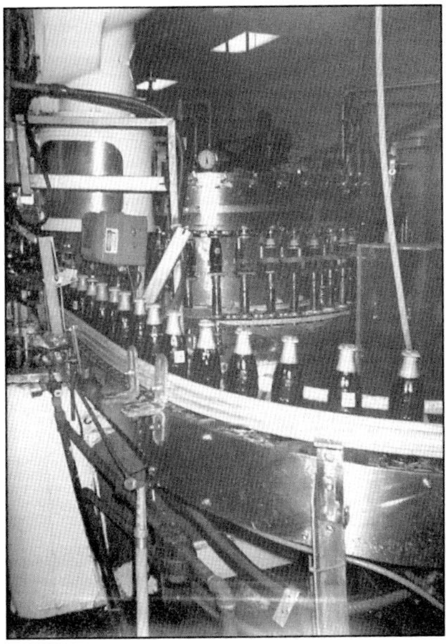

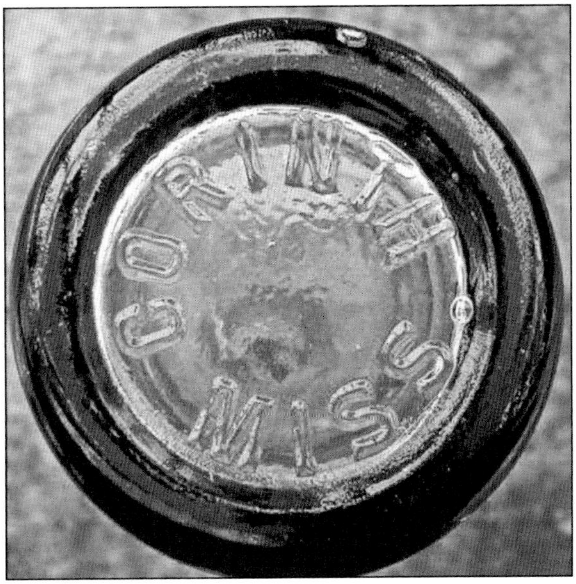


In 1905, Avon Kenneth Weaver bought an interest in a small soda water plant in Corinth, and in 1907 he assumed sole ownership of a company that has remained a family-owned business for over 100 years. Today, the current owners are the fourth generation to run this most American of companies. (Courtesy of Coca-Cola of Corinth.)

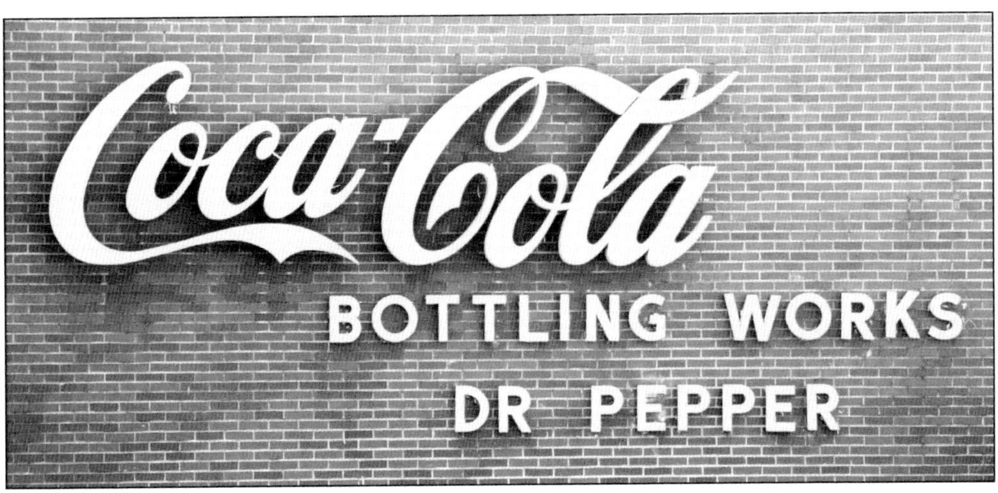

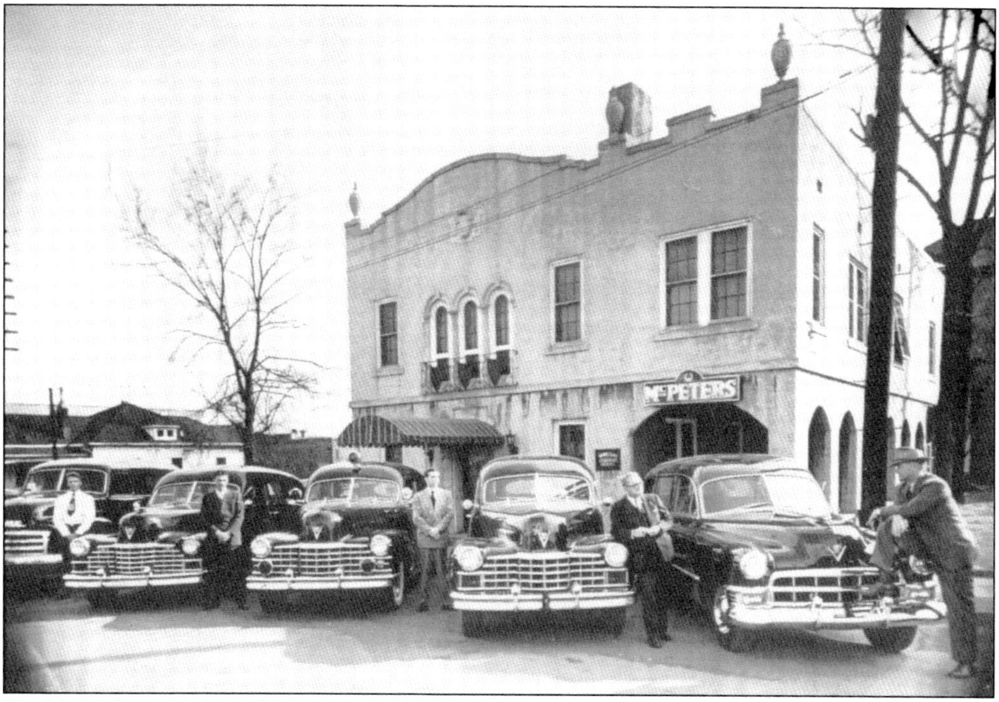


Established in 1905 by the McPeters family and Dave Hindman, McPeters was the first burial association in Mississippi to offer burial insurance and provide a variety of services to the community and surrounding areas. McPeters records show that the least expensive funeral was at a cost of 25¢. In 1954, J.R. "Bill" McPeters assumed sole control of the business.

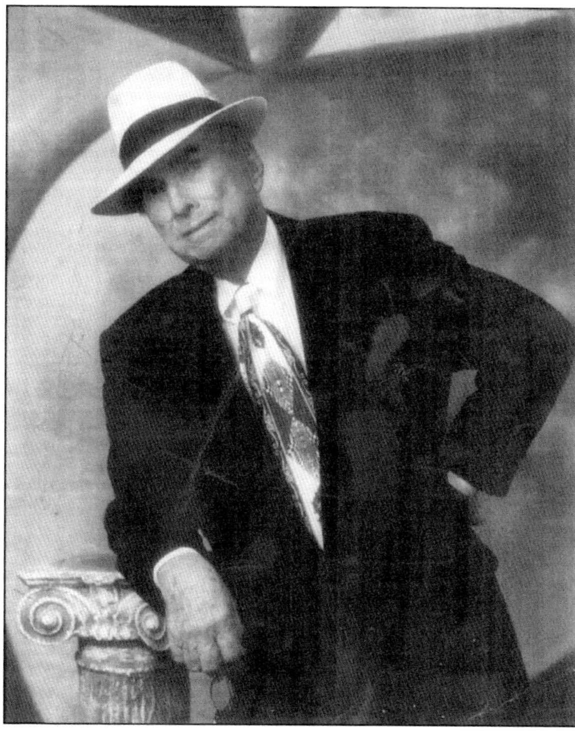

In addition to being a superb and professional funeral director, Bill McPeters has for years been considered by Corinthians to be a beloved town character. One can tell the natives from the newcomers when a remark is overheard, "I just saw a man wearing a tie for a belt and a purple fedora," or countless other fantastical eccentricities, to which the lifelong resident will proudly reply, "Oh, that's just Bill!" (Courtesy of LuAnne Parrish.)

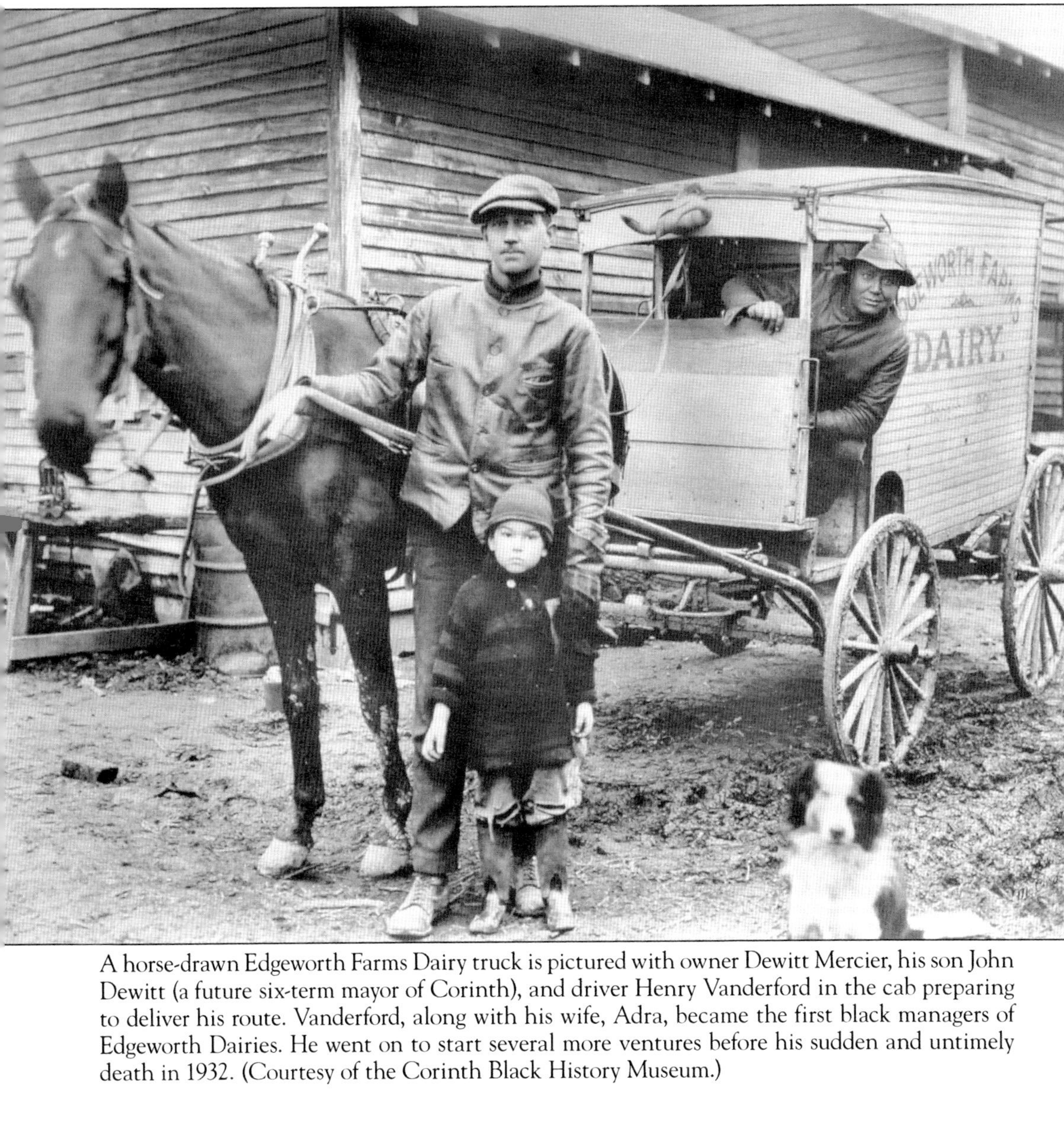


A horse-drawn Edgeworth Farms Dairy truck is pictured with owner Dewitt Mercier, his son John Dewitt (a future six-term mayor of Corinth), and driver Henry Vanderford in the cab preparing to deliver his route. Vanderford, along with his wife, Adra, became the first black managers of Edgeworth Dairies. He went on to start several more ventures before his sudden and untimely death in 1932. (Courtesy of the Corinth Black History Museum.)

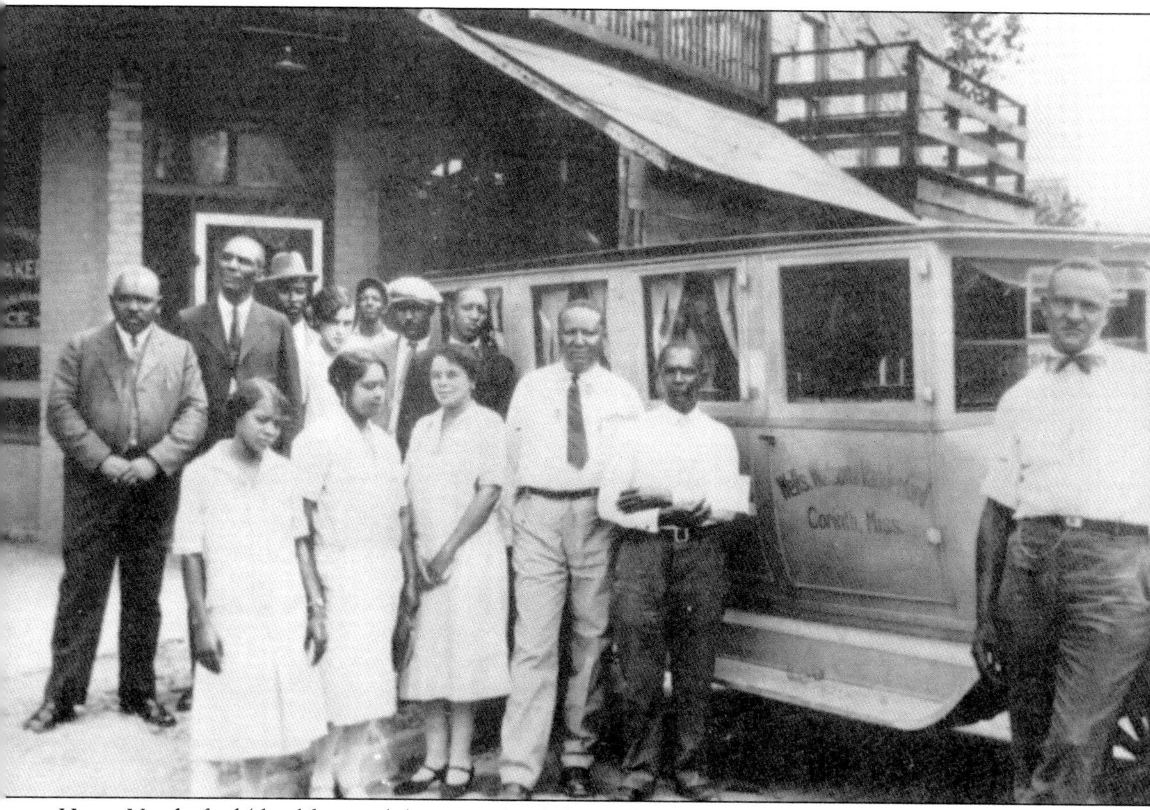

Henry Vanderford (third from right), pictured with his staff, was one of Corinth's earliest undertakers. He began his training in business by overseeing the operations of Edgeworth Farms, and he later joined Goldie Wells and J.P. Watson in an undertaking business serving Corinth's African American community. Upon his death at the age of 45 on Christmas day in 1932, the *Daily Corinthian* heralded him as "the best known member of his race in (the) locality."

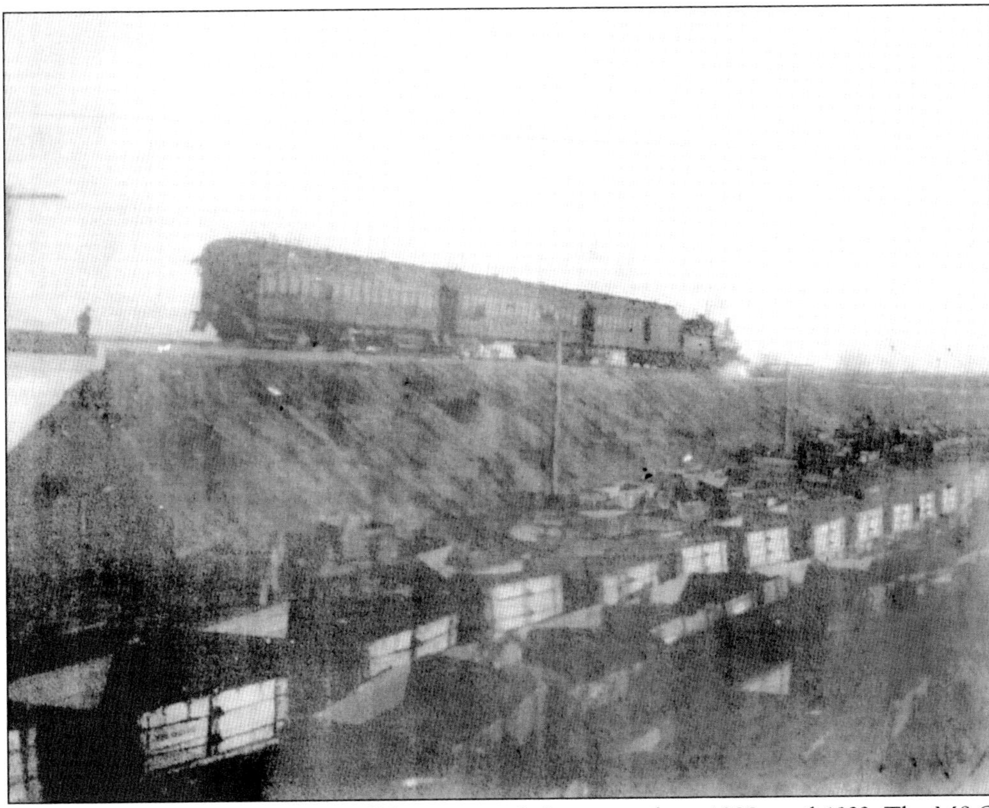

The Illinois Central Railroad *Doodlebug*, pictured above, ran from 1908 until 1933. The M&O *Doodlebug*, pictured below, ran from the 1920s through the 1950s and would even stop long enough for passengers and crew to eat a hasty meal at nearby cafes. Both lines were special accommodation trains that shuttled local travelers between Corinth, Mississippi, and Birmingham, Alabama, with designated stops along the way.

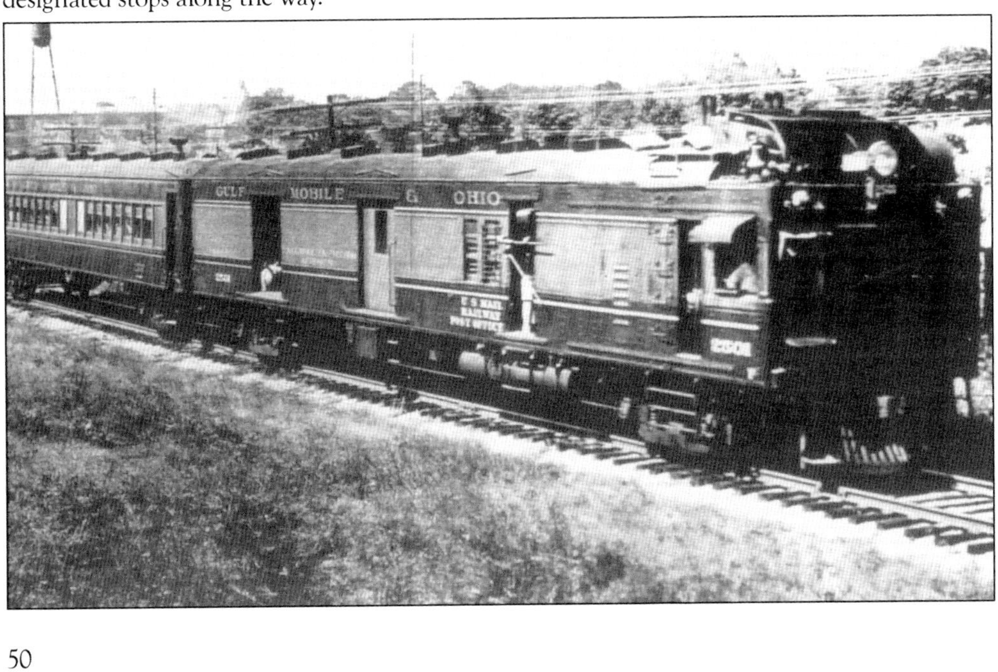

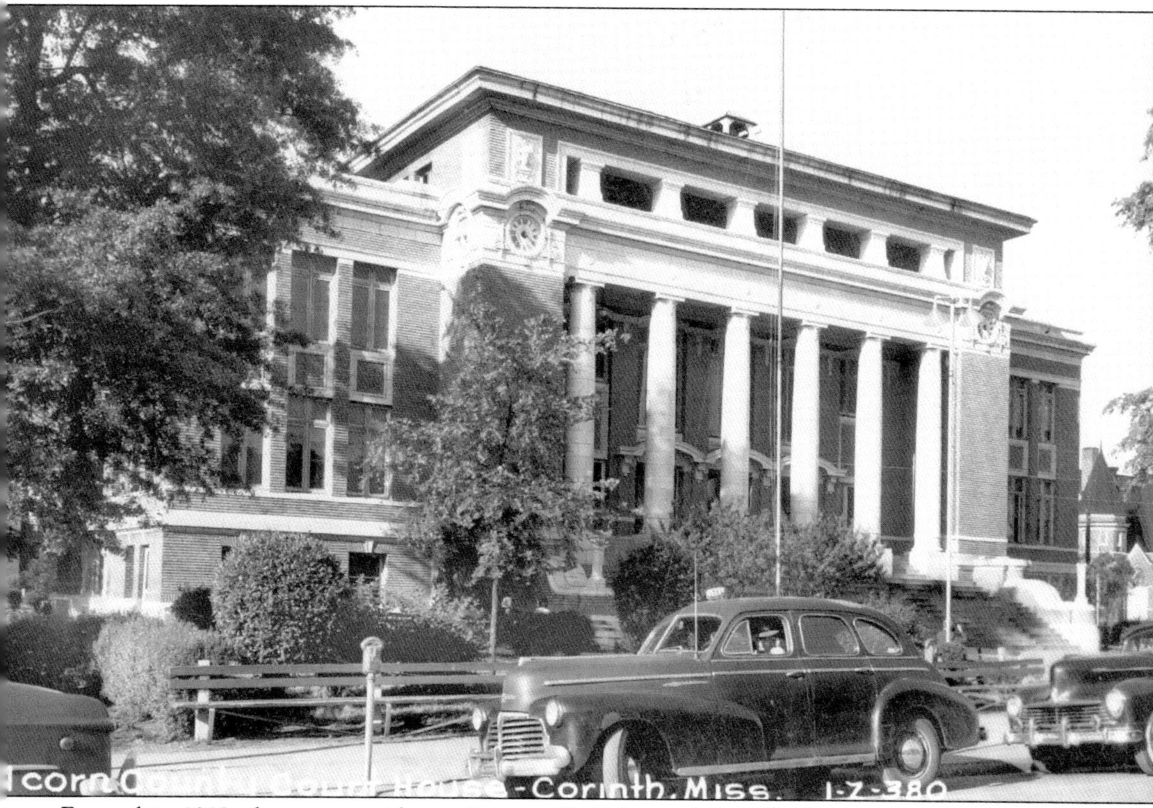

Erected in 1918, the current Alcorn County Courthouse has N.W. Overstreet listed as the architect and E.G. Parish listed as the builder on the bronze plaque located at the entrance. Colonial Revival in style and constructed of tan bricks with white stone trim, this is the third courthouse to occupy court square. The first was a two-story frame structure, but it was replaced by a redbrick structure in 1880, which itself was lost to fire in 1917.

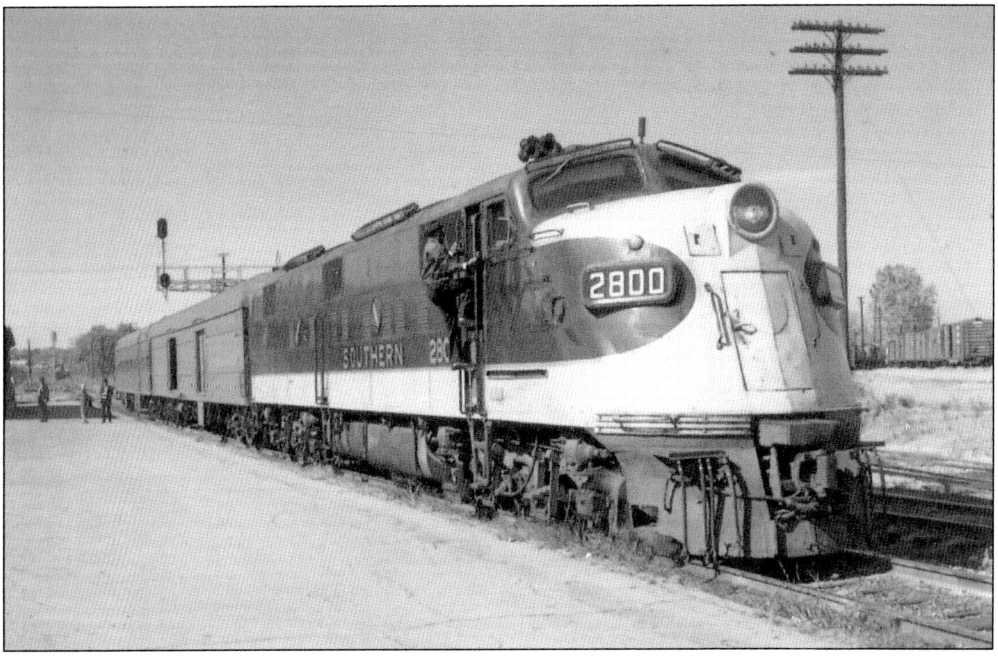


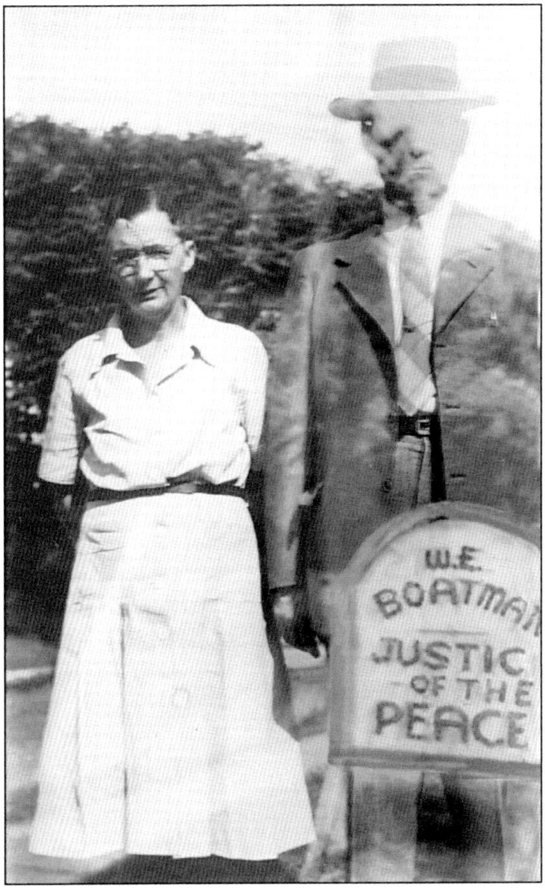


In the golden era of rail travel, Corinth saw a virtual explosion in couples from all points of the compass making Mississippi their matrimonial destination of choice. With no waiting period, no blood tests, and no residency requirements, thousands of couples made Corinth the "marriage capital" of the country. If they arrived by day, the courthouse was a mere four-block walk from the train station. After-hours, a short taxi ride would deliver the couple to the door of the local justice of the peace, who would marry the couple posthaste. Judge W.E. Boatman and his wife pose at left by the sign in the front yard of their residence. In over 20 years holding the position, Judge Boatman performed hundreds of nuptials in front of his living room mantle with Mrs. Luna Boatman serving as witness.

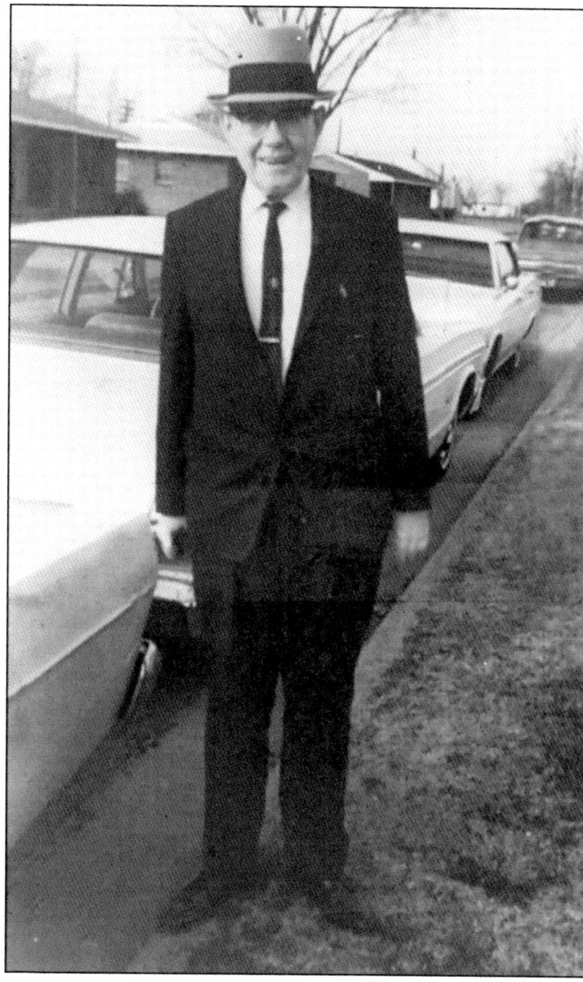

Over his tenure as justice of the peace from the late 1940s until his death in 1969, W.E. Boatman once estimated that he had performed in excess of 5,000 ceremonies. Pictured below is his business card. Instead of posting a set fee for the service, when asked after the ceremony by the newly wedded groom how much he was owed, Judge Boatman would always reply, "Whatever she's worth to you, son!"

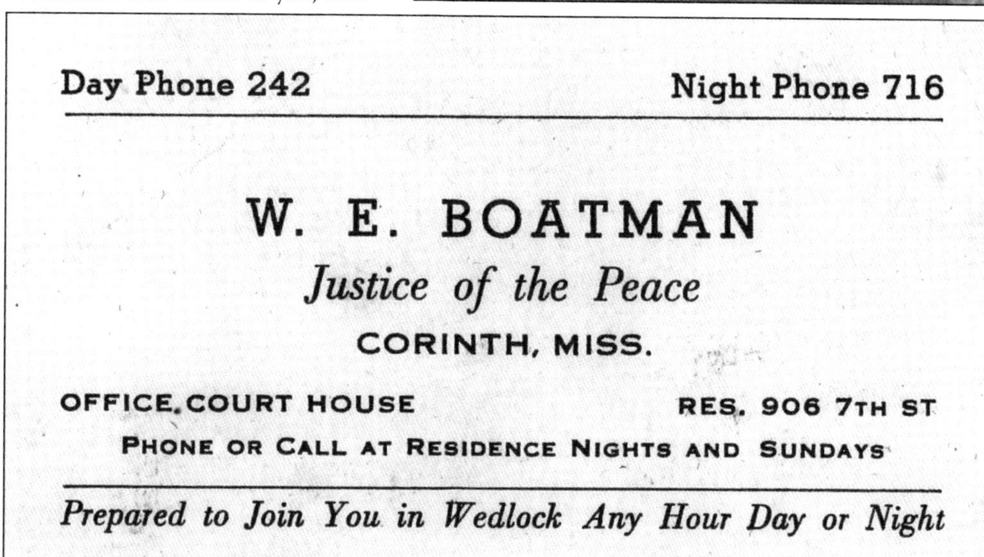

**Day Phone 242** **Night Phone 716**

**W. E. BOATMAN**

*Justice of the Peace*

CORINTH, MISS.

OFFICE, COURT HOUSE RES. 906 7TH ST

PHONE OR CALL AT RESIDENCE NIGHTS AND SUNDAYS

***Prepared to Join You in Wedlock Any Hour Day or Night***

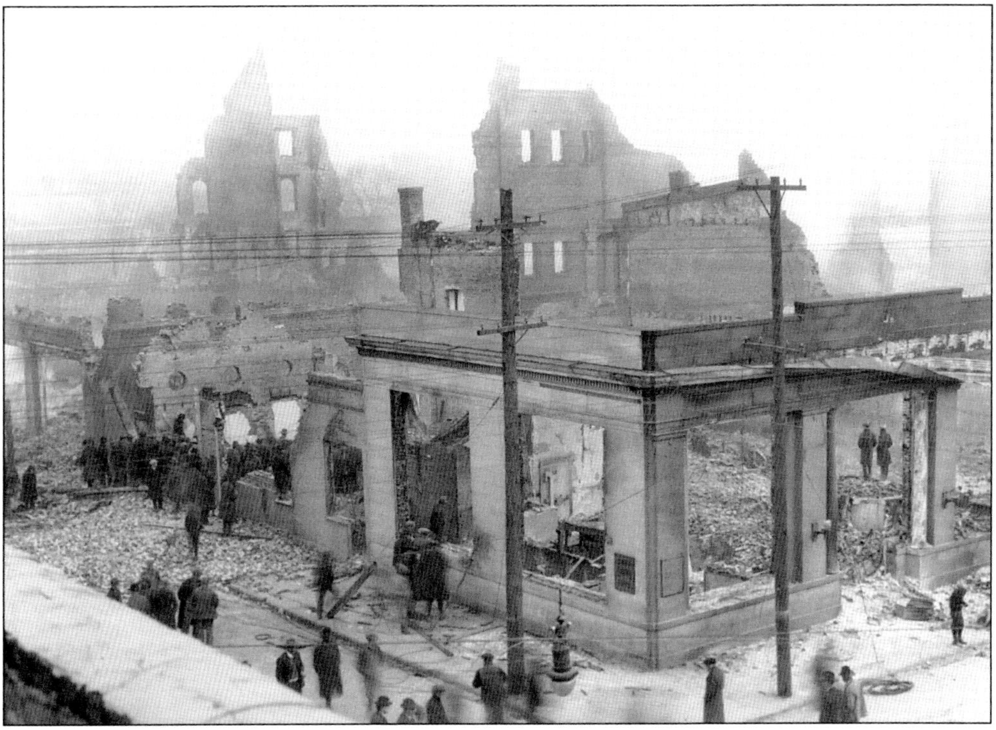

On December 28, 1924, the block bounded by Fillmore, Foote, Franklin, and Waldron Streets was completely destroyed when fire broke out in the early morning hours. A number of downtown businesses, including The Opera Building, were a total loss. The post office across the street was severely damaged, but was ultimately saved by the heroic actions of the Corinth Volunteer Fire Department, the local postmaster, and several of his employees. All told, the damage incurred was estimated to be at least $1.75 million.

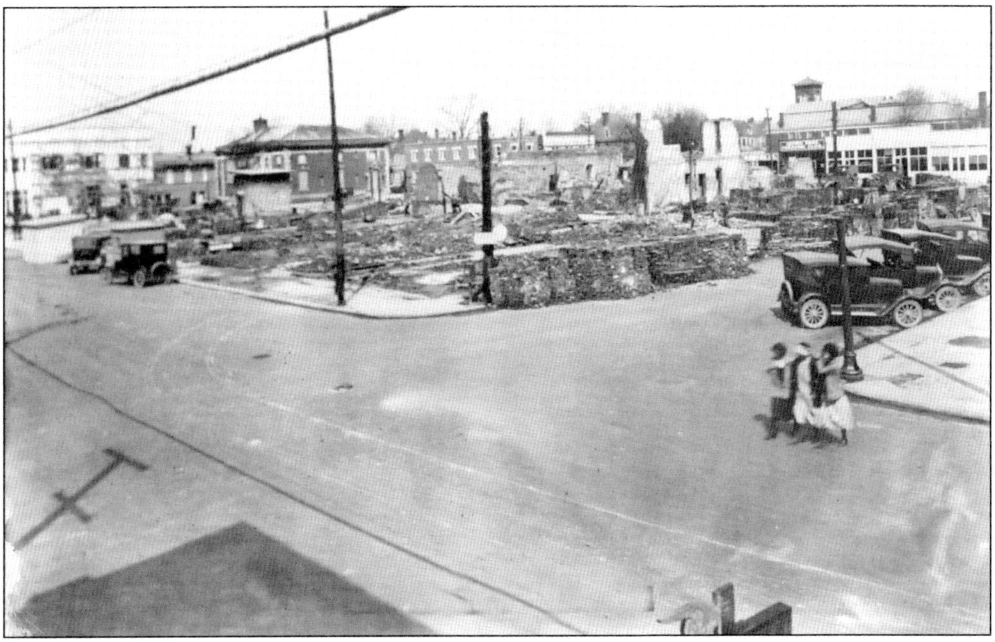

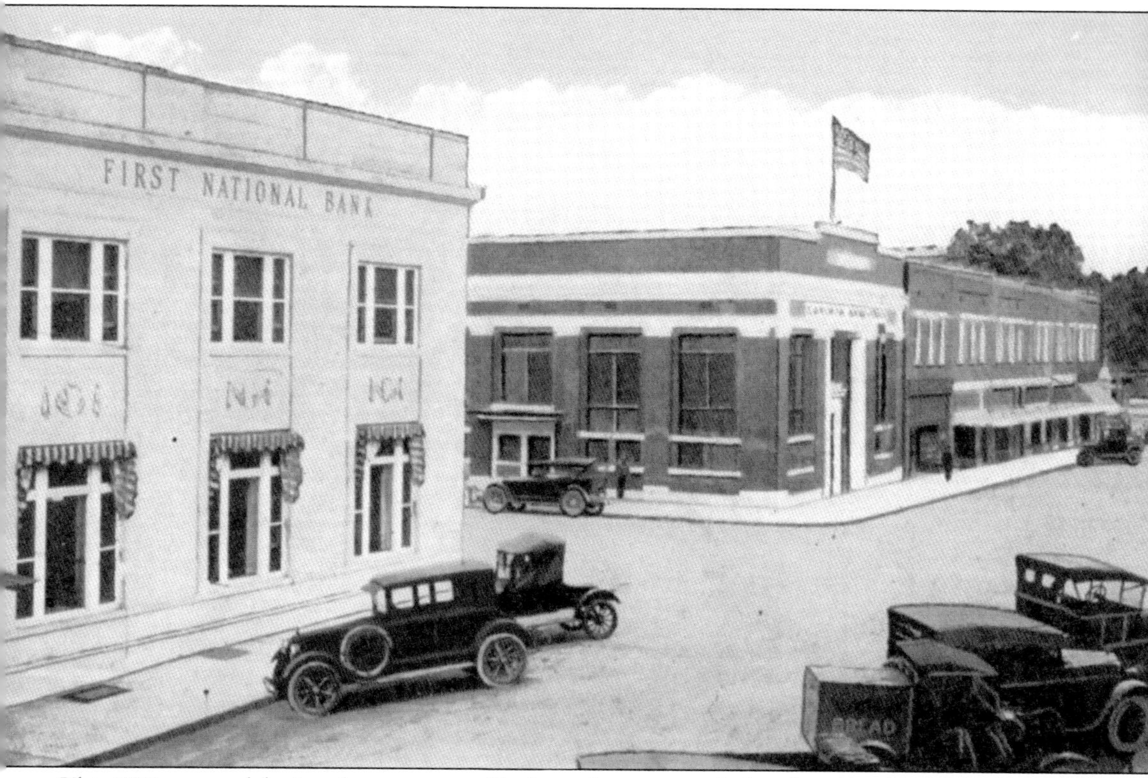


This 1926 postcard depicts the two square blocks as they appeared after they were lost to the Great Fire of 1924. Much like a phoenix rising from the ashes, downtown Corinth once again became a flourishing site of commerce. In time, the First National Bank became the National Bank of Commerce; in later years, the Security Bank (across the street) became Regions Bank and moved across the street from the courthouse. Today, the former Security Bank building is home to the Alcorn County Chancery Clerk's Office. (Courtesy of Dr. William Jackson.)

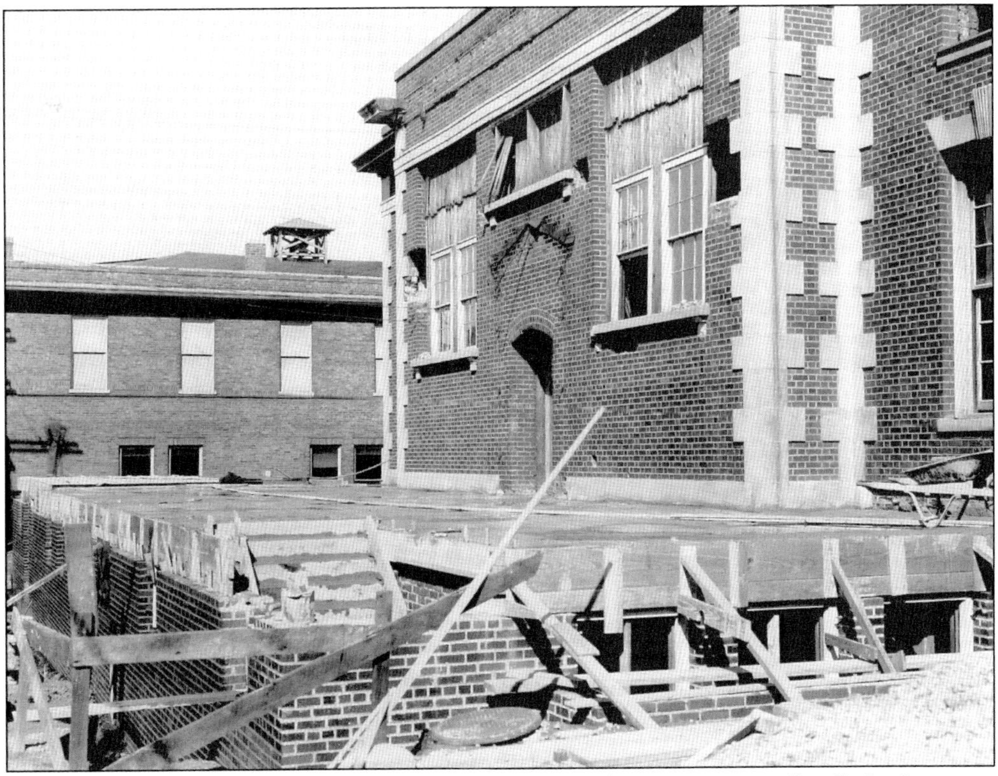

In the Great Fire of 1924, the postal employees managed to save practically all the furniture and carried the mail to safety because of their heroic efforts. The Corinth Post Office was all but gutted and so extensively damaged that a complete restoration was necessary. At that time, the foundation was repaired and substantially strengthened, and a loading dock was added to accommodate the growing mail volume.

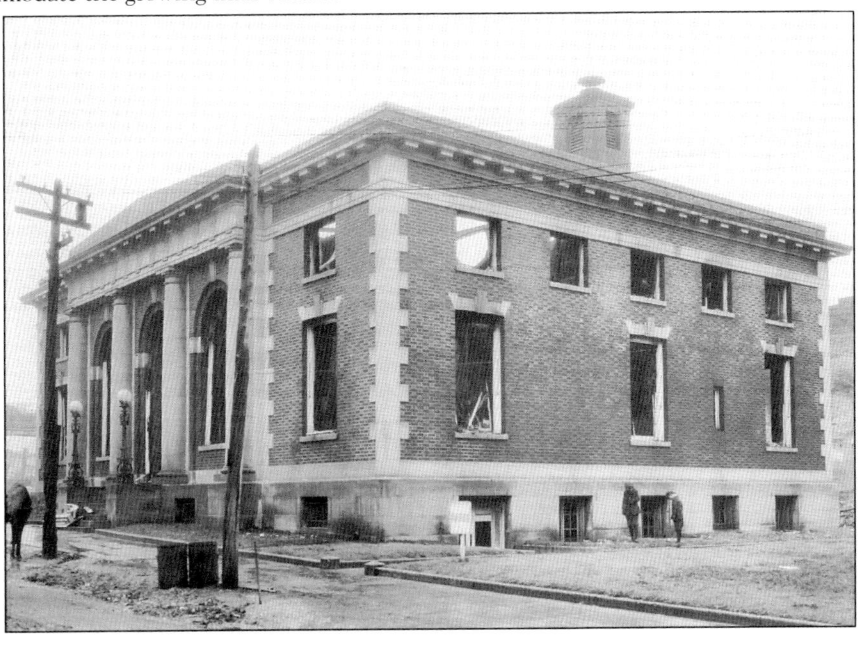

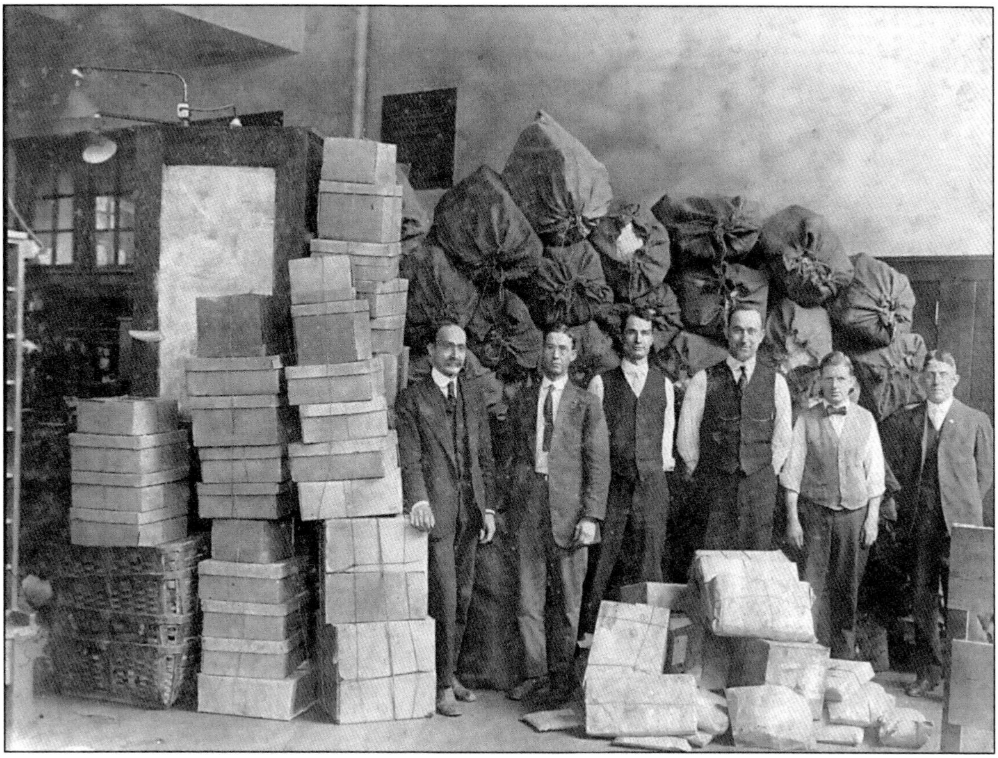

In 503 B.C., Herodotus wrote what would later become the unofficial motto of the US Postal Service, "Neither rain, nor snow, nor heat, nor gloom of darkest night shall stay these faithful couriers from the swift completion of their appointed rounds." Employees in three separate crafts, such as clerks who sort the mail, city carriers who deliver mail on walking routes to city residents, and rural carriers who deliver to patrons outside the city environs by car, worked in the old post office until moving to a larger facility in 1986.

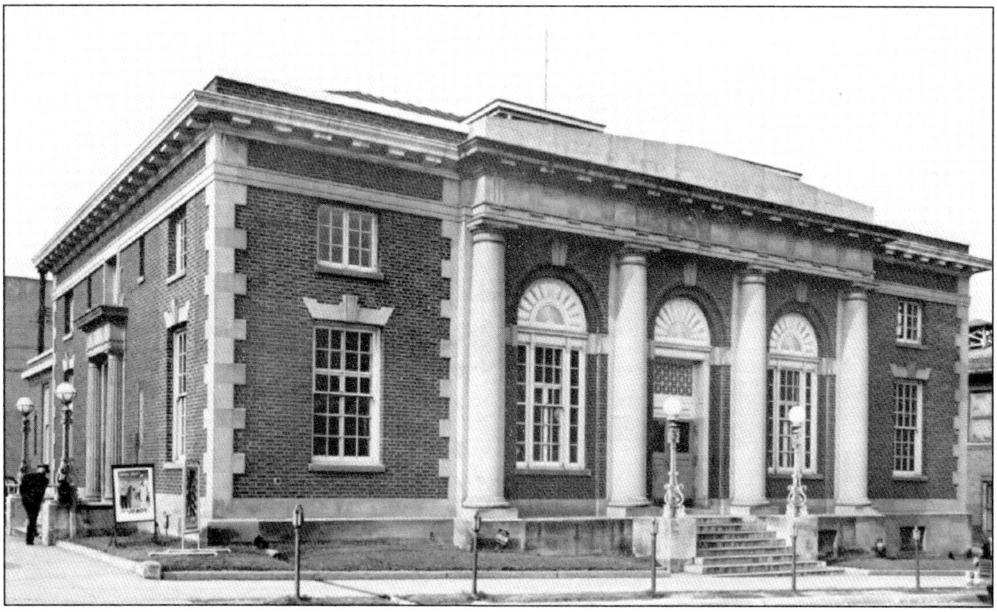

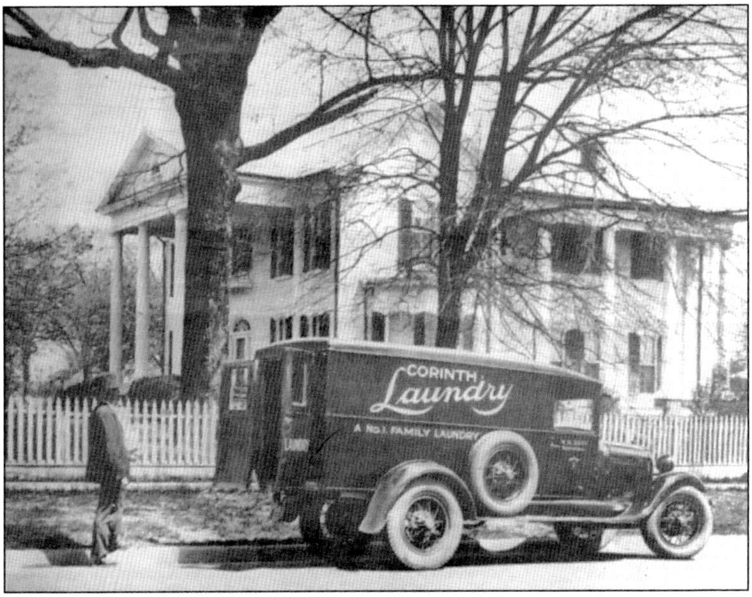


In the mid-20th century, after women began working in local factories like Weaver's Pants Company and before every home had a washer and dryer, several laundry businesses operated in town. Most notable of these businesses was Corinth Laundry, which delivered patrons' clothes freshly washed, ironed, and folded right to their door.

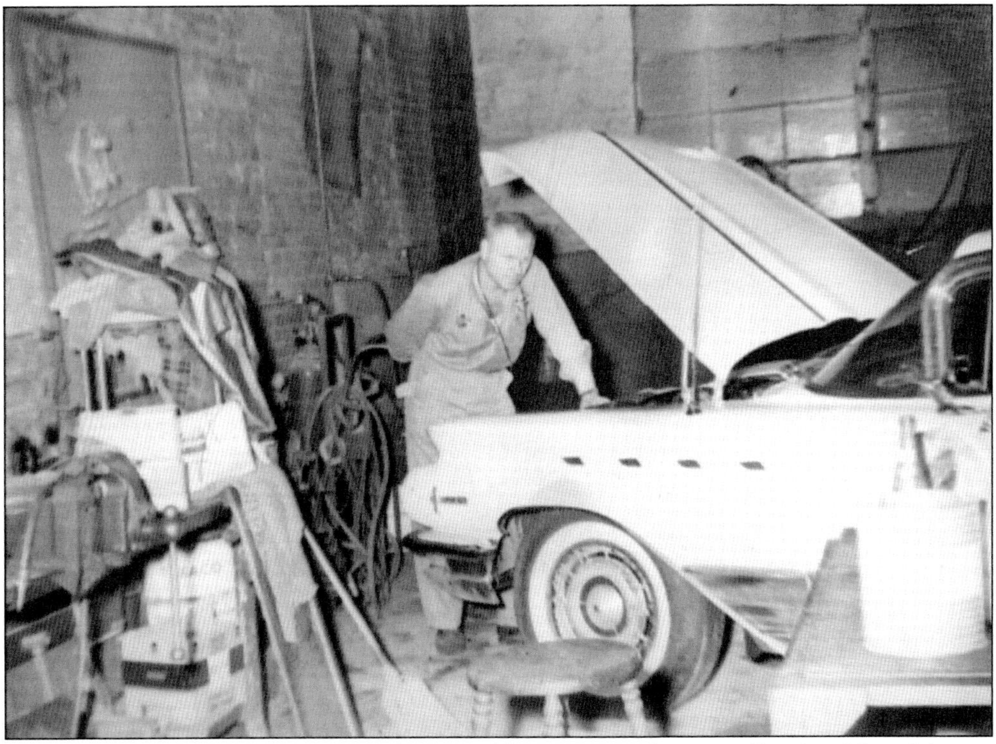

Pictured sometime in the 1950s is mechanic Ackle Garrett working on a Buick at Heyer Motors. As a master sergeant in the Army Air Corps during World War II, Ackle served as crew chief on a B-52 bomber in the Pacific theater. His wartime experience enabled him to moonlight from time to time and work on the airplane engines of local pilots at the Roscoe Turner Airport while maintaining a full-time position at Heyer Motors for over 40 years. (Courtesy of Donna G. Baird.)

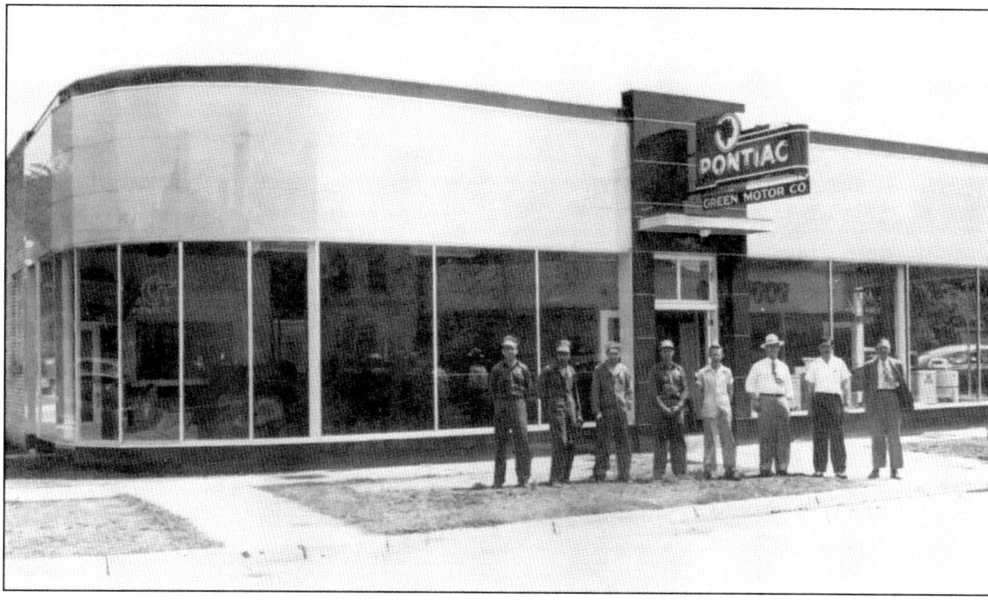


Founded as a Pontiac dealership in 1937 by Hillie Arthur Green, Green Motor Company's Art Deco headquarters stood at the corner of Foote and Webster Streets in the heart of downtown Corinth. Very much a family business, Green Motor saw three generations of Green men doing business at that location. A 1955 photograph shows, from left to right, employees Joe Gurley, Johnnie R. Miller, Warren H. Miller, Rob Doran, an unknown parts man, Hillie's sons John Hillie and Leroy, and founder Hillie Green.

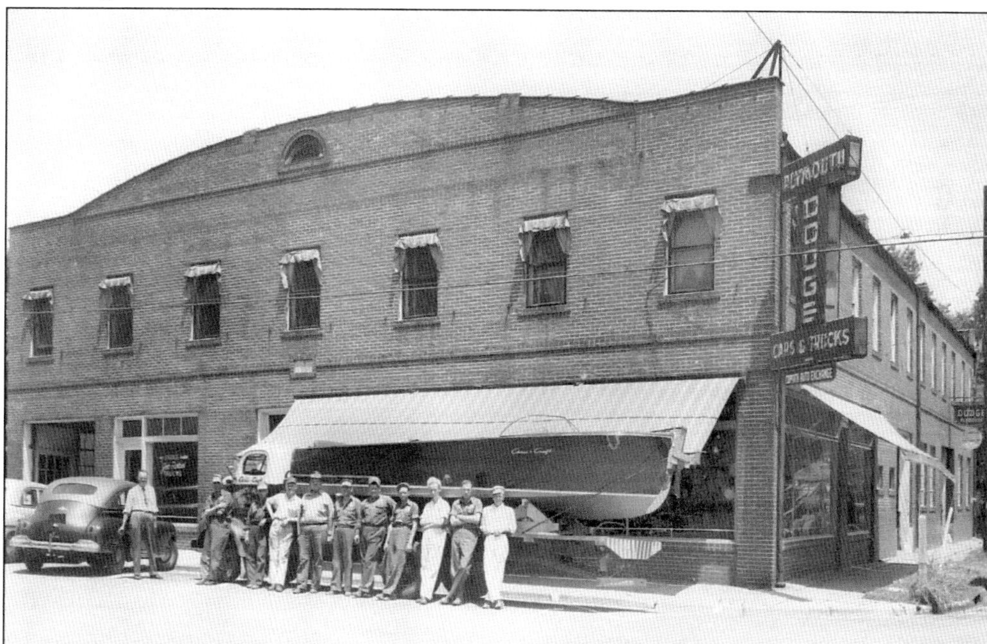


An unidentified group of dealers, mechanics, salesmen, and customers poses by a classic Criss Craft sports boat parked in front of the Corinth Auto Exchange Plymouth and Dodge Dealership. Vice President J.W. "Jimmy" Burns looks on from the far left in this late-1940s photograph. (Courtesy of Donna G. Baird.)

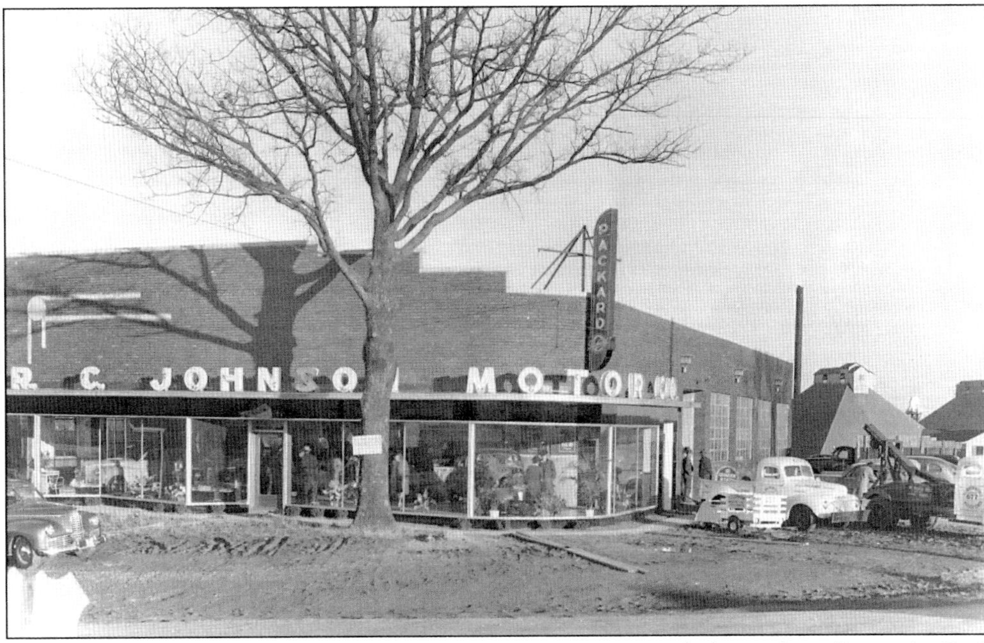


R.C. and Price Johnson were brothers, sometime partners, and always-friendly rivals. Each man had dealerships from the 1930s through the 1960s. In the 1940s, they stood directly across Highway 72 from each other, as seen in the photograph below of the interior of R.C.'s showroom with Price's sign prominently visible through the window. At various times, R.C. sold Ford, Nash, and Packard automobiles, as well as used cars, while Price sold Oldsmobiles and Cadillacs his entire career. Both men would have sons who followed them into the car business: R.C.'s son, R.C. "Buddy" Johnson Jr., and Price's sons, William and V.P. "Dude" Johnson. All of them had successful careers as car salesmen. Nephews Max and Wilford "Bud" Johnson were also brothers and second-generation salesmen. (Courtesy of Steve Johnson.)

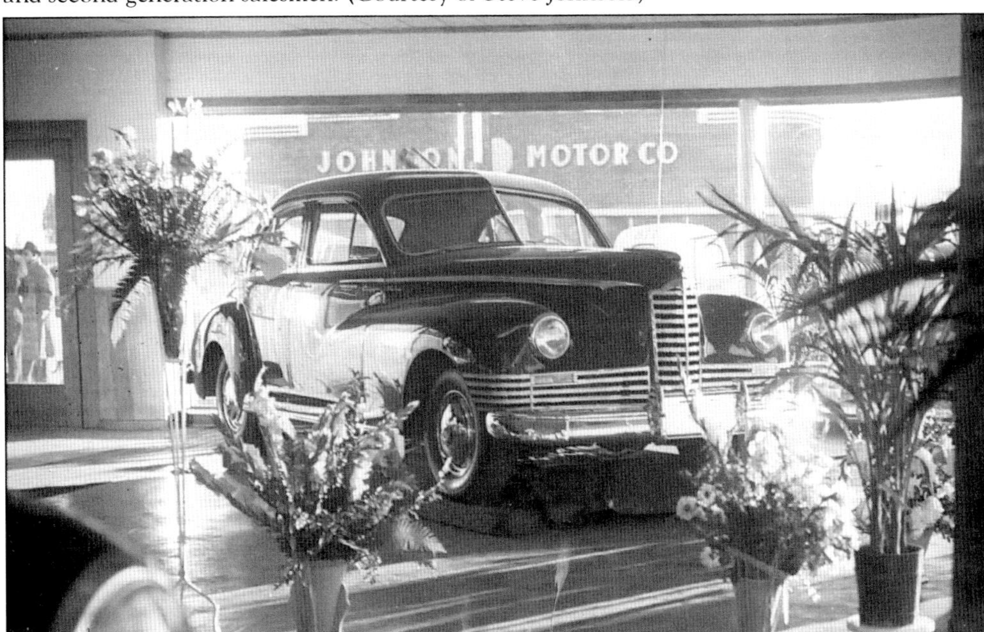

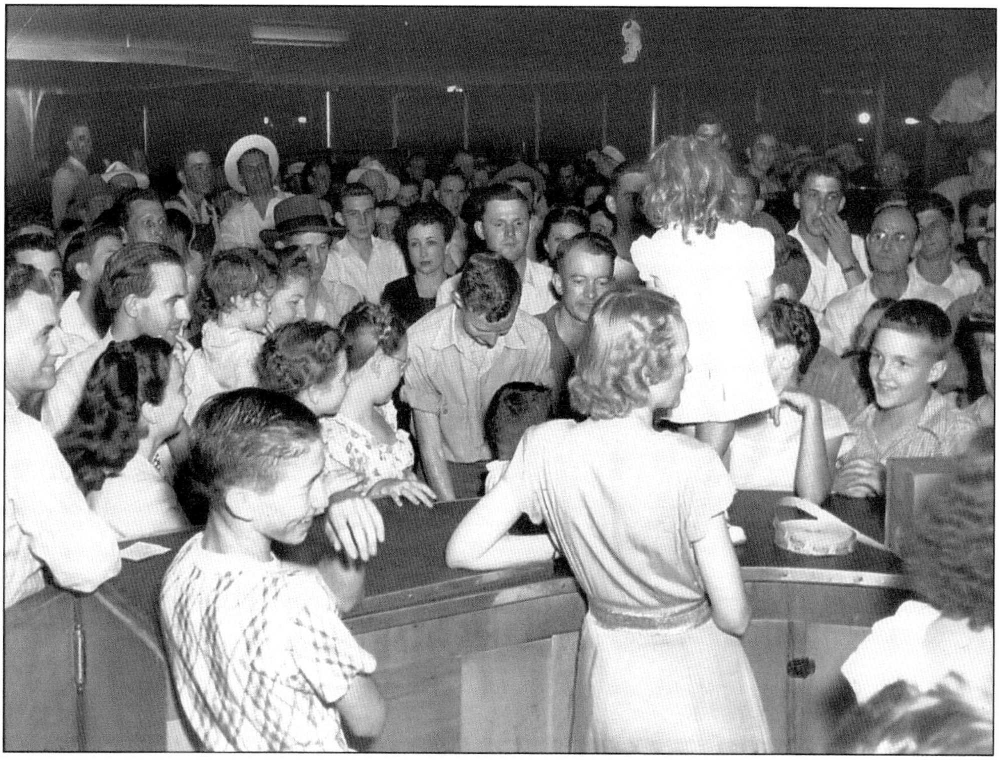

Brothers R.C. and Price Johnson opened identical buildings directly across Highway 72 from each other. R.C. had the Packard dealership while Price sold Cadillacs and Oldsmobiles. Sometime in early 1940, a raffle held to mark the grand opening of R.C. Johnson Motors shows a large crowd eagerly focused on the unidentified little girl standing atop the counter as she prepares to draw the winning ticket. (Courtesy of Steve Johnson.)

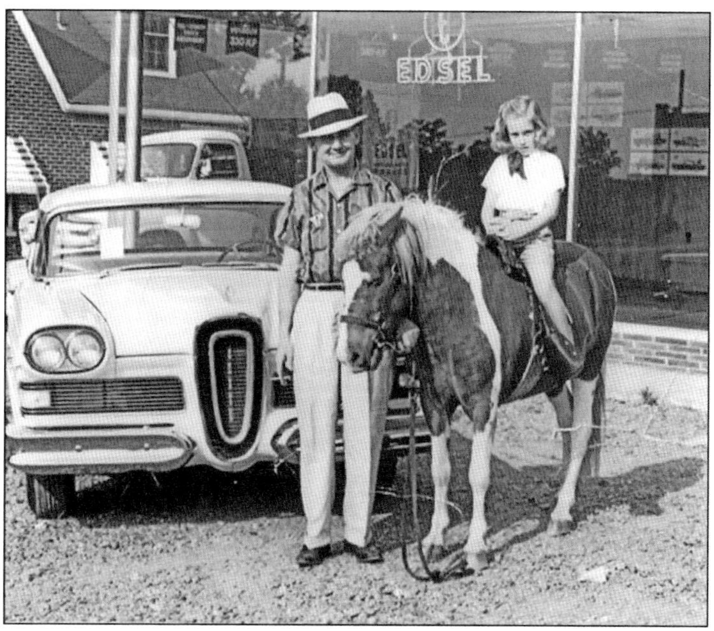


Ever a showman, R.C. Johnson would take almost anything in trade, as evidenced by the pony he accepted as an Edsel dealer. According to his nephew James "Sonny" Boatman, "Uncle R.C. had been known to take goats, pigs, chickens, and just about any other type of livestock you could imagine." In one memorable trade-in, he took worms—although he did not fish—and managed to sell them at a profit to a bait shop. (Courtesy of Steve Johnson.)

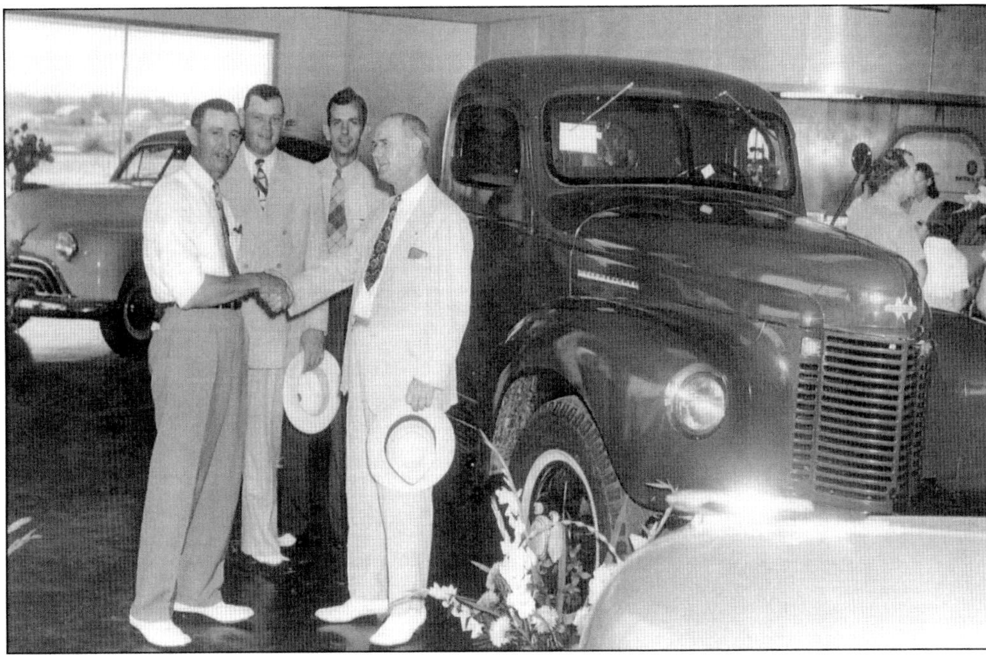

According to family lore, Price was able to stage his grand opening in 1939 by "hijacking" the signage intended for the front of R.C.'s building. When the work crew arrived to install the Art Deco lettering, R.C. was nowhere to be found, so Price instructed them to put the sign on his building instead, thereby stealing a march on his younger brother. Pictured in the showroom at the 1939 grand opening of Johnson Motor Company are, from left to right, Price Johnson, son William, brother-in-law and partner Lew Miller, and unidentified. (Courtesy of LuAnne Parrish.)

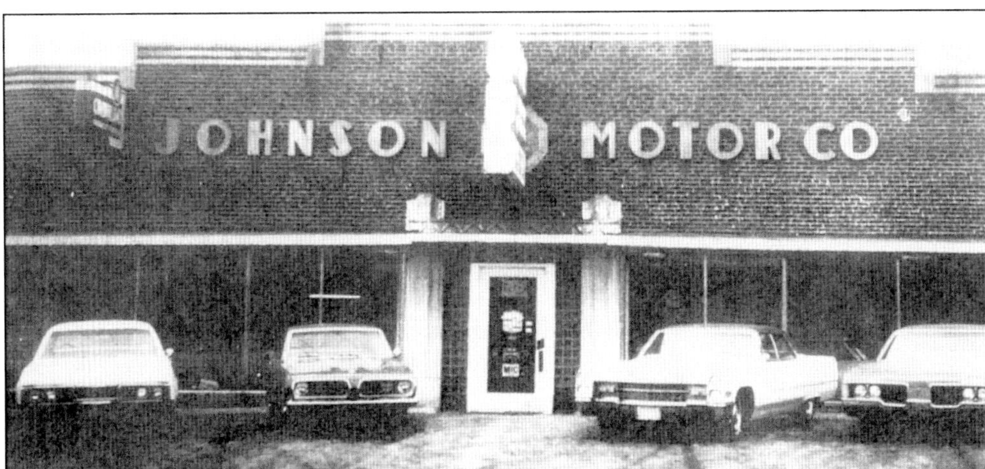

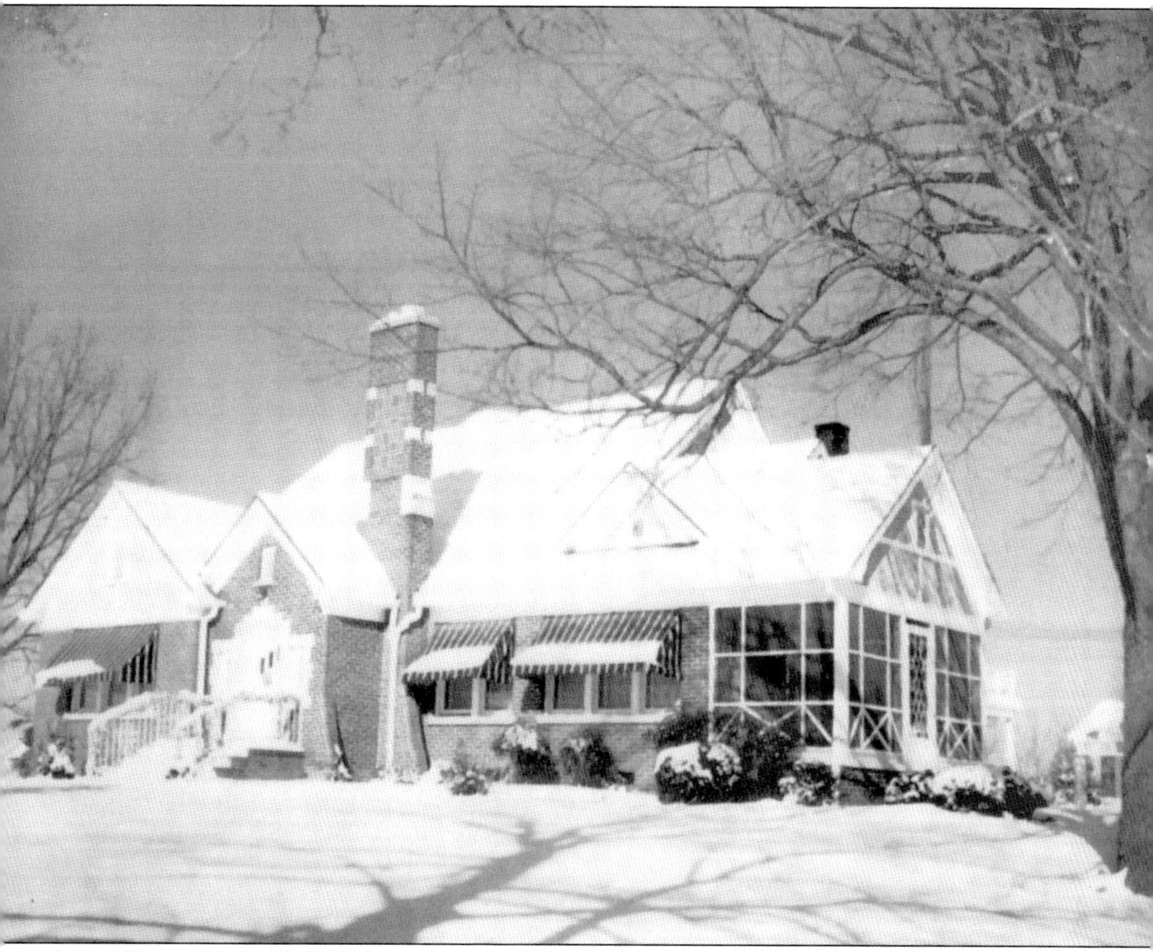

In a February 28, 1985, *Daily Corinthian* article titled "Down Memory Lane," Dr. E.A. "Boogie," White III is quoted as saying, "Well, now, Dude (Johnson) won't tell you this, but his father's house was such an attractive and exemplary Mississippi home, that for years it appeared in the Mississippi History textbooks. They had an example of a 'typical' house—it was anything but typical."

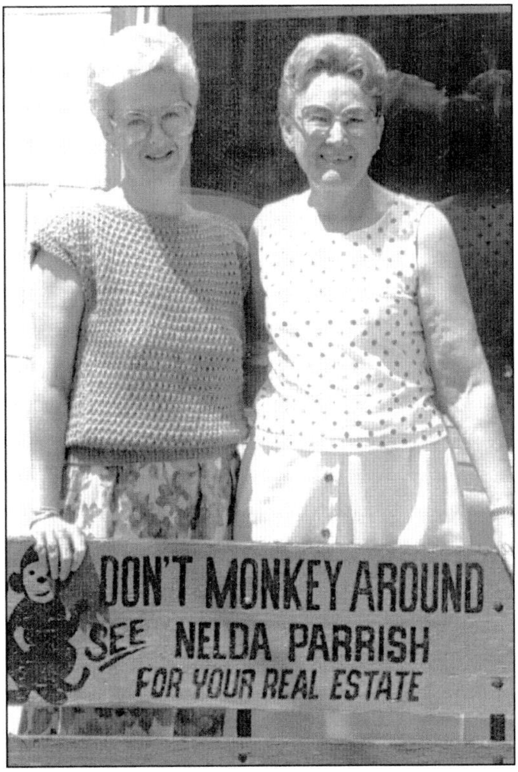


In addition to other varied positions, Corinth's first female realtor, Nelda Parrish, accepted a position with the Alcorn County Vo-Tech to teach an introductory class in real estate throughout the 1970s and 1980s. This weekly night class allowed several hundred locals to educate themselves about real estate and brought a new generation of professionals to the rank of local realtors. When asked once why she would help those who might become her competition, she replied, "The cream will always rise to the top, regardless." If she was going to have competition, she wanted her competition to be knowledgeable, professional, and ethical; therefore, she could think of no better way to insure that goal than to teach them herself. As a result, Bailey Williams, president of the Corinth Board of Realtors at the time, awarded her the sobriquet "Mother of Corinth Real Estate." Pictured are Susanne Kiddy on the left and Nelda Parrish on the right. (Courtesy of LuAnne Parrish.)

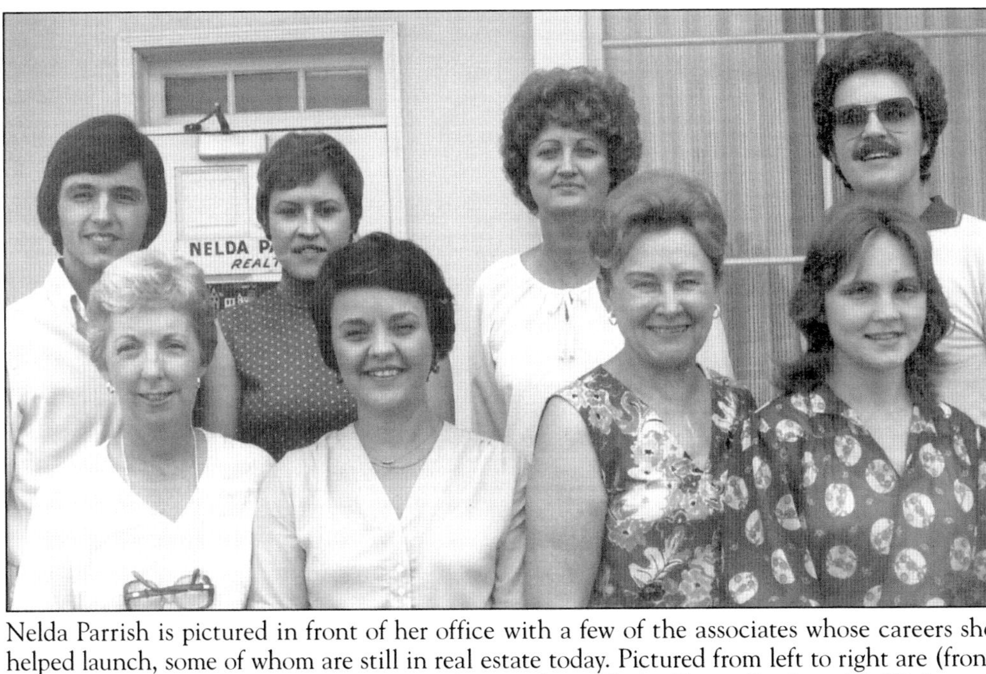

Nelda Parrish is pictured in front of her office with a few of the associates whose careers she helped launch, some of whom are still in real estate today. Pictured from left to right are (front row) Mary Jean Pittman, Ann Castile, Nelda Parrish, and Judy Glenn; (back row) Jeff Johnson, Ladana Hardin, JoAnn Mann, and Truman Dawson. (Courtesy of LuAnne Parrish.)

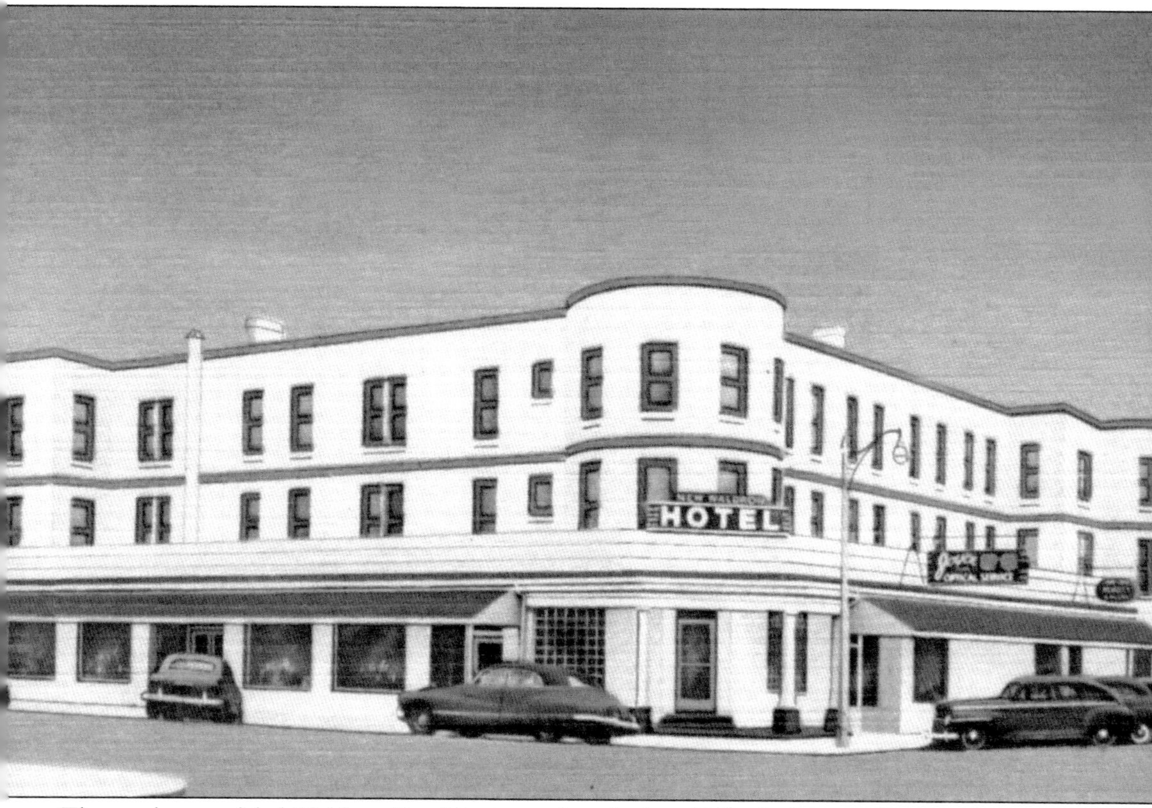


The newly remodeled Waldron Hotel is pictured in the late 1940s. In her recollections from an unpublished memoir, Nelda Boatman Parrish described the Waldron Hotel's ambiance, writing, "It was owned by the McCullar family and stood directly across the street from the courthouse, which was the hub of all activities at this time. It was the 'place to eat' in town and was operated by Mrs. Kate McCullar who tasted all the cooking. You were served on a freshly ironed tablecloth with cloth napkins and a wait staff dressed in crisp white coats. You always felt like you had the very best of service. When I married and moved to California, I learned to cook using the cook book *How We Cook in Corinth* and I always chose Mrs. McCullar's receipts as they assured a good turn out!"

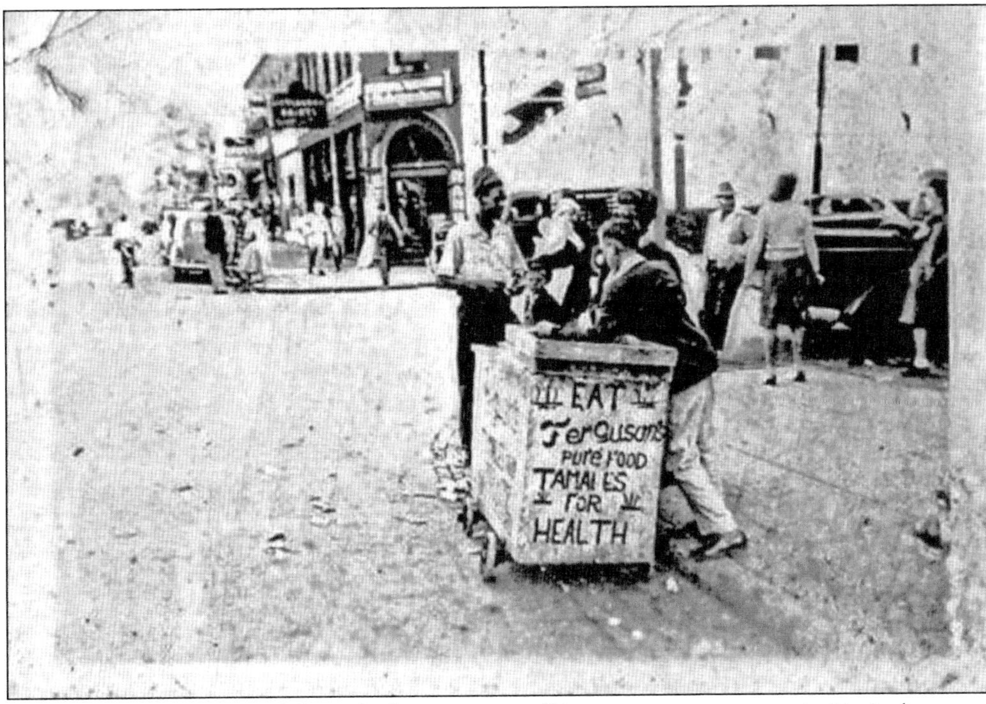


Claiborne Ferguson, one of the early downtown small-business entrepreneurs in Corinth, owned and operated a fish market and one of the city's earliest hot tamale stands. Ferguson was in fierce competition with other vendors selling sandwiches, fried chicken, and a myriad of other delicacies to passengers on the trains regularly stopping as they passed through town.

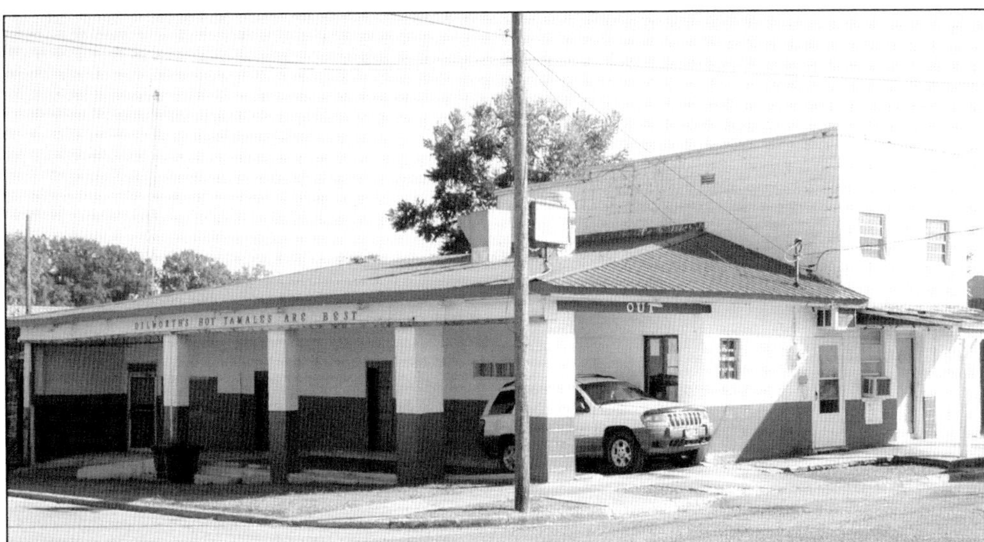


Although Ferguson's Tamale Wagon has joined passenger trains as a fond memory of a bygone era, Corinthians still have a place to go for homemade tamales whenever the craving strikes. In its current location for several decades and operated by generations of the family, Dilworth's Tamales even offers customers the convenience of a drive-thru window when nothing will satisfy but a Dilworth's Tamale.

Right in the beating heart of downtown Corinth, hard by the railroad tracks, stands the city's oldest and most unpretentious cafe. Since 1959, Corinthians from all walks of life have come to indulge their taste buds with the "Big Harold" burger and some of Miss Peggy's world-renowned banana pudding. (Courtesy of Katie Briggs.)

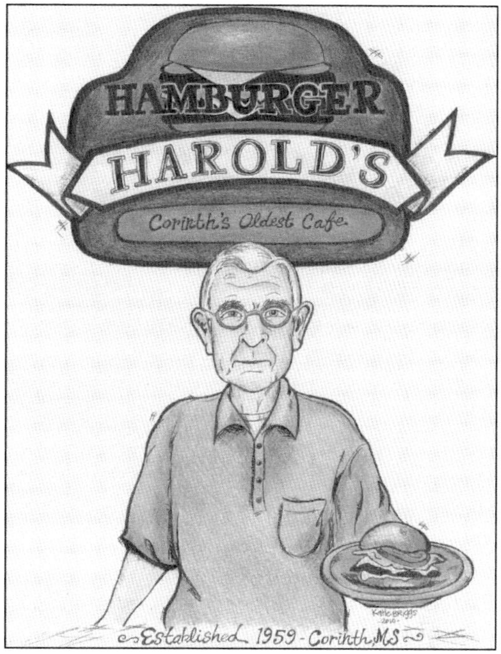


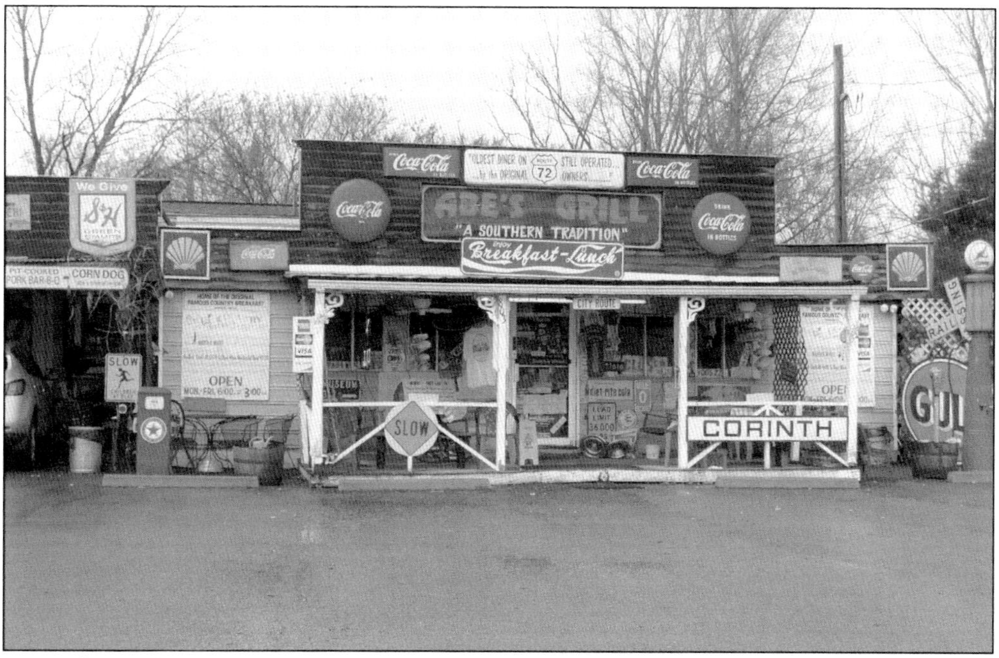


Located near the juncture of Highways 45 and 72, Abe Whitfield has been serving Corinthians for almost 50 years. He and wife, Terry, are perennial winners of the "Corinth's Best" distinction, awarded yearly to the best in Corinth cuisine as voted by the public. "Favorite Biscuit" and "Favorite Breakfast" signs are so numerous and so frequently awarded that they could be used as wallpaper. Also on the walls one will find signed photographs of famous folks, from movie actors to well-known musical performers who have visited Abe's when passing through town. They can sometimes even be found in person at the counter, shoulder to shoulder with locals who have been in on the secret for over half a century. (Courtesy of Abe Whitfield.)

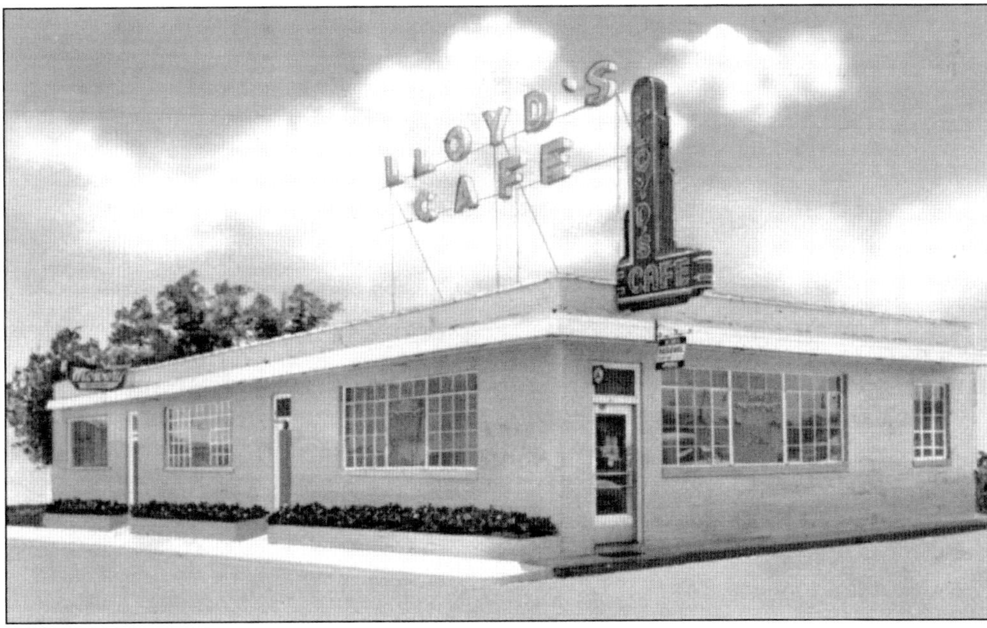


Lloyd's Café was located directly across the highway from Mildred's Restaurant and offered travelers a welcome place to take a break, whether the trip was across town or across the country. The interior shot showing (from left to right) owner Lloyd Gann and countermen Bruce Brown and Smith Davis was taken in the early 1930s when the café was located downtown on Waldron Street, where the young men hung around outside in front and watched the girls walk by. (Courtesy of Dr. William Jackson.)

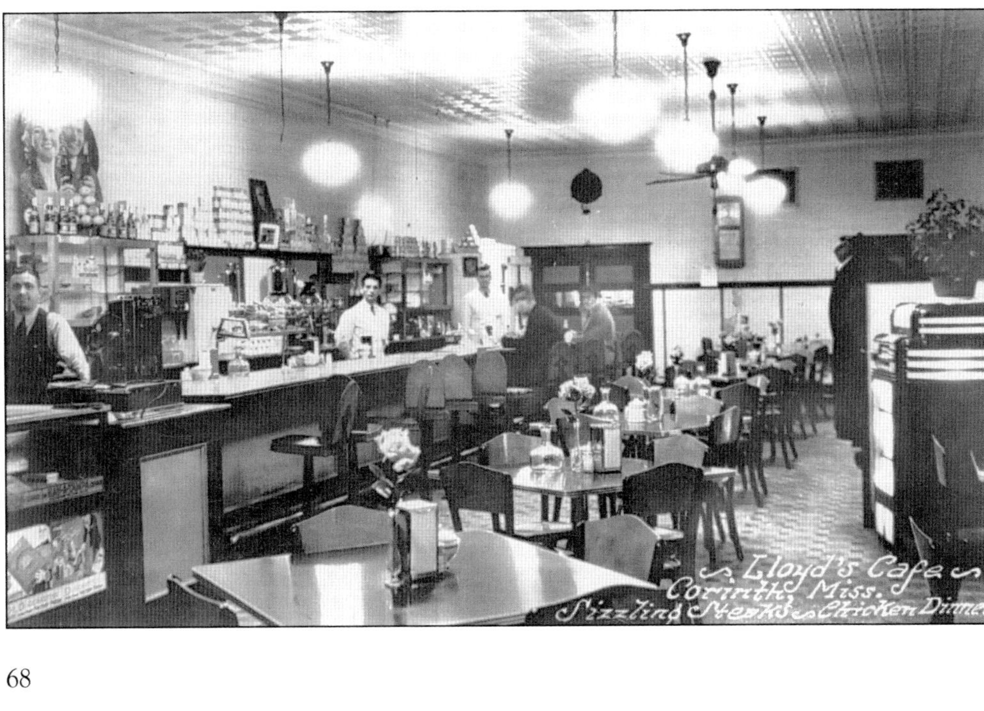

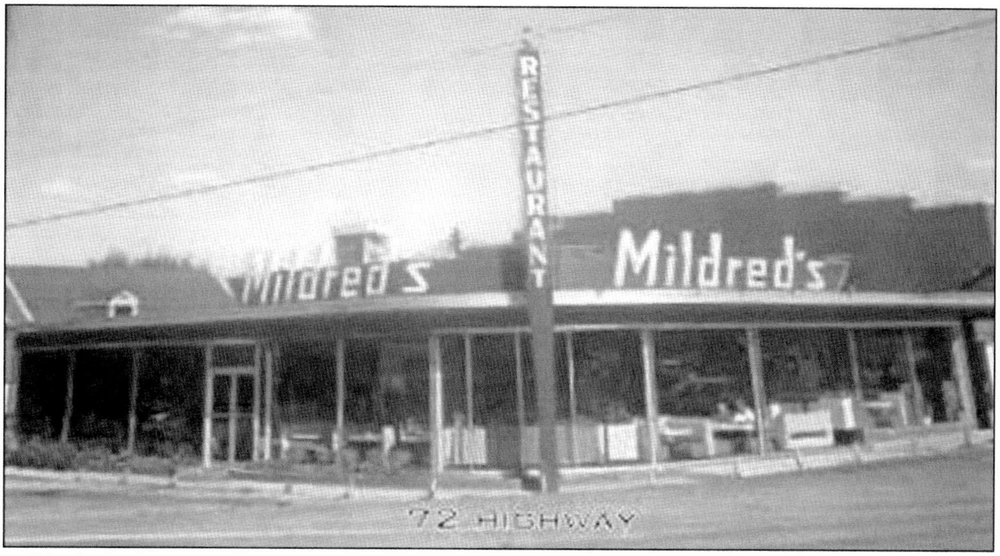

Mildred's Restaurant was strategically located at the juncture of Highways 72 and 45 in the old R.C. Johnson Building and run by Mildred Doyle in the 1960s and 1970s. Be it tourist, truck driver, or traveler, everyone seeing the bright neon sign atop Mildred's knew they were in for some of the best down-home Southern cooking this side of the Mississippi. (Courtesy of Dr. William Jackson.)

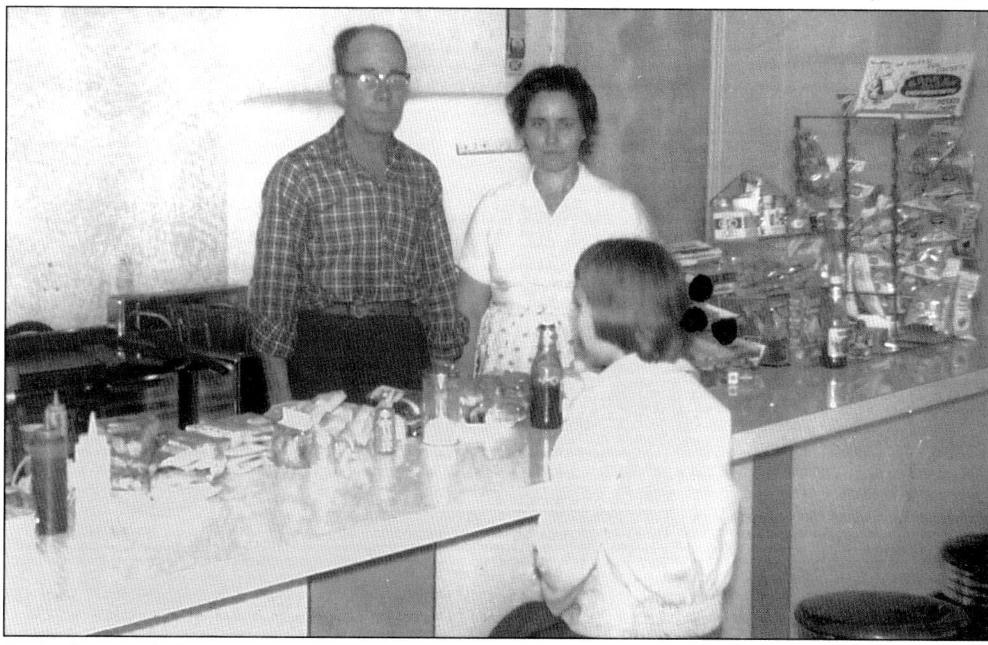
In the heart of what was colloquially known by all as "the Shiloh Road Strip," or just "the strip," generations of local teenagers spent every weekend endlessly looping around a half-mile stretch of blacktop trying to see or be seen. Before there was a McDonald's or Burger King, before there was any such thing as fast food, there was Byrd's Dixie Queen on the strip. Upon entering, each patron was greeted by Mary Byrd with the same three-word query, "What fer ye?" Home of the best soft-serve custard in the universe, Byrd's was a frequent stop for youngsters out cruising on weekends. Pictured here are owners Doss and Mary Byrd with daughter Janet seated at the counter. (Courtesy of Carter and Judith Byrd.)

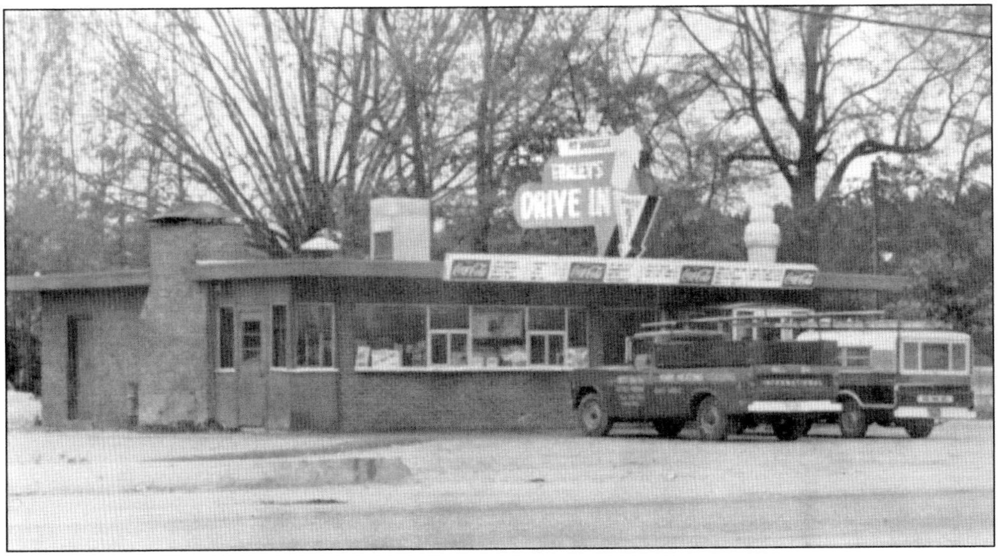


At the epicenter of the strip was Fraley's Drive-In, purveyor of the best pit barbecue this side of Memphis, Tennessee. Scores of Corinth baby boomers had their first date in one of the booths at Fraley's. Mark Fraley, son of owners Leck and Bernice, is seen perched atop the roof of Fraley's for a CHS yearbook photograph in 1972. (Courtesy of Greta and Bernice Fraley.)

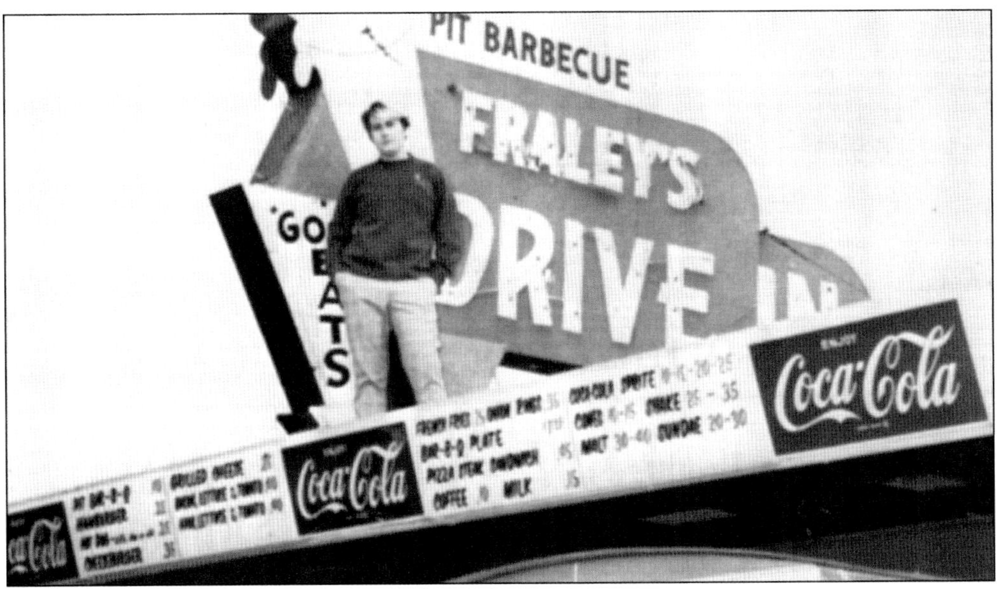

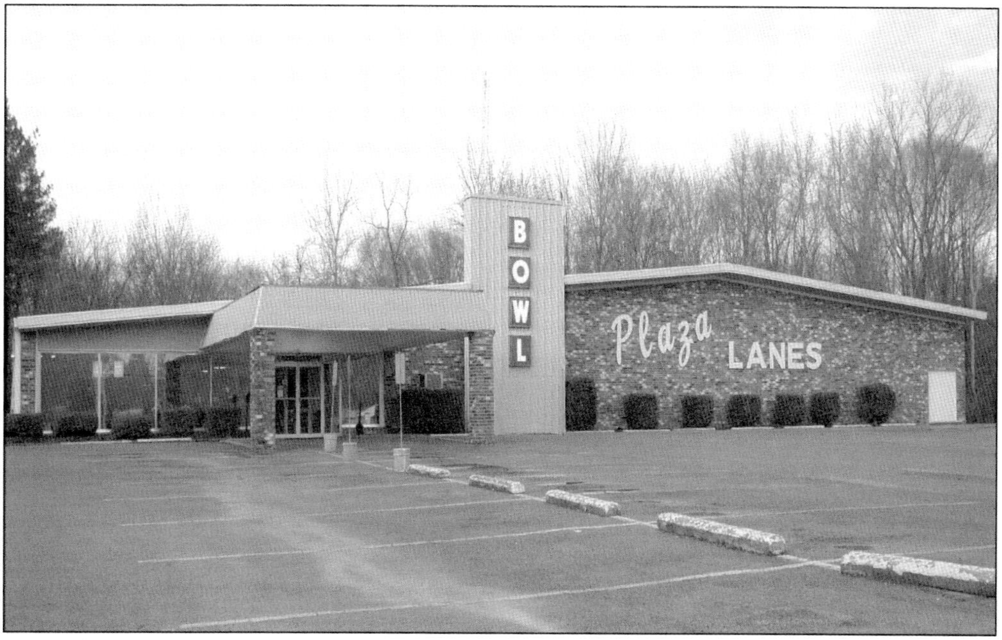


Opened in August 1960, Gateway Lanes, "the bowling alley" as it was universally known by one and all, is the sole survivor of the iconic businesses that once graced "the strip." In the mid-1960s, the name changed to Plaza Lanes, but very little else has been altered according to current owner David Curry. David, who began working for previous owner Ralph Strickland in 1967, did so "so I could bowl whenever an empty lane was available" and became the owner in 1978. He proudly states that he is still using the original seats, ball racks, and pinsetter machines, while the hardwood floors and lanes have also remained untouched. The restaurant looks much the same as it did when it opened half a century ago with the same tables, chairs, and counter. The game room, once filled with pinball machines and the pinball wizards of a bygone era, are no longer there, but the same original Brunswick pool tables continue to see plenty of action and are still going strong.

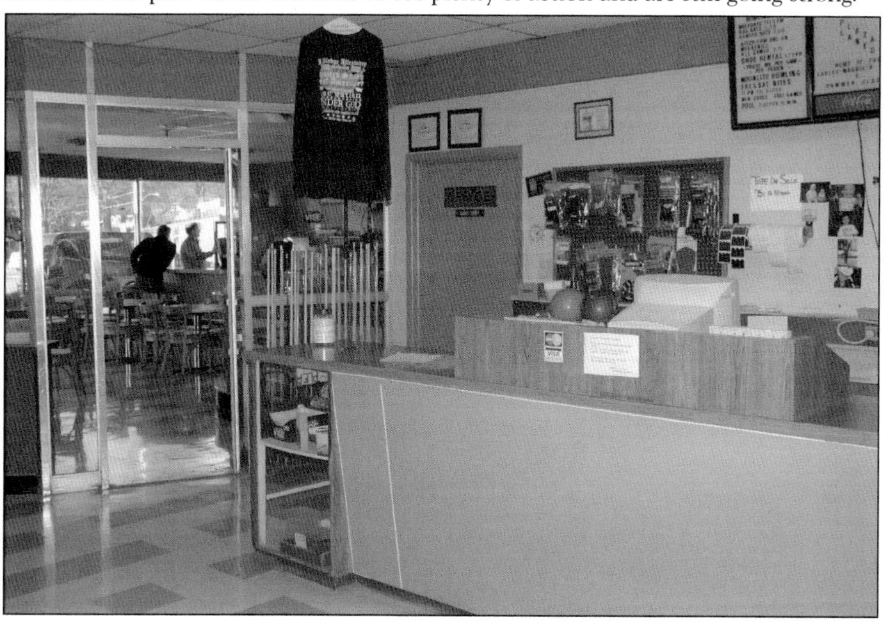

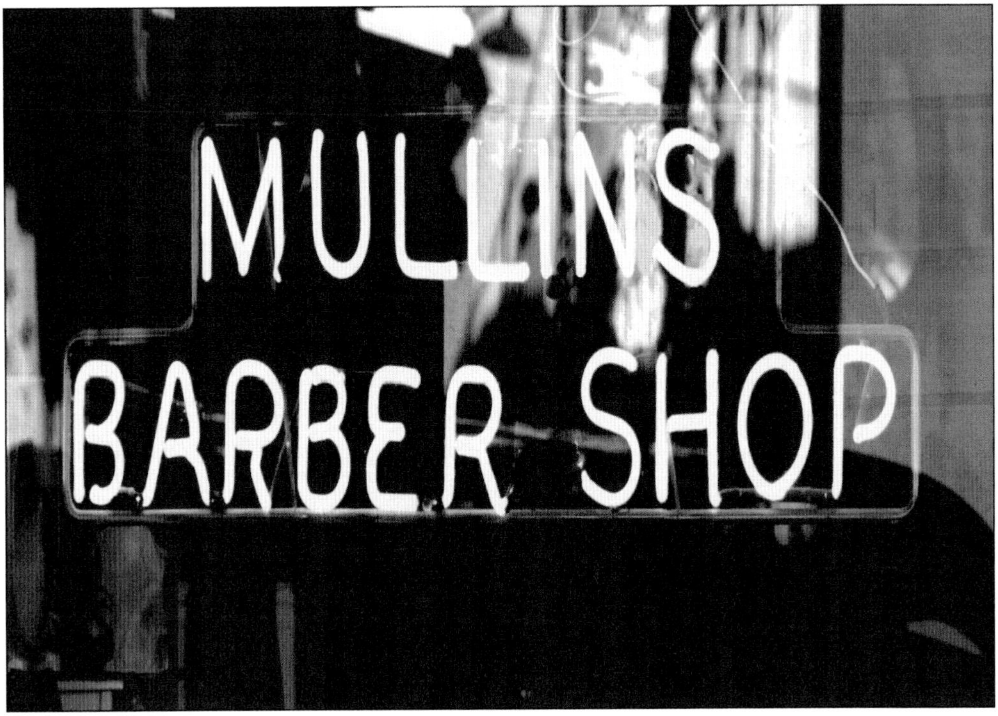


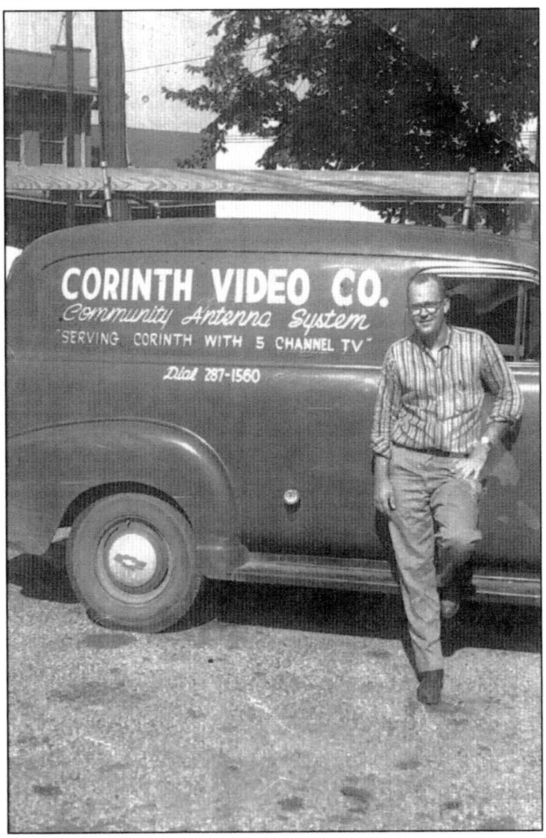


Known to all as a Corinth institution since 1957, Audry C. "Moon" Mullins has been responsible for the tonsorial needs of several generations and countless heads of male Corinthians, large and small and young and old (as well as the occasional small girl in need of a tomboy cut).

Long before some of the country's largest cities sported anything but "rabbit ears" and rooftop antennas, Corinth had cable. Corinth Video Company owner and manager Bob Campbell is shown with his service truck in 1962. For the bargain price of $4.95 a month, customers received all five available stations: three were from Memphis, one from Tupelo, and one from Jackson. Each one came in crystal clear.

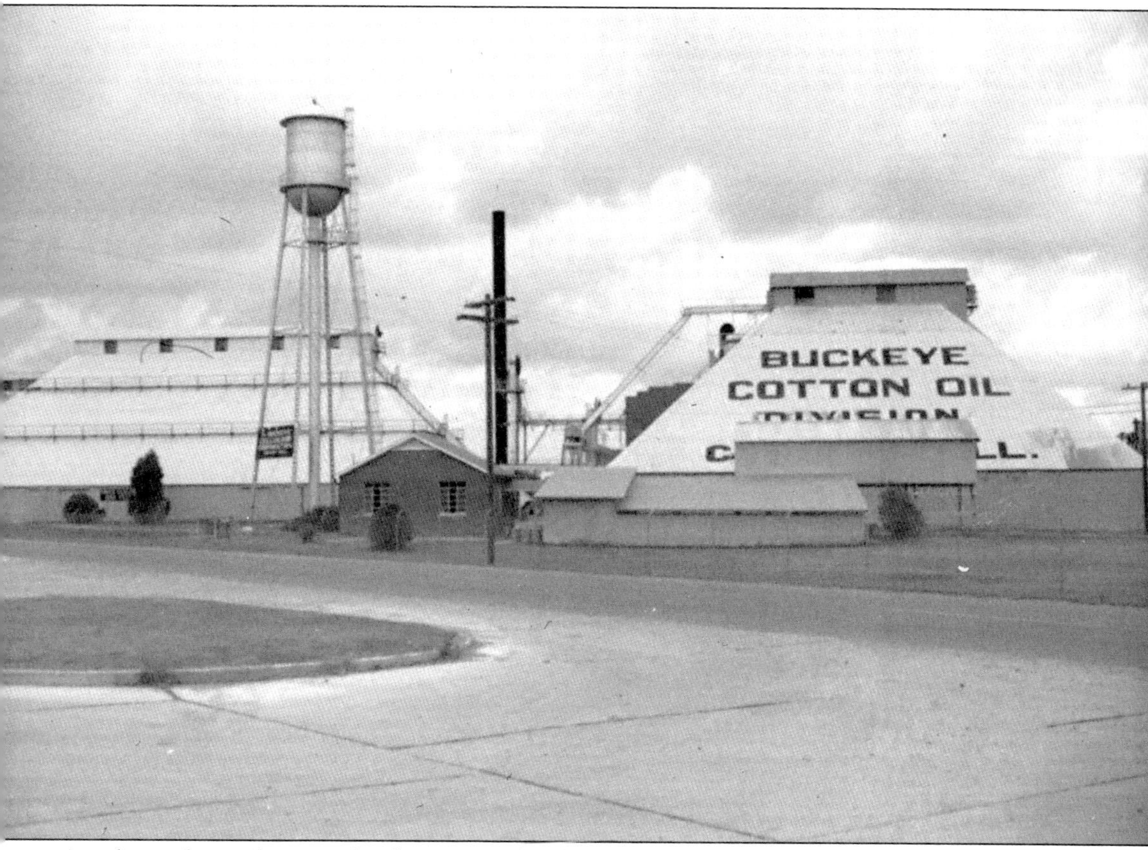


Another industry that was closely associated with the cotton trade was the Buckeye Cotton Oil Mill, where cottonseeds were processed. After the first and second lint and hulls were removed from the cottonseeds, they were pressed until all of the oil was extracted and formed into "cake," which was subsequently ground into meal. (Courtesy of Donna G. Baird.)

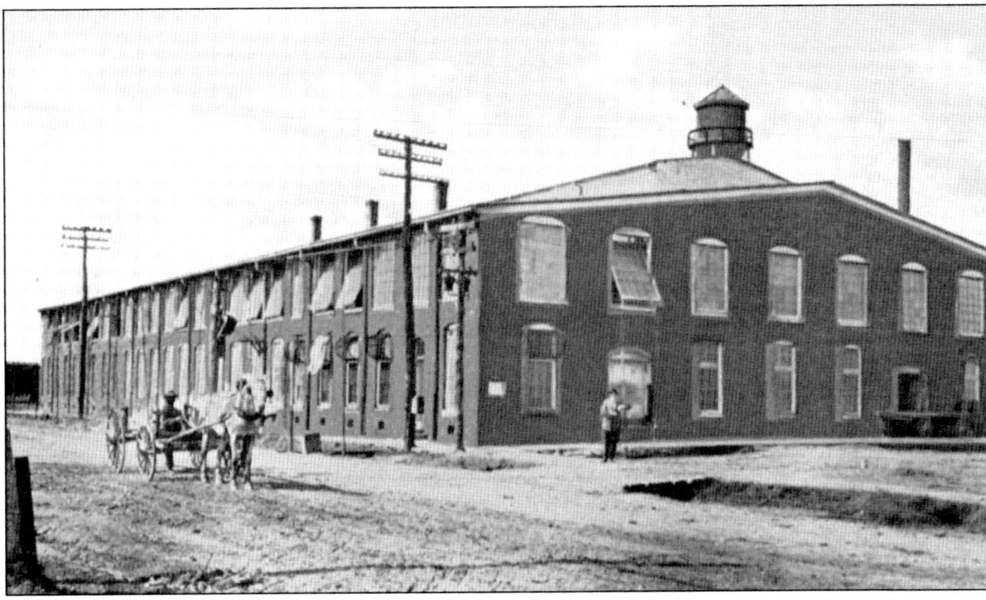

Founded at the turn of the 20th century and originally located in The Opera Building downtown, Weaver Pants Company virtually established the city's reputation as an apparel-manufacturing center when Admiral Byrd ordered Weaver-made pants for his second Antarctic expedition. The company moved to the location pictured above in 1908. In her unpublished memoir, Nelda Boatman Parrish recalled, "One time they paid in silver dollars to make the people of Corinth know what this factory meant to Corinth's economy." (Courtesy of Dr. William Jackson.)

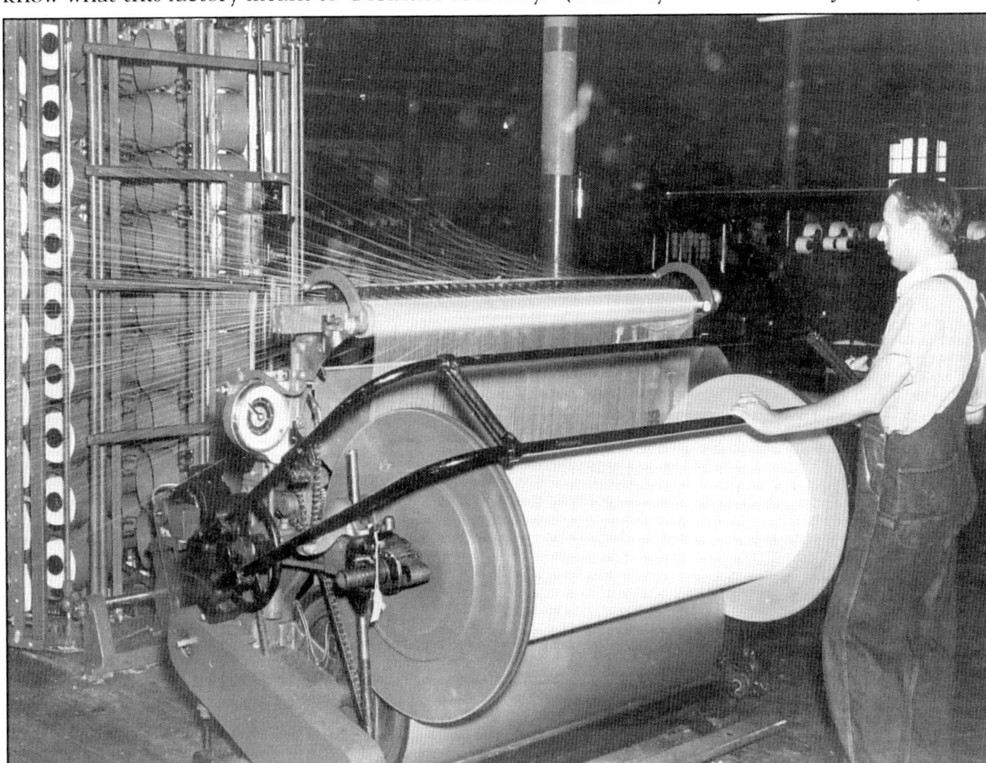

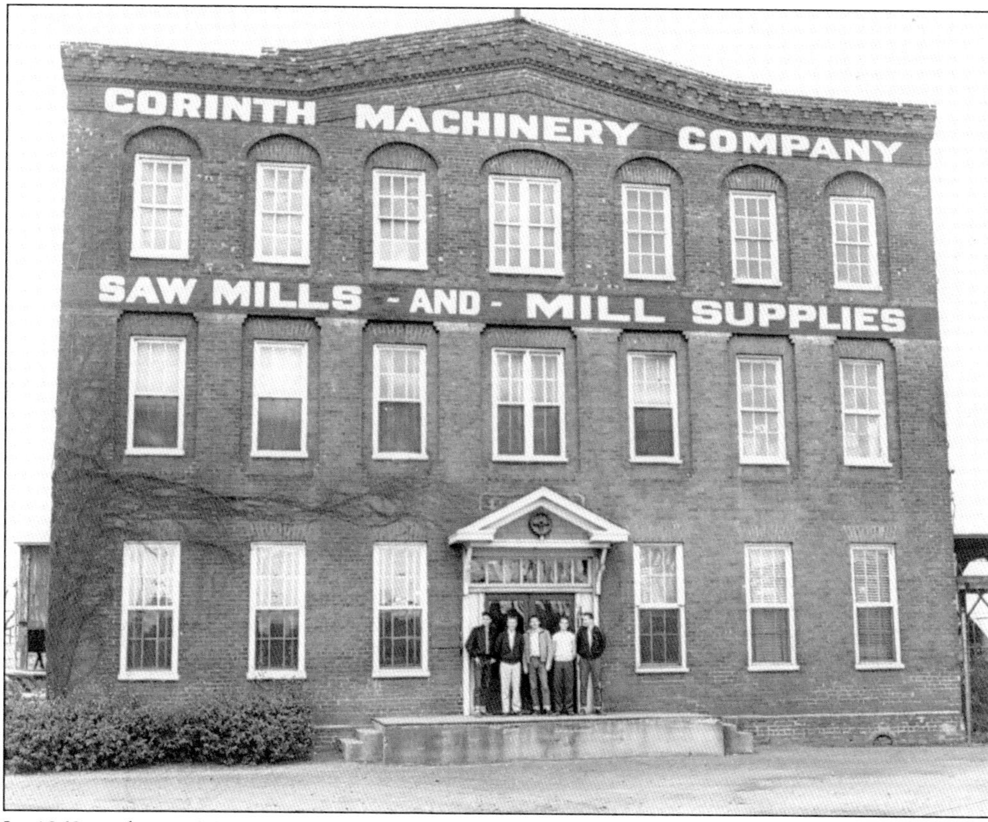


In 1869, architect Martin Seigrist and builder Robert W. Richie erected the building pictured above. It is the oldest documented factory in Mississippi according to an article appearing in the December 6, 1997, edition of the *Daily Corinthian* entitled, "A Look Into Corinth's Industrial Past," by Stephanie Sandy. In 1907, Hugh E. Ray organized Corinth Machinery Company, and soon the company's sawmills gained worldwide recognition for the quality of their products. (Courtesy of Tommy Ledbetter.)

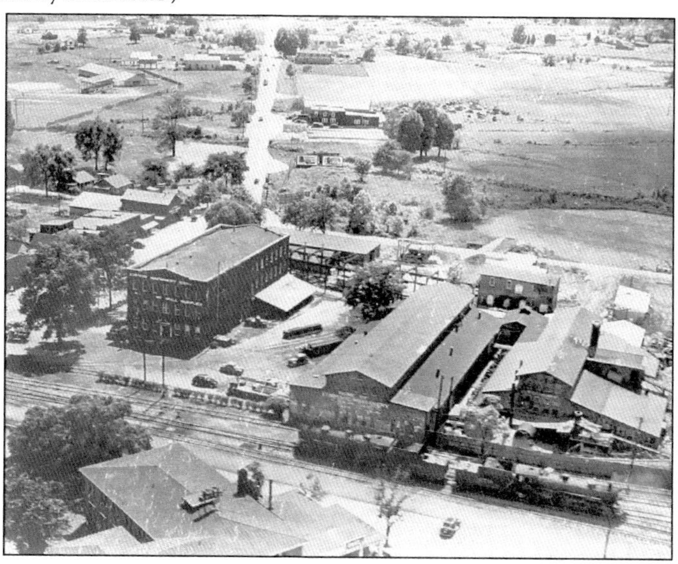

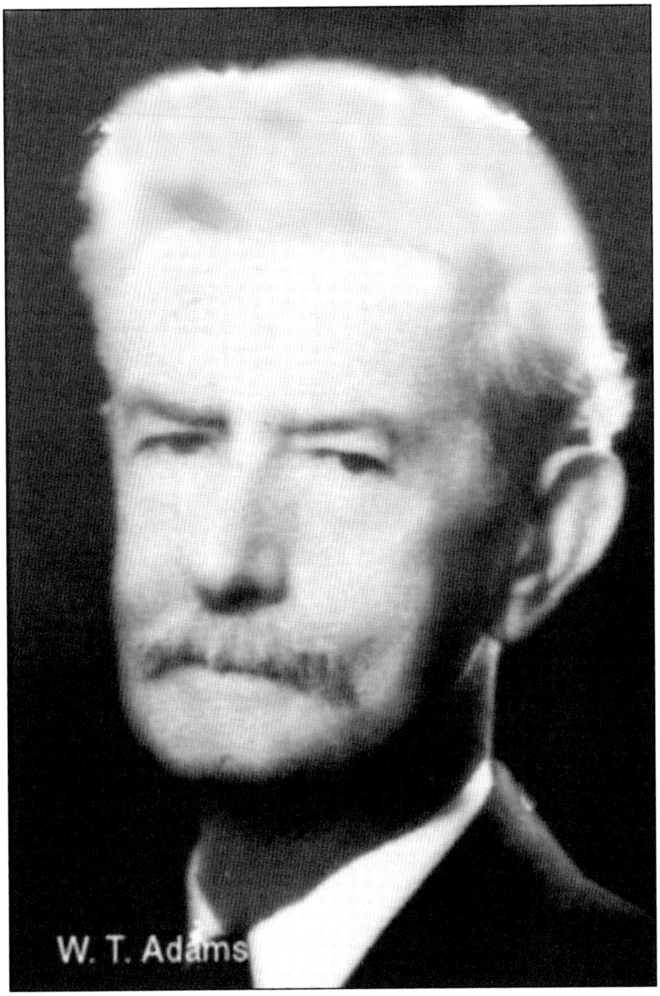


W.T. Adams was one of Corinth's most successful and well-known industrialists and philanthropists. For a number of years, he furnished the citizens of Corinth with a free public library. In 1879, he organized the W.T. Adams Machine Company, which soon became the largest industry in the city, employing over 500 men at its peak. For the next 40 years, the company manufactured steam engines, boilers, sawmills, and other related items.

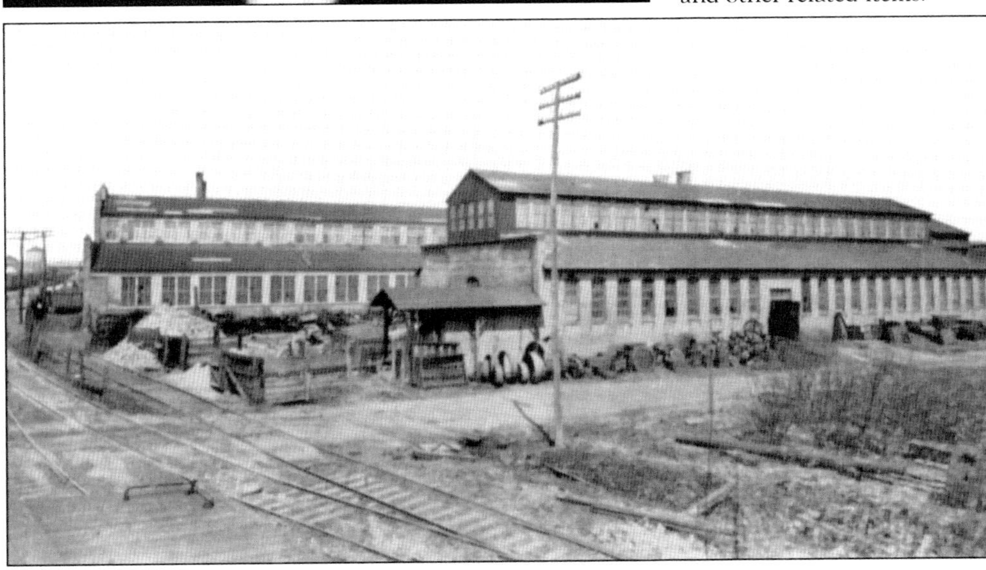

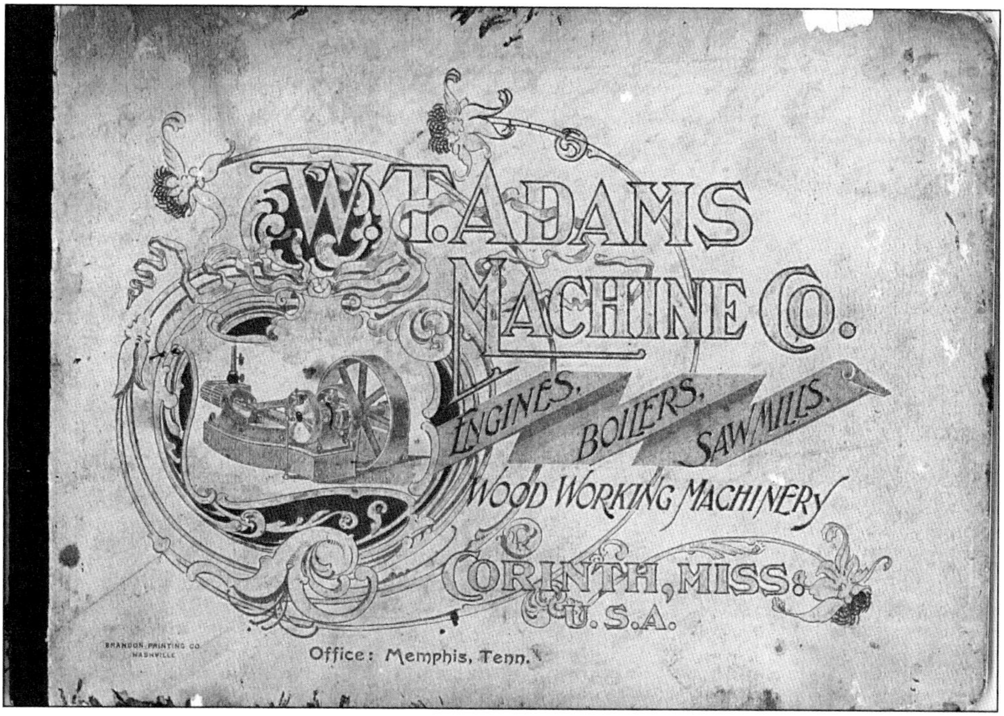


By the turn of the 20th century, the W.T. Adams Machine Company was one of the leading manufacturers of its kind in the world. Pictured above is the cover of the *Adams Catalogue* that all potential customers would receive. Below is a photograph of the company's booth as it would have appeared at trade shows, exhibits, or expositions across the nation. W.T Adams is pictured at a desk with an unknown customer in the lower right-hand corner.

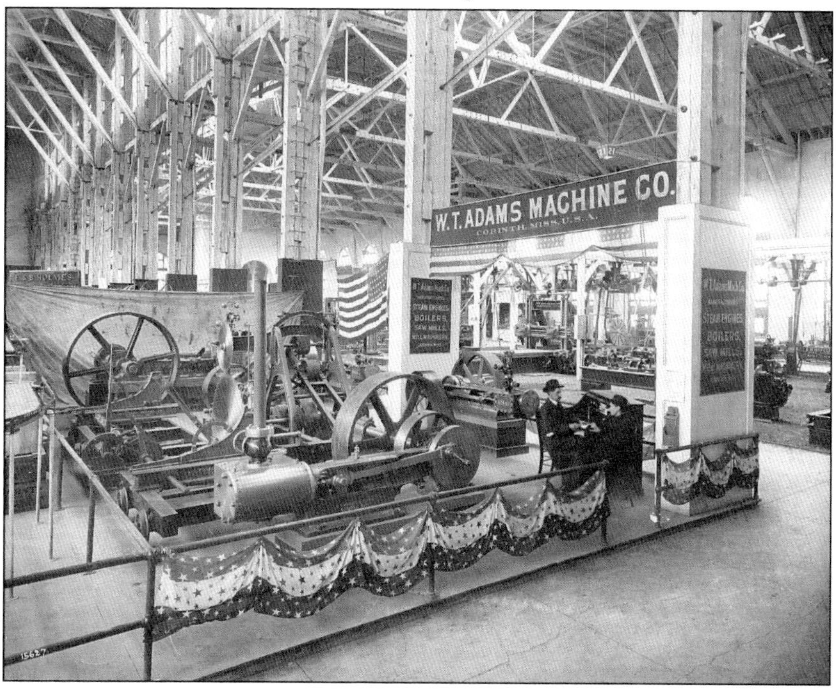

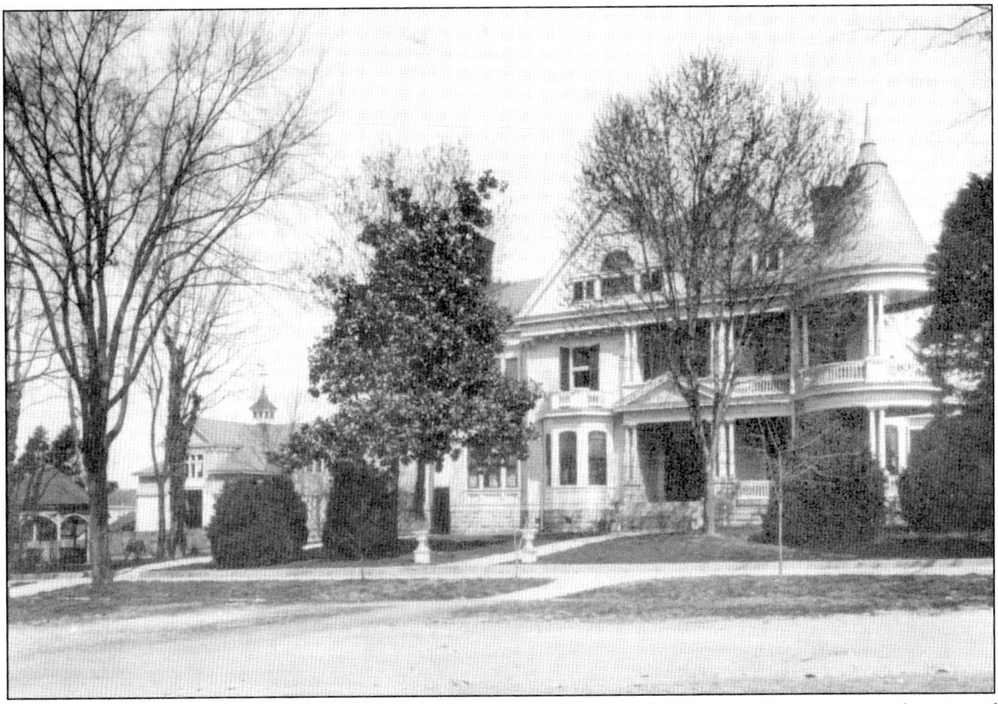

The W.T. Adams home was located on the corner of Main and Fillmore Streets, now the site of the First Baptist Church. The interior boasted all of the flounces and furbelows typical of the late Victorian era. It was said that Adams could walk out of his front door and go straight down Fillmore Street directly to the front door of his office.

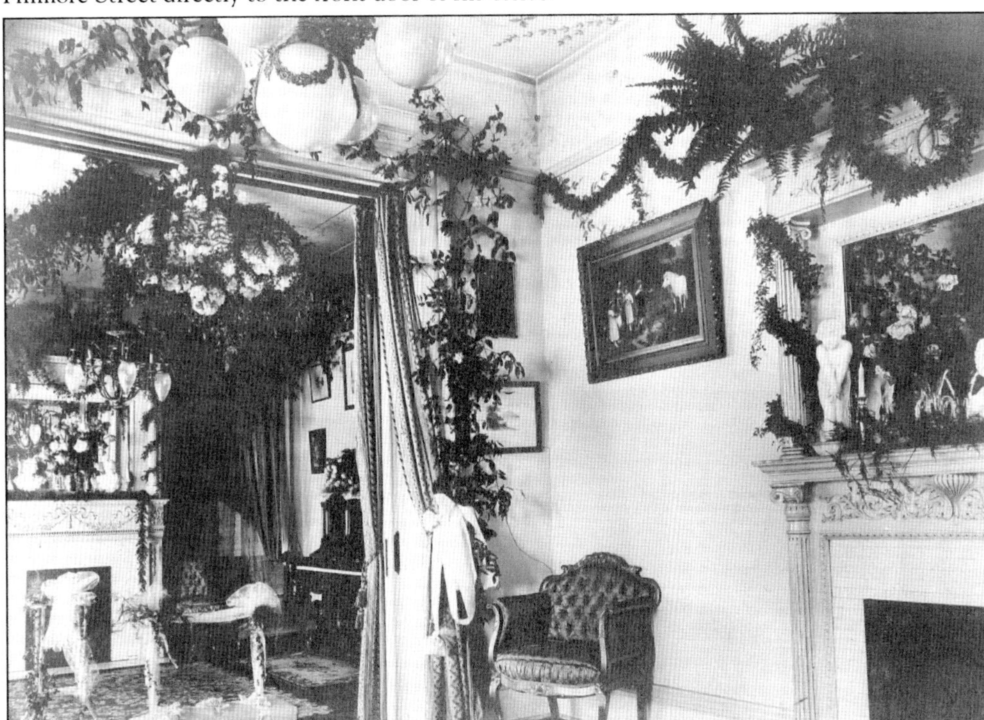

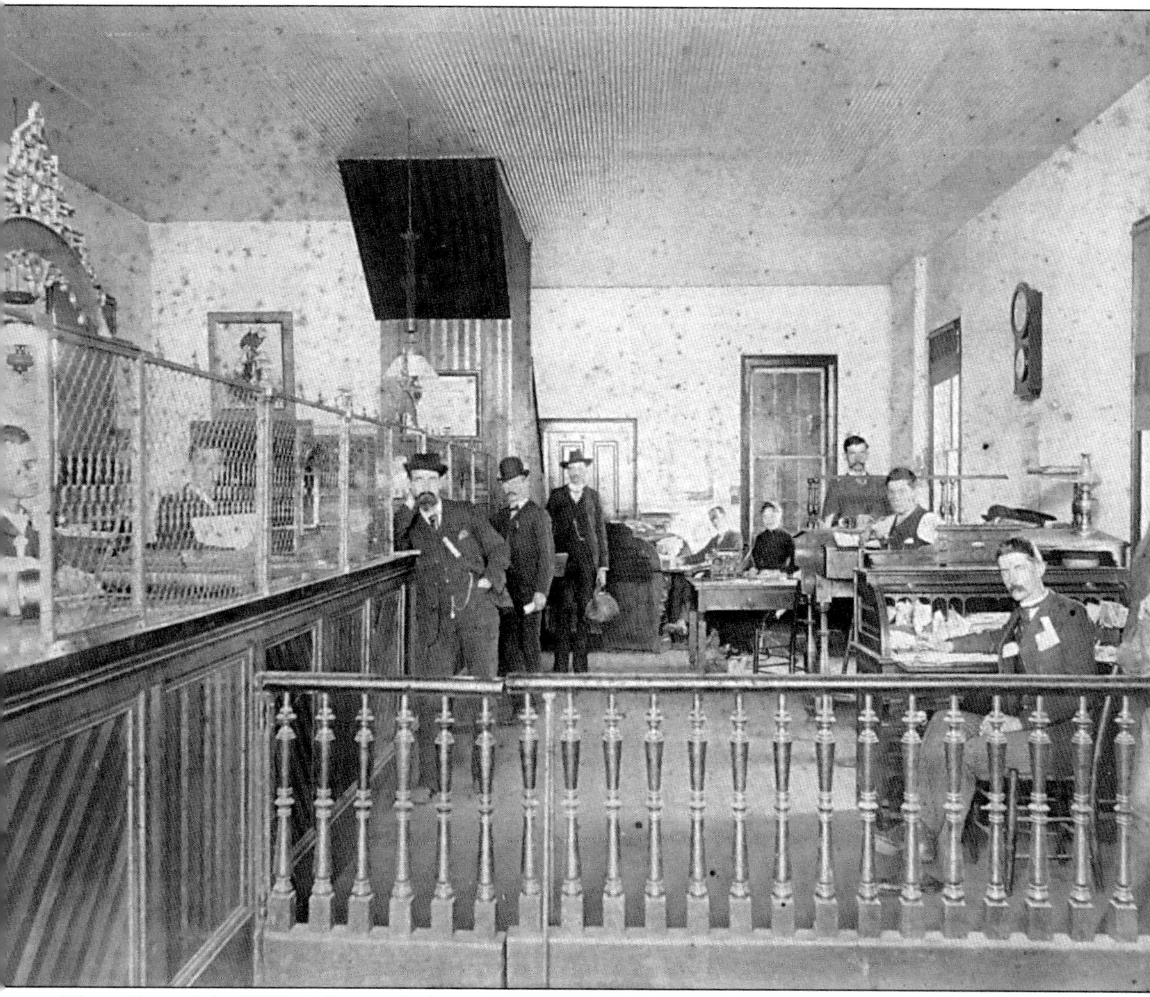

The office of the W.T. Adams Machine Company was located a short and pleasant walk down Fillmore Street in the center of the business district of downtown Corinth. In this photograph of his office, customers and clerks stop doing business long enough to strike a pose on either side of the elaborately decorated and caged counter. Adams is pictured seated at his desk in the lower right-hand corner, and no other individual is identified.

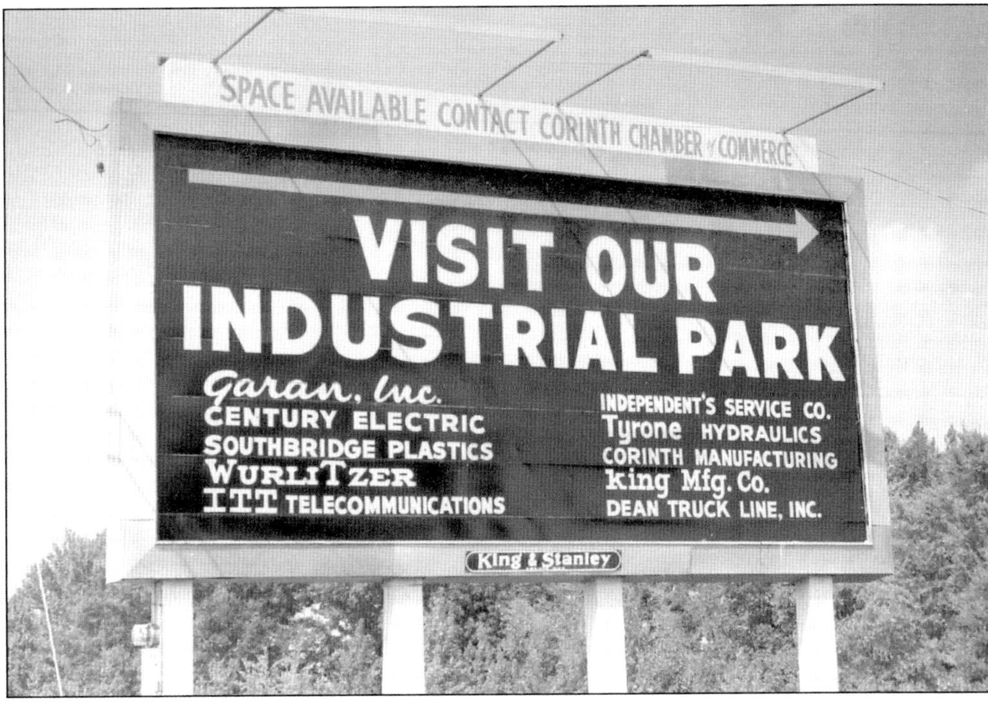


In the early 1950s, Corinth and Alcorn County launched a major solicitation to attract new industry when 40 local businessmen put up $1,000 each to buy the old 900-acre Whitfield plantation for the purpose of establishing a new industrial park. The city leaders added the extra incentive of tax abatements and a stable workforce to attract new industry. By the end of the decade, a dozen plants had made the Corinth Industrial Park their home.

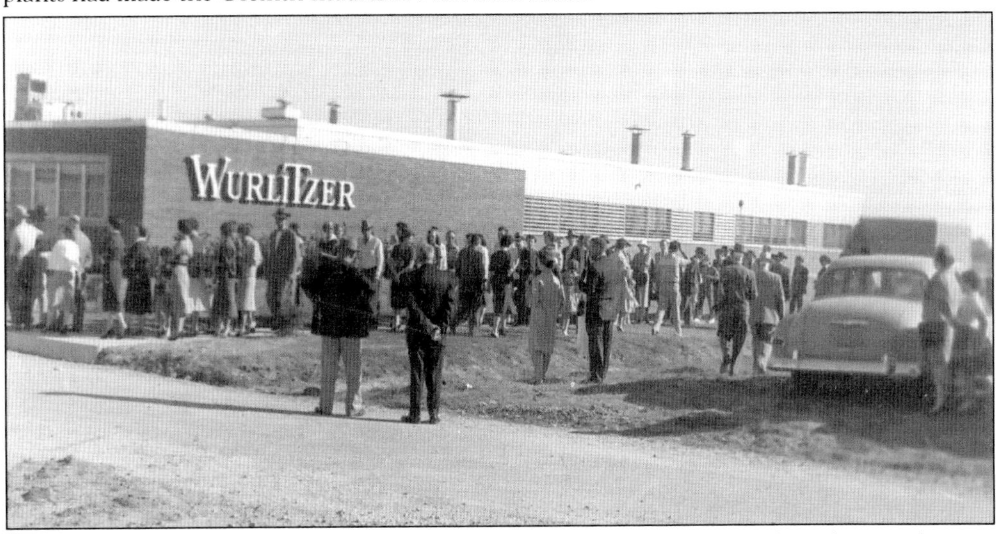


Marketed by the Rudolph Wurlitzer Company and manufactured in Corinth and Towanda, New York, the Wurlitzer electric piano was manufactured in a variety of models. Its electric pianos were used by everyone from ordinary music lovers for their own amusement to world-renowned bands such as the Beach Boys, the Carpenters, and Supertramp. Potential employees are pictured in the mid-1950s lined up at the newly built Wurlitzer plant to submit their applications. (Courtesy of Donna G. Baird.)

Using the most cutting-edge computer technology of the day, C.R. Parrish is pictured putting a hydraulic part to the test and examining the results in his capacity as a quality control inspector at Tyrone Hydraulics (later Dana Corp.), which was a company that was a leading manufacturer of hydraulic motors, pumps, and valves for over 30 years. (Courtesy of LuAnne Parrish.)

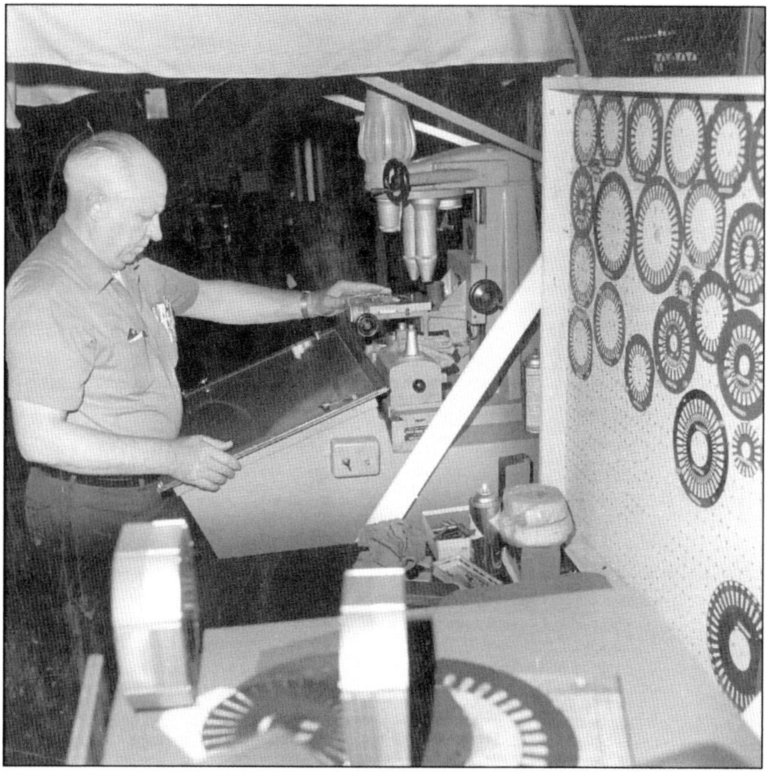

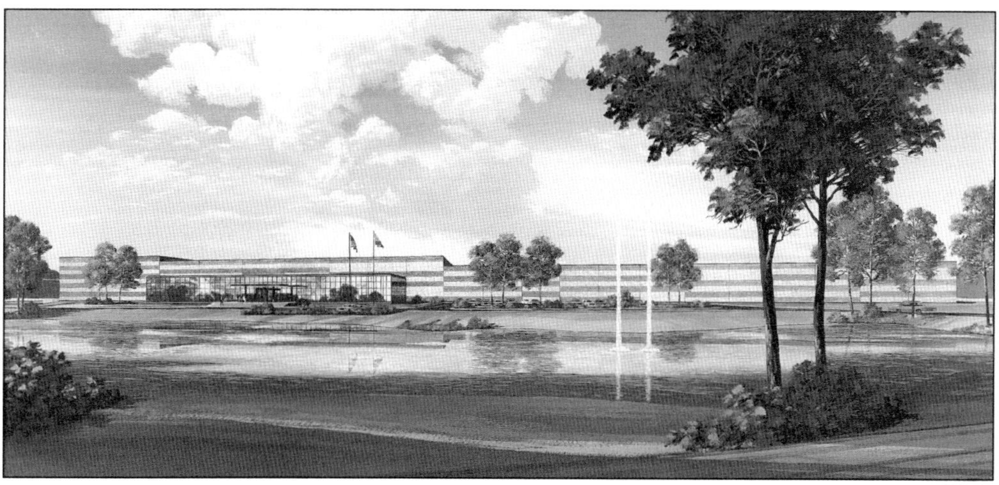

In 1977, Hall of Mississippi, which printed *National Geographic*, *Jet*, *Ebony*, *Ebony Man*, and many other magazines, relocated to the Corinth Industrial Park, becoming second in the number of workers employed. Its printing plant used the rotogravure process, a system using a rotary press with intaglio cylinders. The name "Hall" would be succeeded by a variety of others; throughout the succession, though, Corinthians were proud to claim the distinction of being the only plant where *National Geographic* was printed.

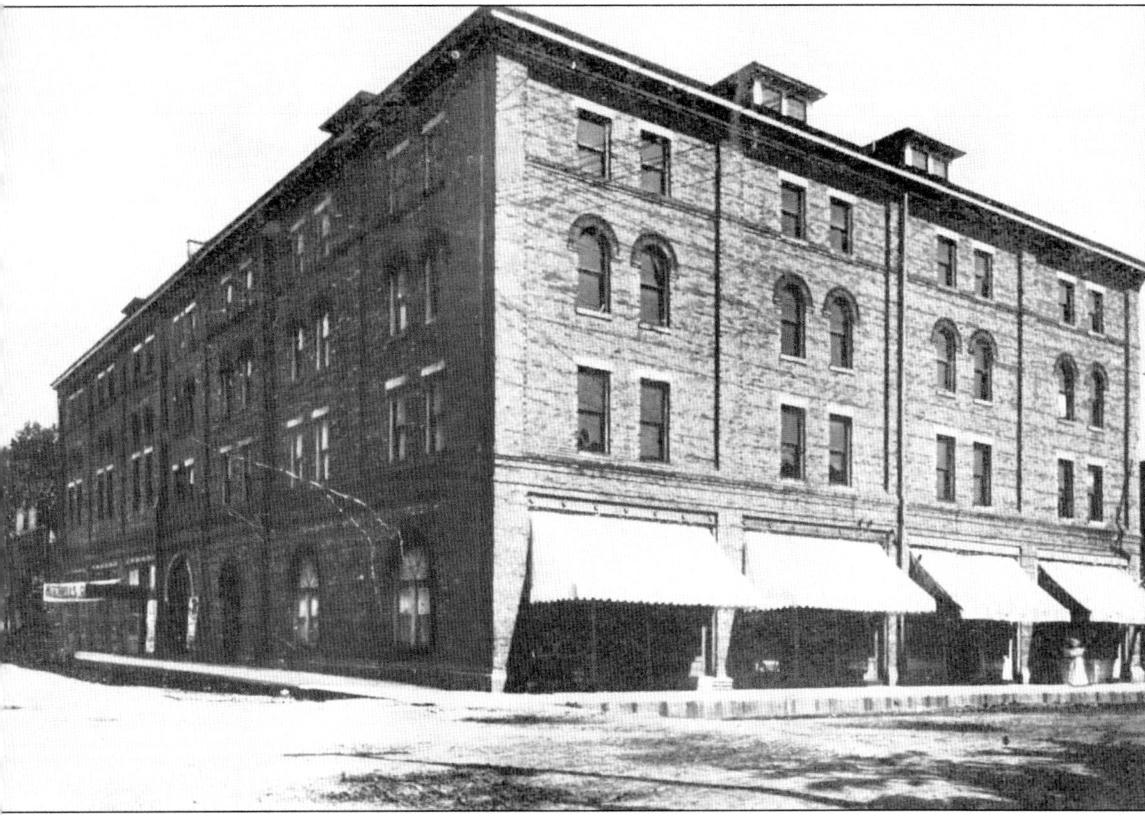

H.T. McGee, who later designed the Pink Palace in Memphis, was the architect for The Opera Building erected at the turn of the century. Road companies traveling between Knoxville and Memphis were regularly booked for performances, along with various homegrown talents. At various times, the building also housed fledgling businesses such as the Weaver Pants Factory. (Courtesy of Dr. William Jackson.)

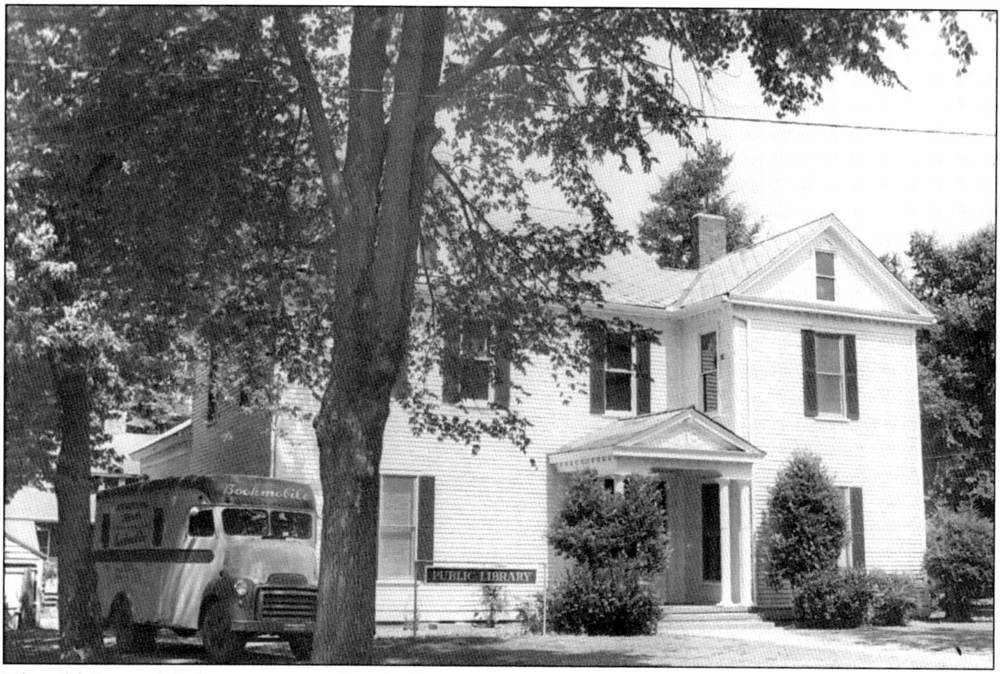


The old Corinth Library, pictured with the bookmobile parked beside it, was originally established in 1938 in the courthouse basement, where it remained until it was moved to this location in 1943. The bookmobile service began in 1939 when the Works Project Administration (WPA) furnished a panel truck for the "demonstration of library services." It was replaced in 1945 by a new van, and in 1952 another bookmobile was added. As the ability to access the library grew and schools had increasing funds for books, the need for the bookmobile decreased until it was discontinued in the 1960s. In 1967, the original library building was torn down and replaced by a sleek, modern, 22,460-square-foot brick building that was dedicated on February 8, 1970, by Congressman Jamie L. Whitten.

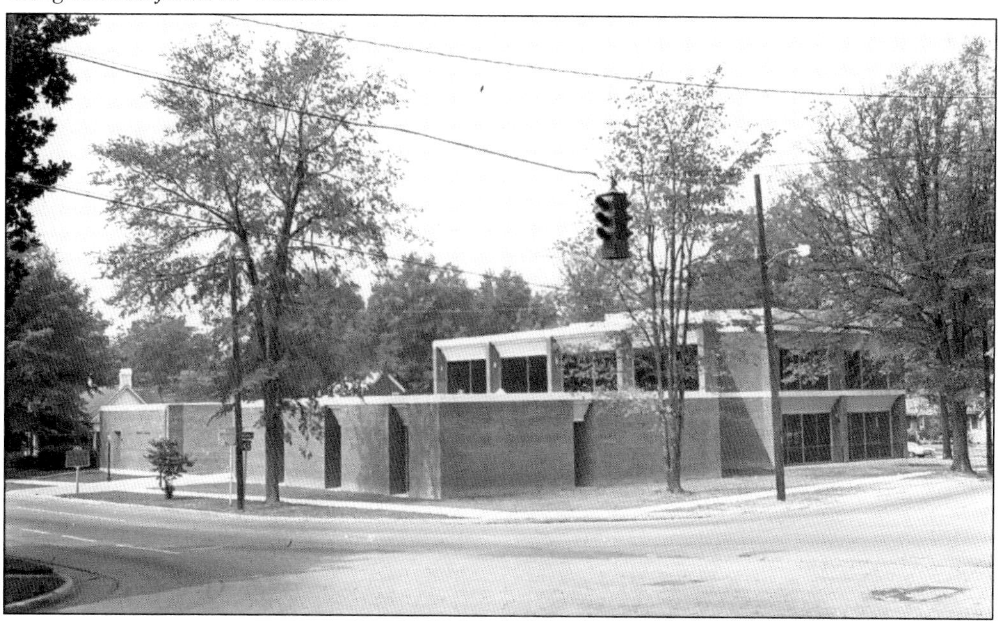

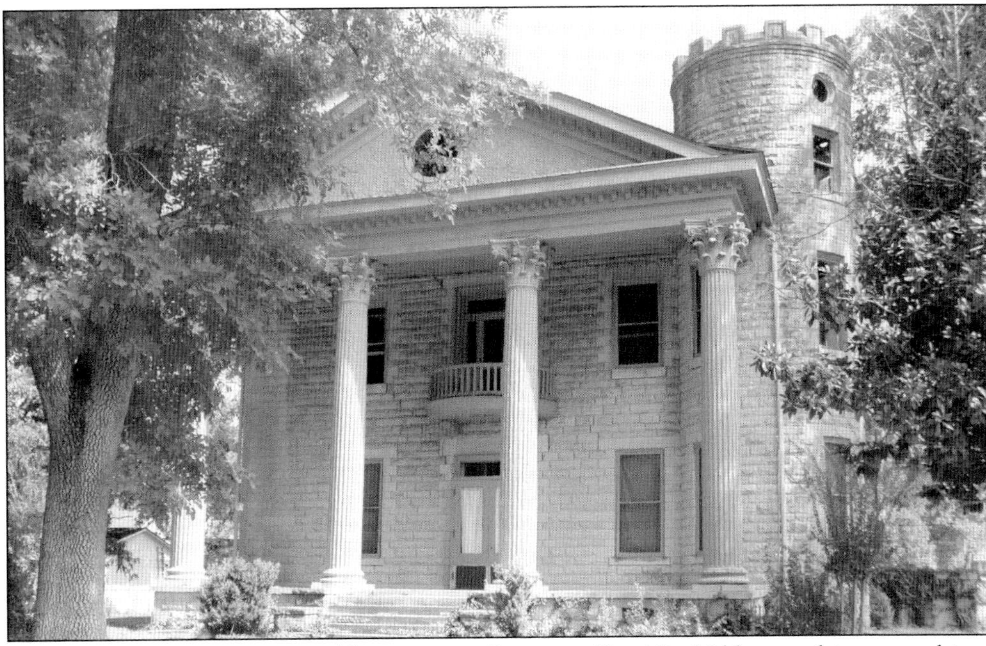

Noted builder, entrepreneur, and businessman Benjamin Franklin Liddon was his own architect when he had this palatial home erected in 1907. He was a pupil of Corinth public schools and had stints at Millsap's College, Princeton, and Cornell. Upon his return to Corinth, he worked as a teller and bookkeeper from 1899 to 1903 for the Tishomingo Savings Institution until he determined to strike out on his own. As a self-taught architect, generations of Corinthians have worked, played, and been entertained in buildings and structures that he created. Though some of his unique contributions have passed into fond memories, many still exist. Below, he is pictured on the front porch of his home with his only grandchild, Shirley McCullar Simmons, and her new husband, Frank Simmons, on their wedding day, November 21, 1941. (Courtesy of Alan McCullar Simmons.)

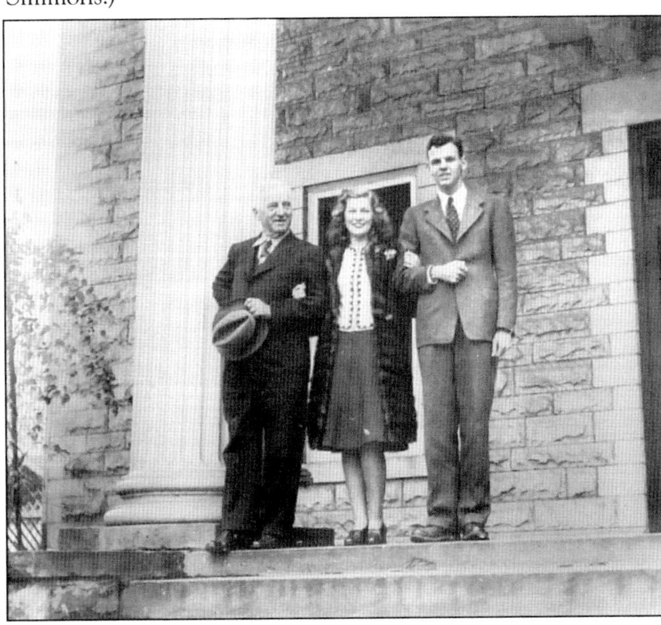

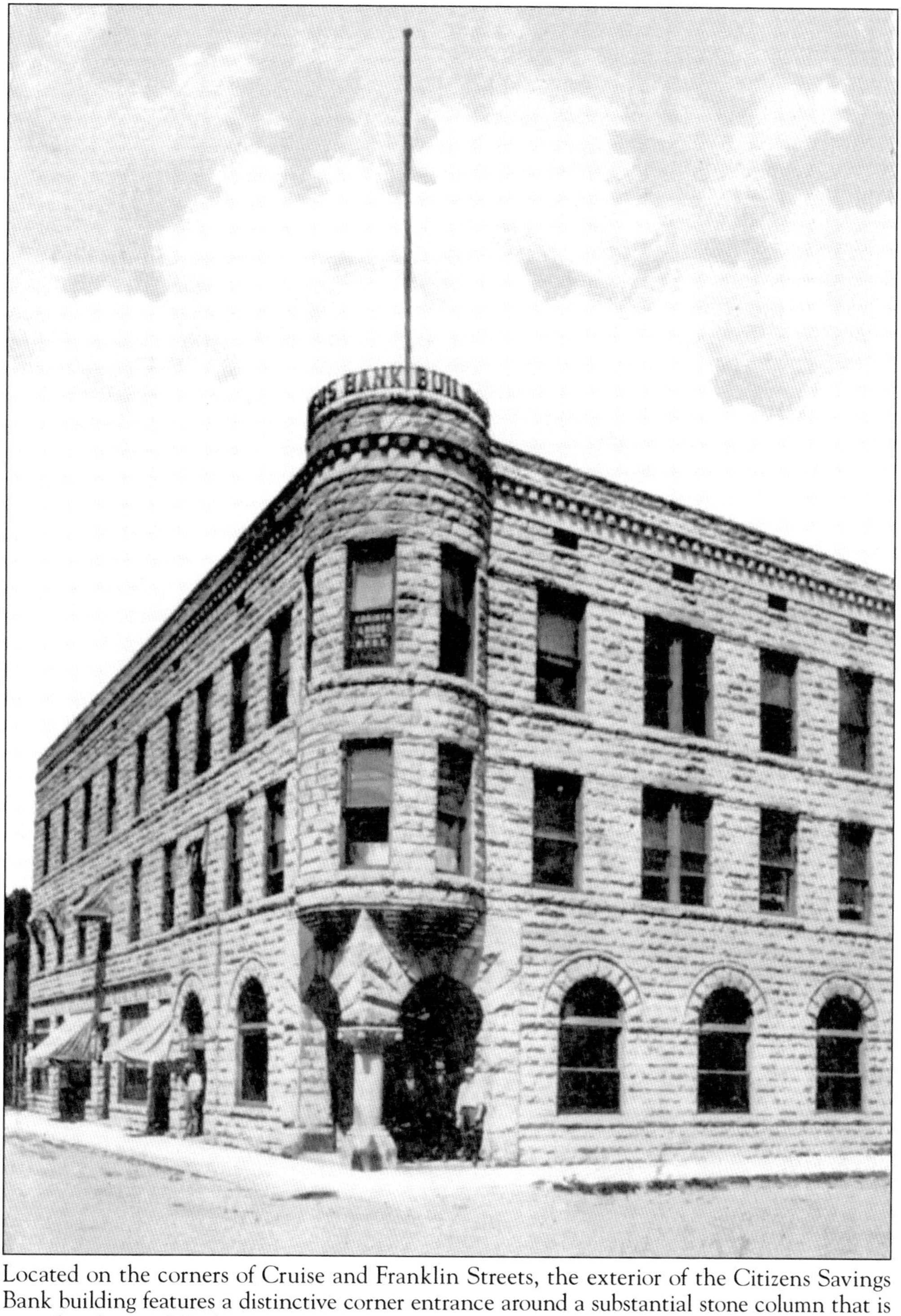

Located on the corners of Cruise and Franklin Streets, the exterior of the Citizens Savings Bank building features a distinctive corner entrance around a substantial stone column that is considered one of the best examples of Richardson Romanesque style in Mississippi. Both his home and the bank building were constructed of Alabama limestone, cut and fitted on the site. (Courtesy of Alan M. Simmons.)

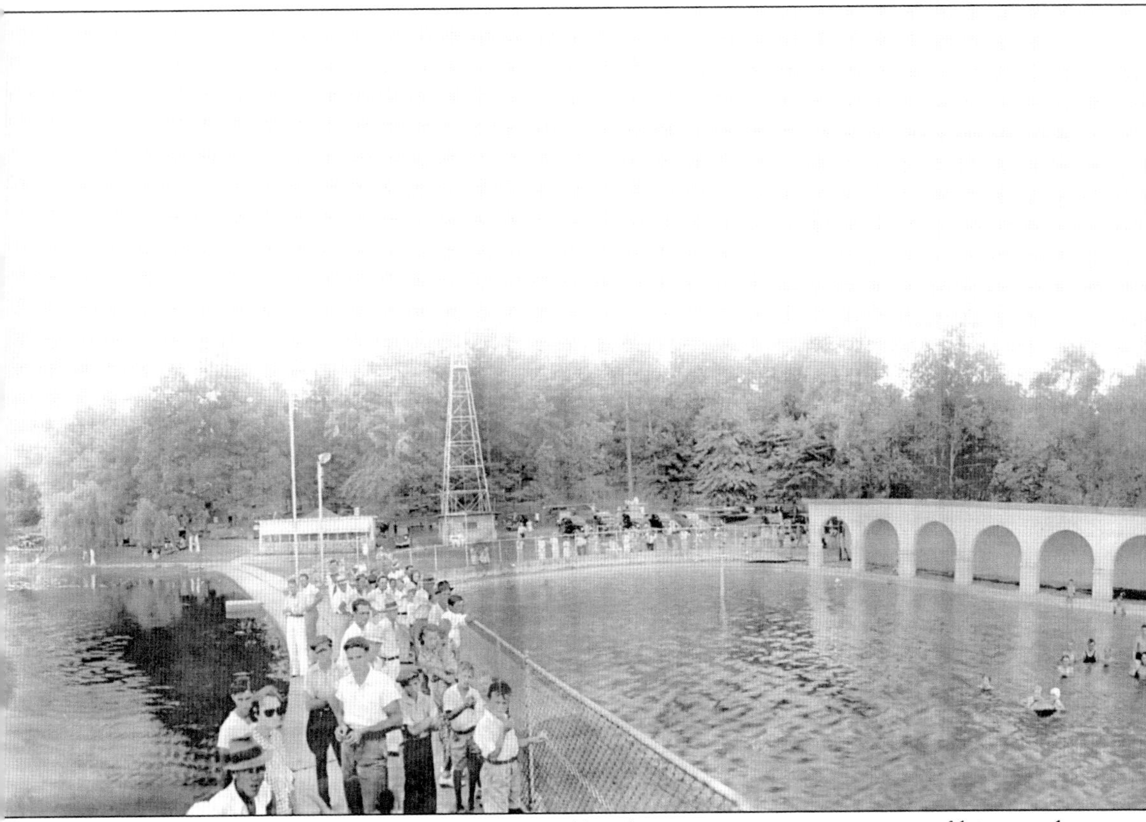

A firm believer that it pays to play, B.F. Liddon began construction on one of his grandest achievements, Liddon Lake Amusement Park, in 1912. Upon completion, the property consisted of five man-made lakes for fishing, which were fed by artesian wells; a land-based boat for parties and dances he named the *Viking*, located on the edge of one of the lakes; and the largest swimming pool in the state, which was 225 feet long and 55 feet wide with a covered gallery for spectators. All of these features were situated between two large lakes that were surrounded by sidewalks for

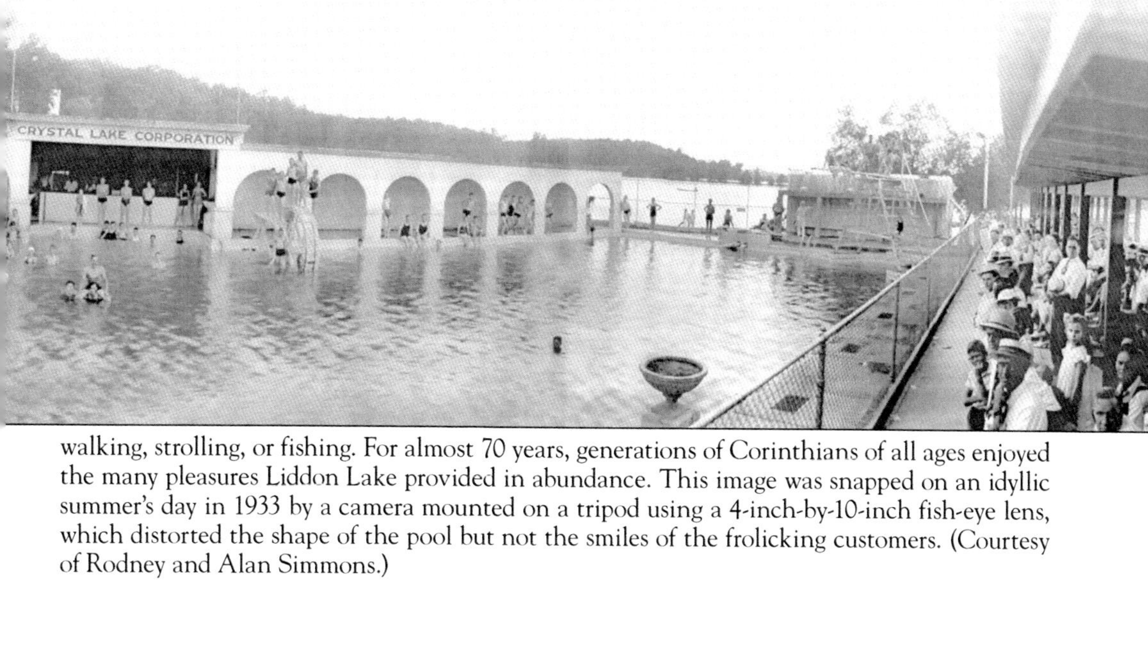


walking, strolling, or fishing. For almost 70 years, generations of Corinthians of all ages enjoyed the many pleasures Liddon Lake provided in abundance. This image was snapped on an idyllic summer's day in 1933 by a camera mounted on a tripod using a 4-inch-by-10-inch fish-eye lens, which distorted the shape of the pool but not the smiles of the frolicking customers. (Courtesy of Rodney and Alan Simmons.)

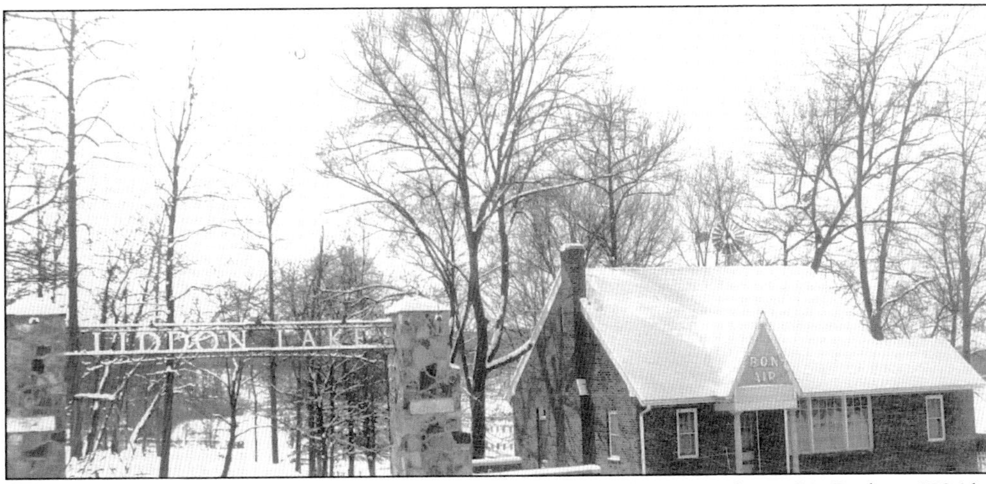

The Bon Aire Café was located at the entrance to Liddon Lake on Highway 72. Built in 1936 by B.F. Liddon as a restaurant and gathering place for his granddaughter and her friends, it was also the site of gatherings of all types from birthday parties to bridal and baby showers. (Courtesy of Alan McCullar Simmons.)

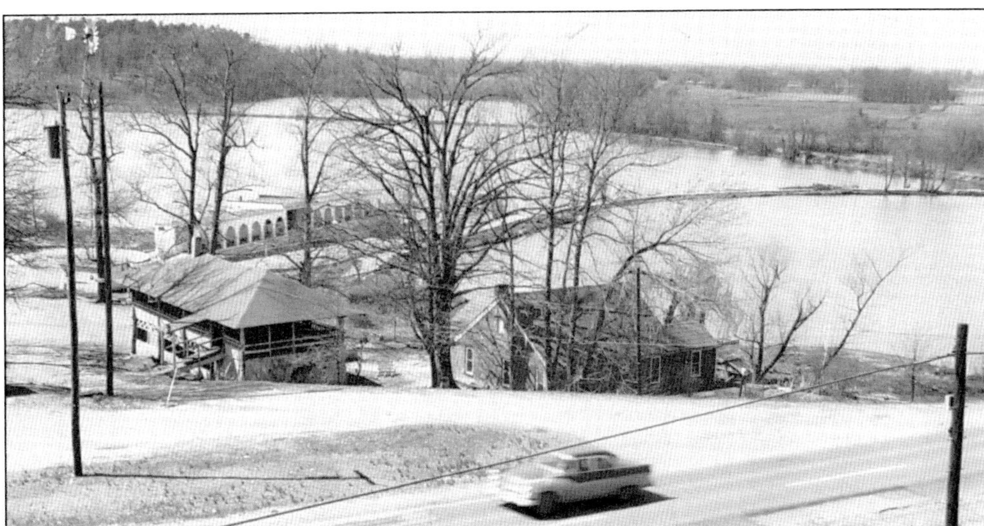

Pictured here in the aftermath of the ice storm of 1951, a lone car is traveling cautiously up the hill on Highway 72 with Liddon Lake pictured in the background. Seen in the foreground are the large pavilions for family reunions and other types of gatherings and the Bon Aire, which overlooks the lake. (Courtesy of Alan McCullar Simmons.)

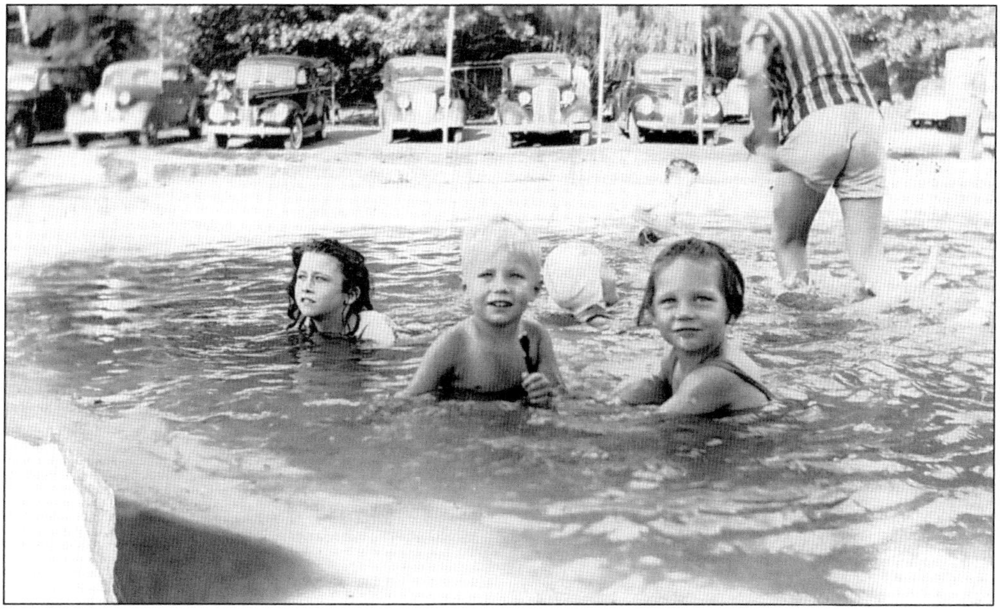

Besides the lakes and the swimming pool, Liddon Lake offered tennis courts, a children's playground, and kiddy pool free of charge. In addition to the sidewalks abutting two of the lakes, the area was equipped with lights, thus allowing for maximum enjoyment in the summer months. Pictured in 1941 in the children's pool are, from left to right, unidentified, Johnny Timlake, and Johanna Timlake (Smith). (Courtesy of Johanna Timlake Smith.)

Kelley Johnson takes a running leap into the Liddon Lake pool in the summer of 1981 as one of the last of a long line of pint-sized Corinthians to learn how to swim there. Shortly after this photograph was taken, Liddon Lake was closed and eventually sold for development. No child or adult who was fortunate enough to grow up in Corinth will ever forget the wonders of this magical place. (Courtesy of Donna G. Baird.)

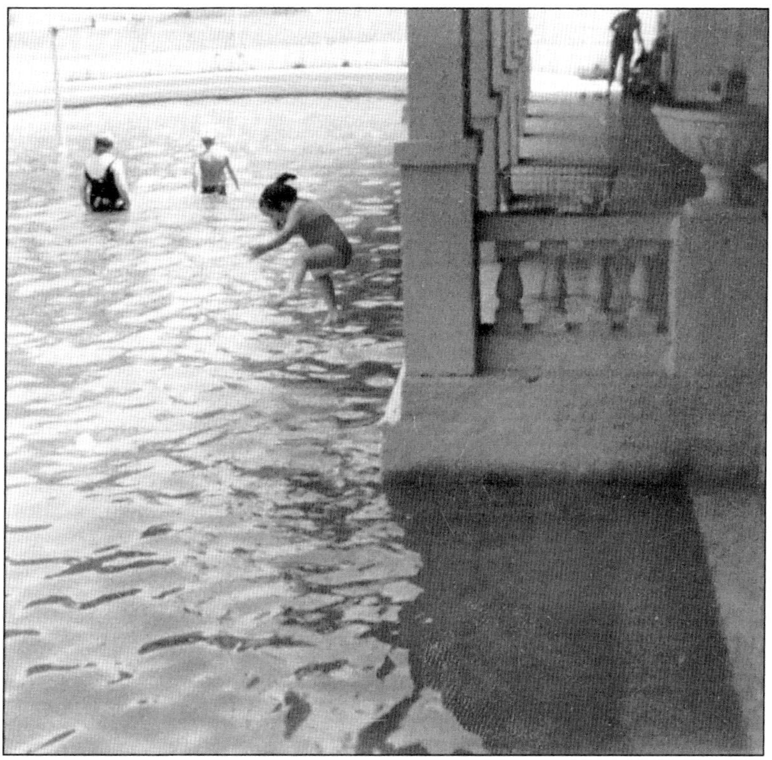

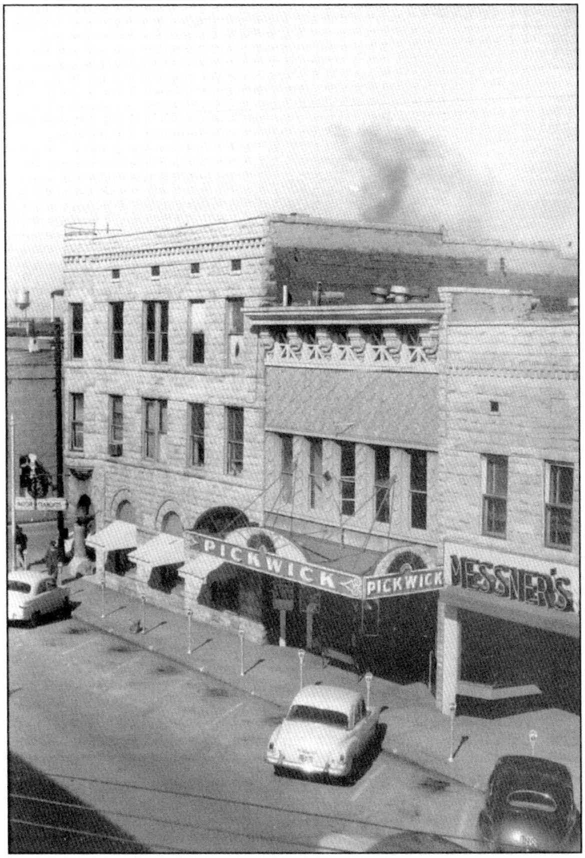


B.F. Liddon entered the "moving pictures business" in 1913 when he opened the Gem, located next door to the Liddon Building, and charged 5¢ admission. Closed in 1924 when he opened the Coliseum Theater, he later reopened it in 1935 as the Pickwick Theater, named for the newly completed Pickwick Dam in nearby Pickwick, Tennessee. By this time, admission price had risen to 10¢. As with his various other projects, he served as his own architect and builder. (Courtesy of Alan McCullar Simmons.)

In an era when equal service for African Americans was almost nonexistent, the Pickwick Theater provided a segregated, upper balcony that also served concessions. Ollie Chambers is pictured beside the Pickwick Popper at the entrance to the balcony seats; popcorn was 5¢ a bag. The Pickwick closed in 1961—another casualty of the television era. (Courtesy of Alan McCullar Simmons.)

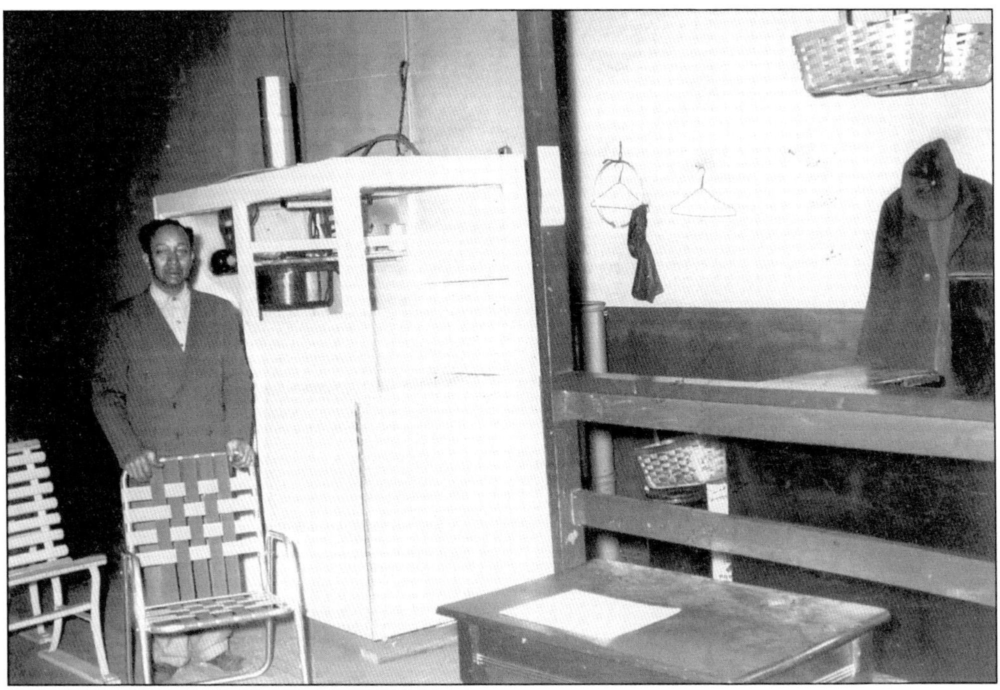

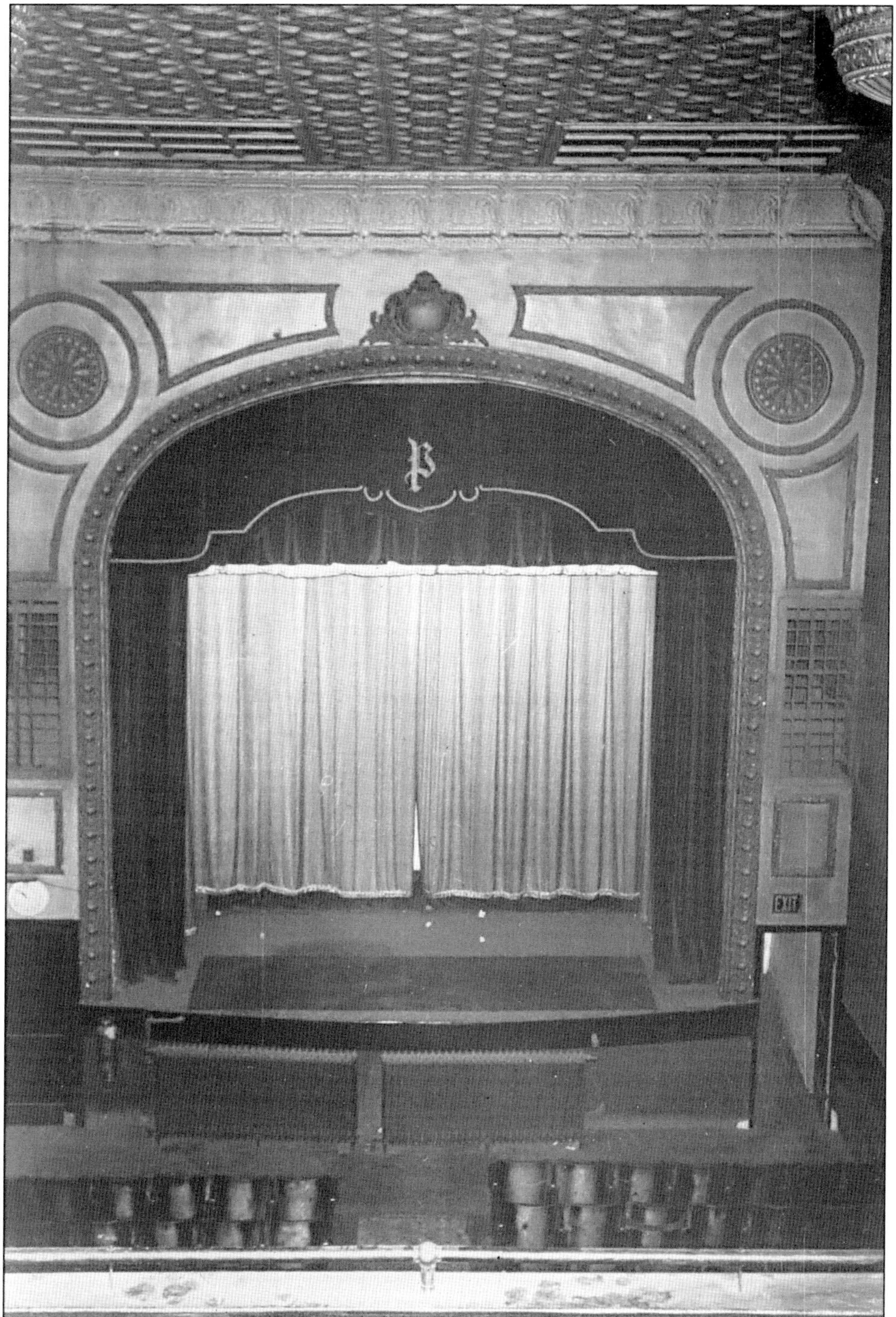

In addition to the opulent velvet curtain that artfully draped in front of the movie screen, the interior of the Pickwick Theater featured a monogrammed velvet curtain above the proscenium, a fully functional stage, and many other ornamental touches, like the rococo medallions flanking the stage. Originally known as the Gem, it truly was one. (Courtesy of Alan McCullar Simmons.)

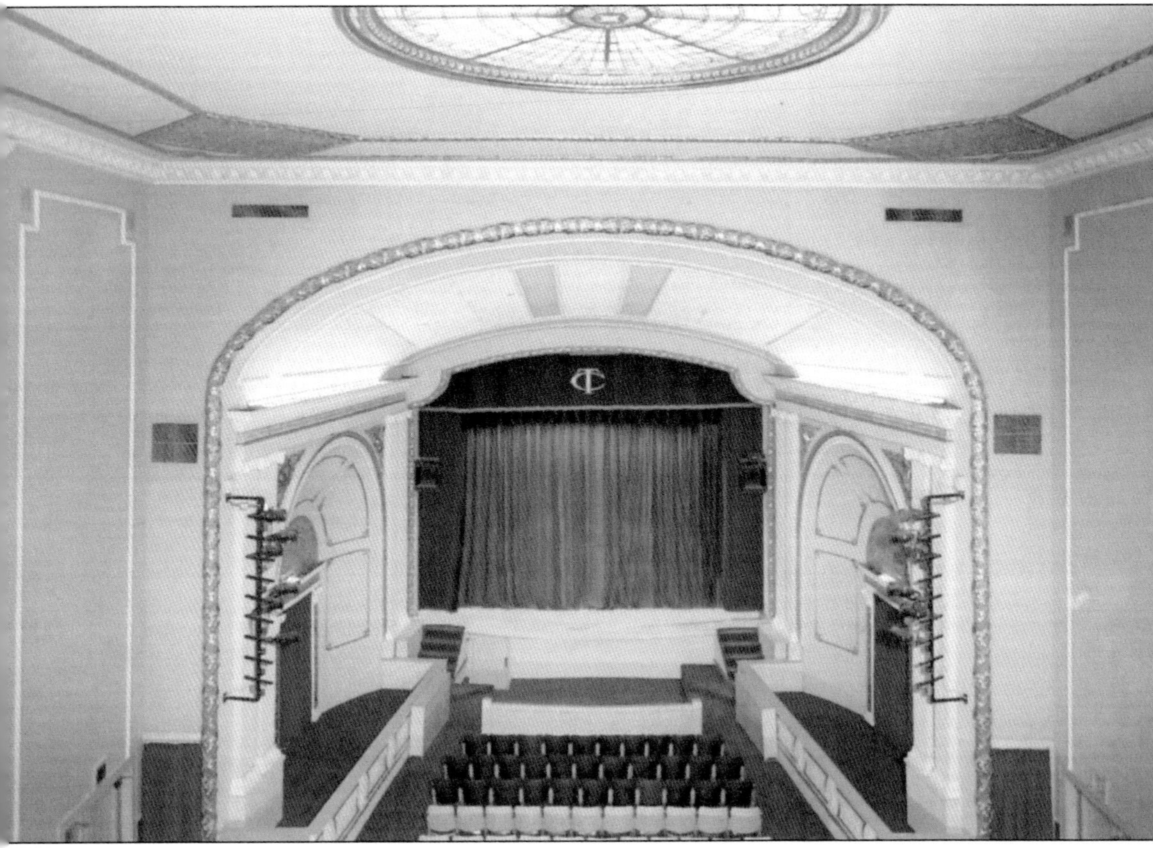

Opened on the Fourth of July in 1924, the Coliseum Theater was Ben Liddon's masterpiece, utilizing tile, marble, beautiful plaster ornamentations, and a stunning stained-glass ceiling. It seats 900 and has two upper balconies. In addition to the movie screen, it has a fully equipped stage that saw some of Elvis Presley's earliest performances. An acoustically perfect building, countless plays, movies, concerts, and other cultural fares have been performed on its historic stage. (Courtesy of Alan McCullar Simmons.)

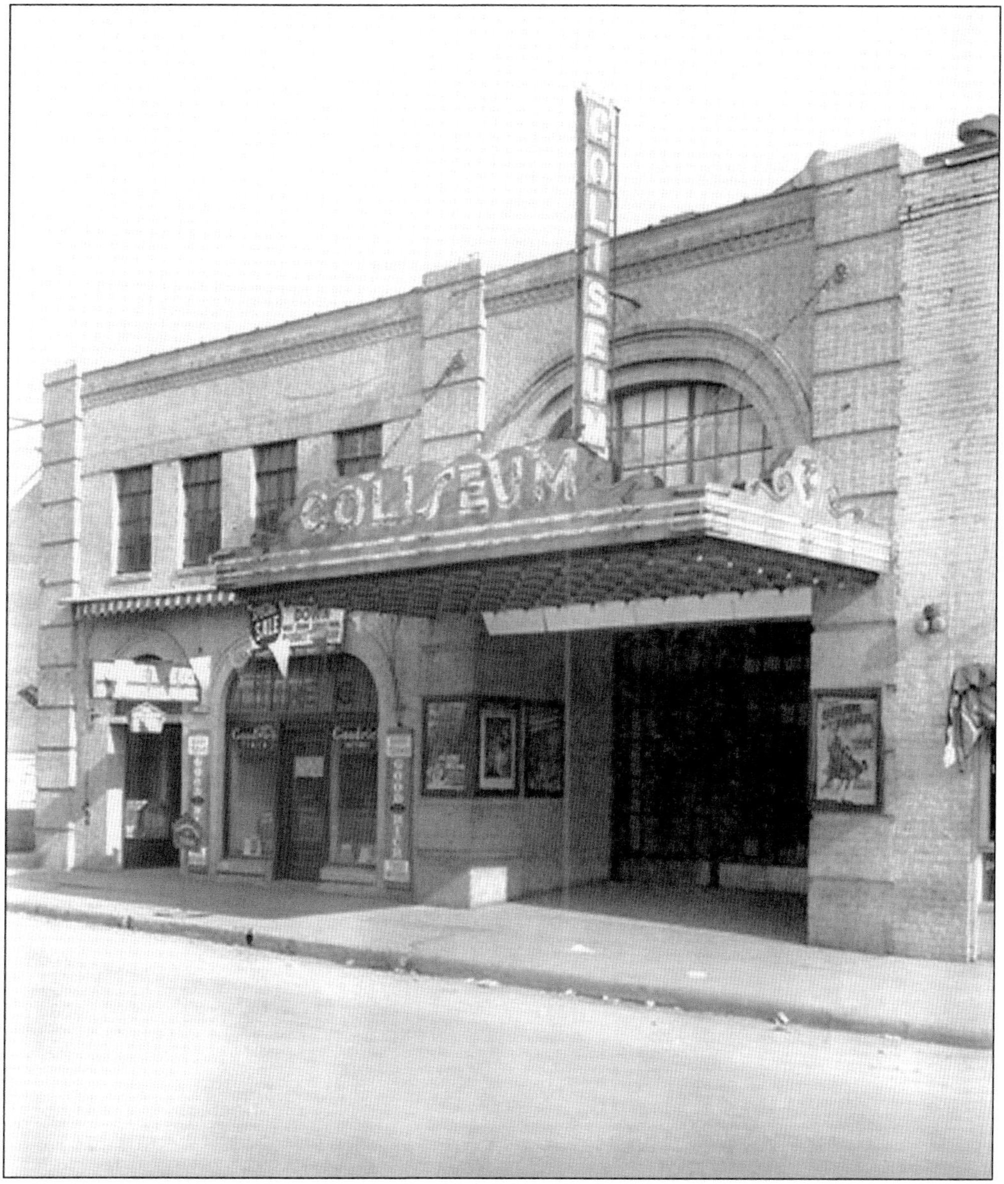


In 1981, Herbert Welch deeded the Coliseum to the City of Corinth, at which time it came under the oversight of the Corinth Area Arts Council. Renamed the Coliseum Civic Center, it had assumed its rightful place as the cultural heart of the city. It also serves as home to the Corinth Symphony Orchestra and hosts other musical events, recitals, school performances, pageants, and receptions. (Courtesy of Alan McCullar Simmons.)

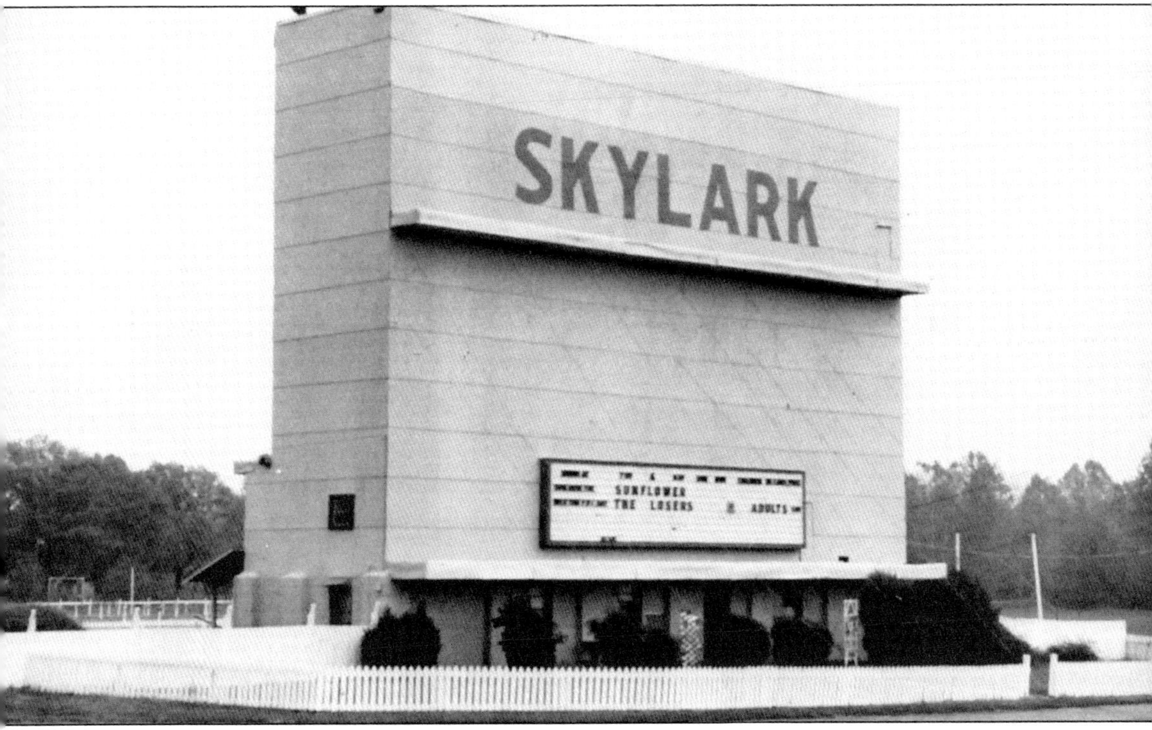


Designed and built in 1949 when Mr. Liddon was 73, the Skylark Drive-In was Corinth's first open-air movie theater. Admission was 25¢, and there was a free children's playground directly under the screen. Parents could bring their children dressed in pajamas and enjoy a movie while the kiddies fell asleep in the back seat. Many small boys and girls grew up watching first-run movies, playing on the slides and swing sets, eating the concession stand's slaw dogs, being protected from mosquitoes by slow-burning coils perched on the dash, and later receiving their very first kiss at the incomparable Skylark. Sadly, the Skylark was sold and demolished in 1986, but it will live on in the fond memories and recollections of aging baby boomers throughout Corinth, Alcorn County, and wherever they may have roamed. (Courtesy of Alan McCullar Simmons.)

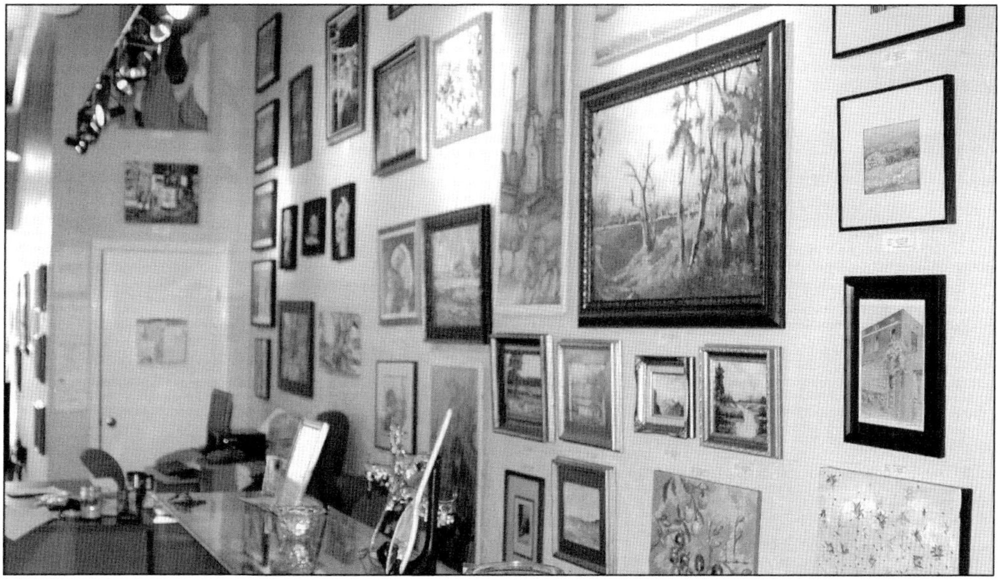

Created in 2003 as a place for local artists to showcase their work, the Corinth Artist Guild Gallery is an ideal place for local artists and craftsmen to receive support, encouragement, and recognition of their creative work from other artists and art lovers. Periodic workshops are made available for all ages and skill levels in a variety of media. Two months out of the year are dedicated to display local students' artwork. The rest of the year, an opening reception is held monthly to introduce the new, featured adult artists and their works. The guild's stated purpose is to encourage "excellence in workmanship and as well as freedom of artistic expression for people of all ages in Corinth and the surrounding area." (Courtesy of James E. "Sonny" Boatman.)

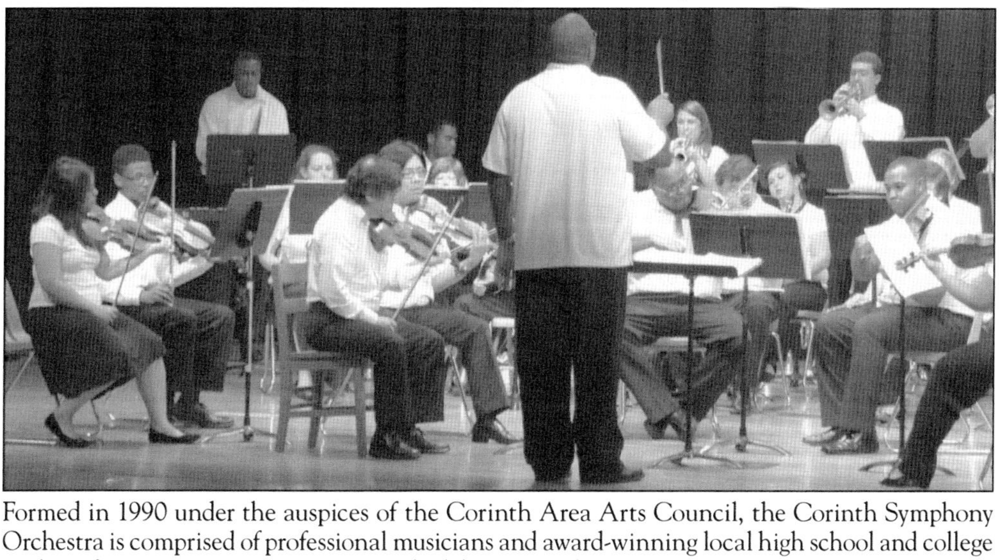

Formed in 1990 under the auspices of the Corinth Area Arts Council, the Corinth Symphony Orchestra is comprised of professional musicians and award-winning local high school and college students from Mississippi, Tennessee, and Alabama. For the past several years, CSO has been under the most capable baton of maestro Maurice Weatherall. The high point of any season is the free Fourth of July extravaganza held annually in the parking lot of the North Mississippi Museum at the old depot. A former Army veteran who played with the US Army Band during his service, "Let Freedom Ring" is the maestro's and his orchestra's gift to Corinthians and the people of the surrounding area—but most importantly to the servicemen and women who sacrifice so much.

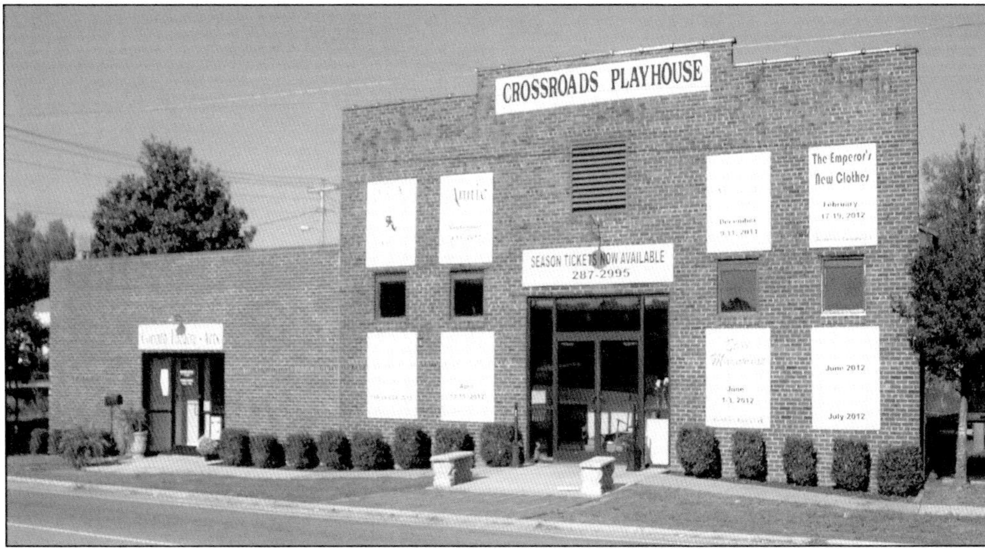


Organized in March 1968 by civic-minded Corinthians whose aim was to have the finest amateur theater in the tri-state area, the Corinth Theatre-Arts is a well-equipped little theater recognized as one of the best of its kind in the entire mid-South. In the beginning, CT-A plays were staged in local school auditoriums until 1972, when the city gifted the theater with the old Tri-State Fair exhibit hall. Since then, a myriad number of directors, playwrights, and poets, both amateur and professional, have cut their teeth and honed their skills on CT-A's stage. Countless Corinthians have "trod the boards," provided musical accompaniment, constructed sets, and worked backstage in a labor of love that is open to anyone who wants to volunteer and become part of a community tradition of excellence that has continued for nearly 45 years.

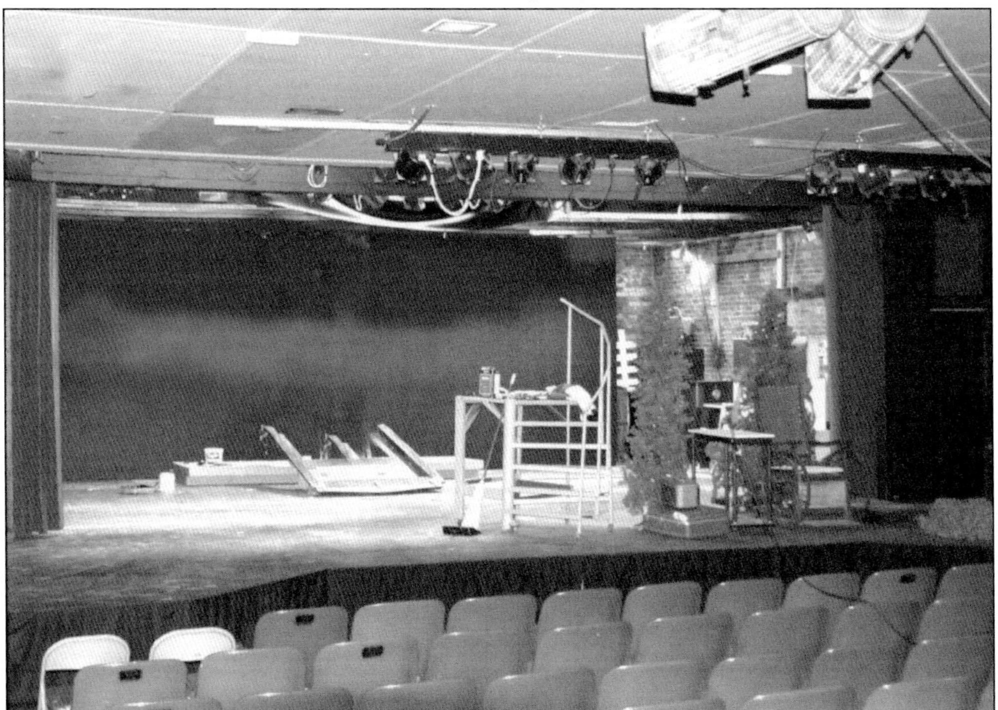

# *Three*

# Celebrities, Celebrations, and CHS

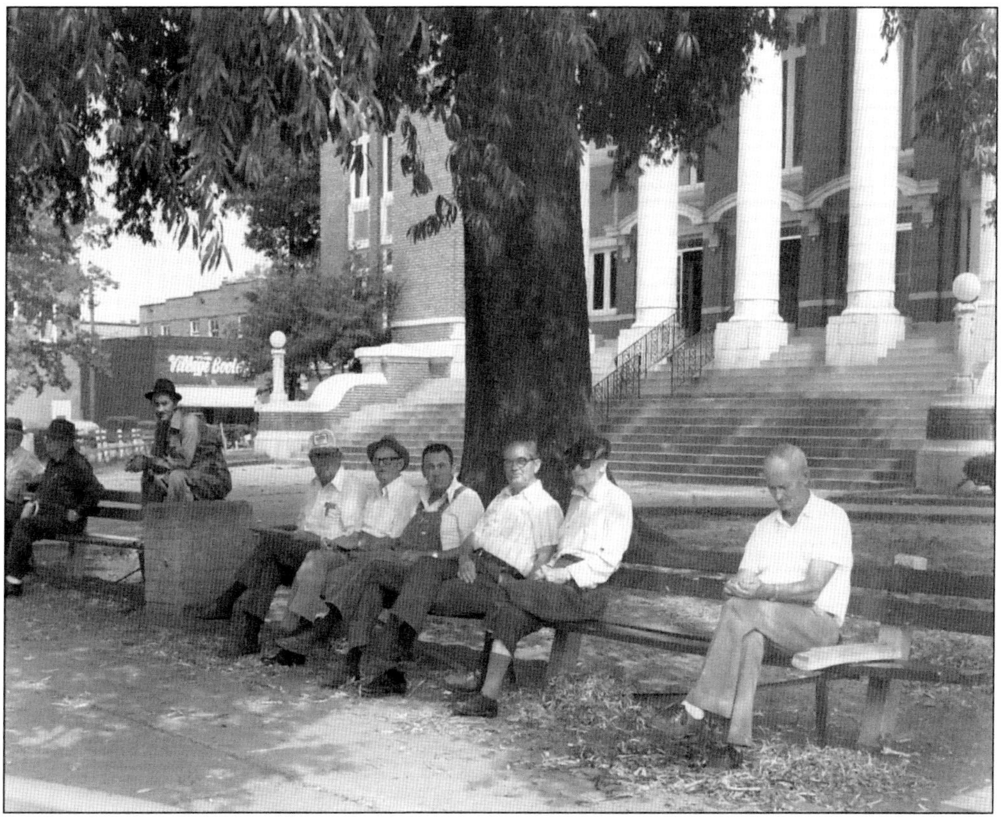

The courthouse has served as the heart of Corinth since 1854, witnessing parades, celebrations, and events since the days of dirt streets. One of the most constant and familiar sights in front of it has been a bench filled with old men turning big sticks of wood, mostly cedar, into shavings. The only change throughout the years is the identity of the whittlers. Always up for an event, whether it is to mark a historic anniversary, welcome home a famous native, or celebrate a rite of passage, the average Corinthian finds plenty of time to celebrate the joys of small-town living.

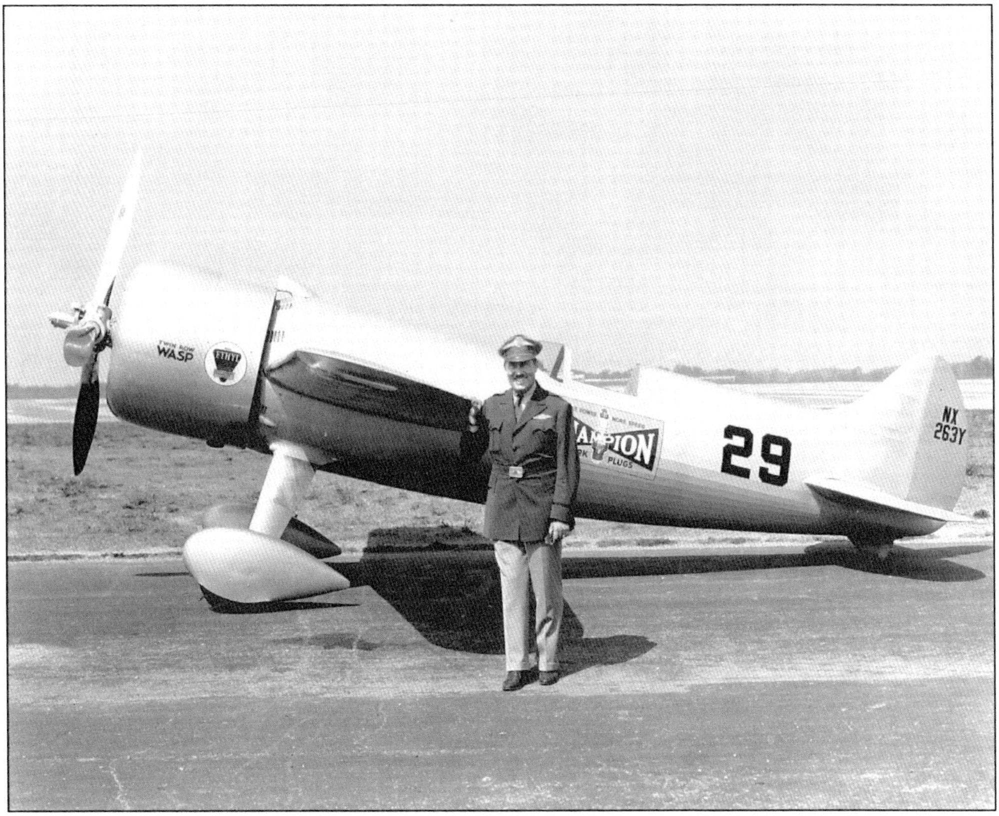


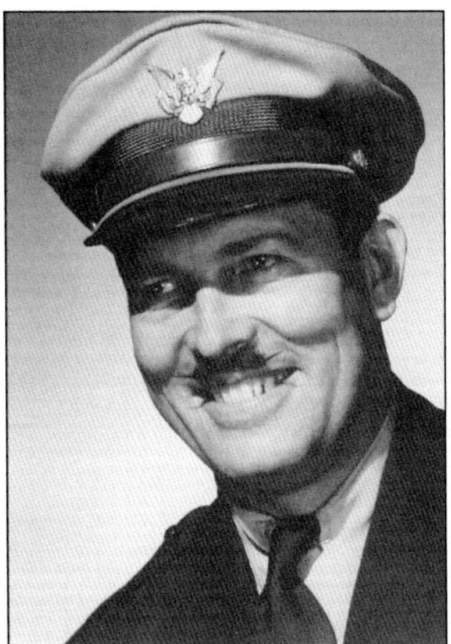

The National Cyclopedia of American Biography

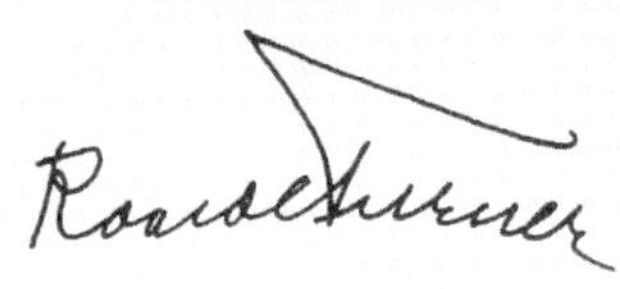

Roscoe Turner broke speed records nearly every time he flew. The premier aviator of his time, he was considered the number-one speed pilot of the 1930s. In a decade when air races were second only to baseball in attendance, he won the Harmon Trophy, the Bendix Trophy, and was the only three-time winner of the Thompson Trophy. Along with Jimmy Doolittle, he was the only pilot to win both the Thompson and Bendix Trophies.

As a result of his amazing career and the fame it brought, one of Roscoe's planes and many personal items have a permanent home in Washington, DC, at the Smithsonian Institution. As one of Corinth's most famous and beloved native sons, the local airport is named in his honor.

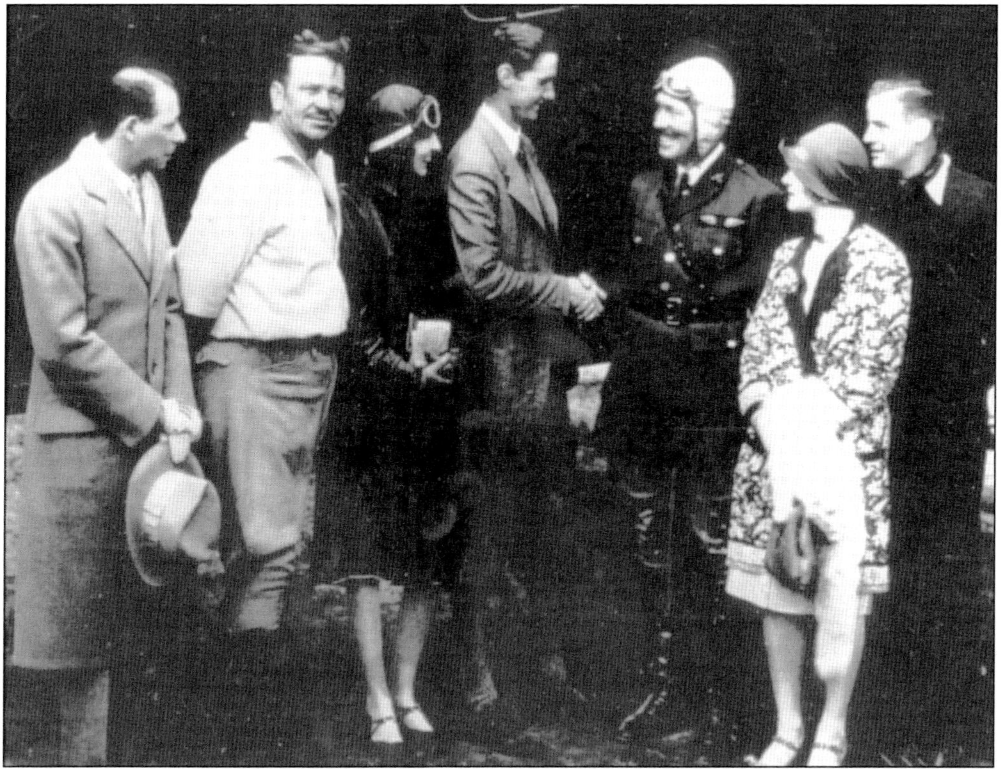

In the late 1920s, long before he became a reclusive billionaire, Howard Hughes decided to make the definitive movie on aerial combat. He therefore hired Roscoe Turner to fly in his epic World War I movie *Hell's Angels*. Pictured from left to right are Lucien Prival, Wallace Beery, Roscoe's wife, Carline, Howard Hughes, Roscoe Turner, Greta Nissen, and John Darrow.

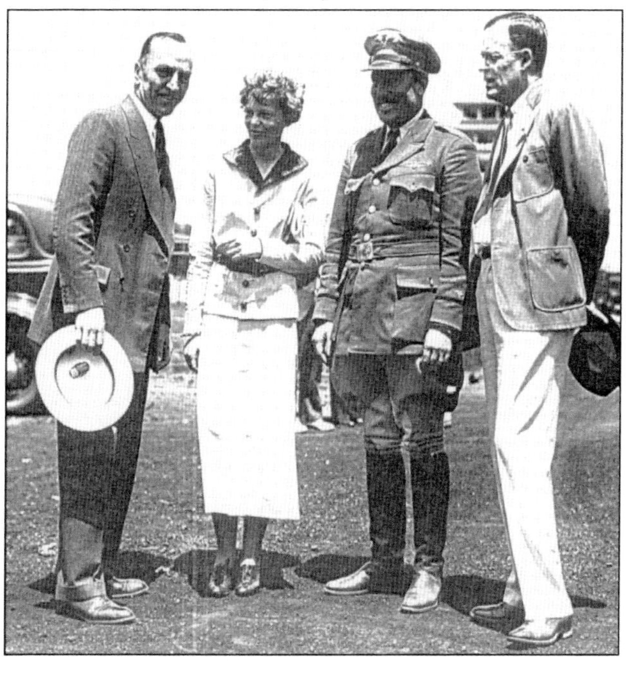

In the 1930s, there was no better-known pilot than Col. Roscoe Turner, and no other pilot won more awards or broke more speed records. A flamboyant showman both inside and outside the cockpit, Roscoe regularly rubbed elbows with the most famous Hollywood stars of the day and was featured in a Hollywood movie, *Flight at Midnight*. He took Clark Gable and Fred MacMurray on their first airplane rides, among other famous stars. He was equally as famous as other well-known pilots of the day. Pictured from left to right are World War I ace Eddie Rickenbacker, famed female aviatrix Amelia Earhart, Roscoe Turner, and Earhart's husband George Putnam.

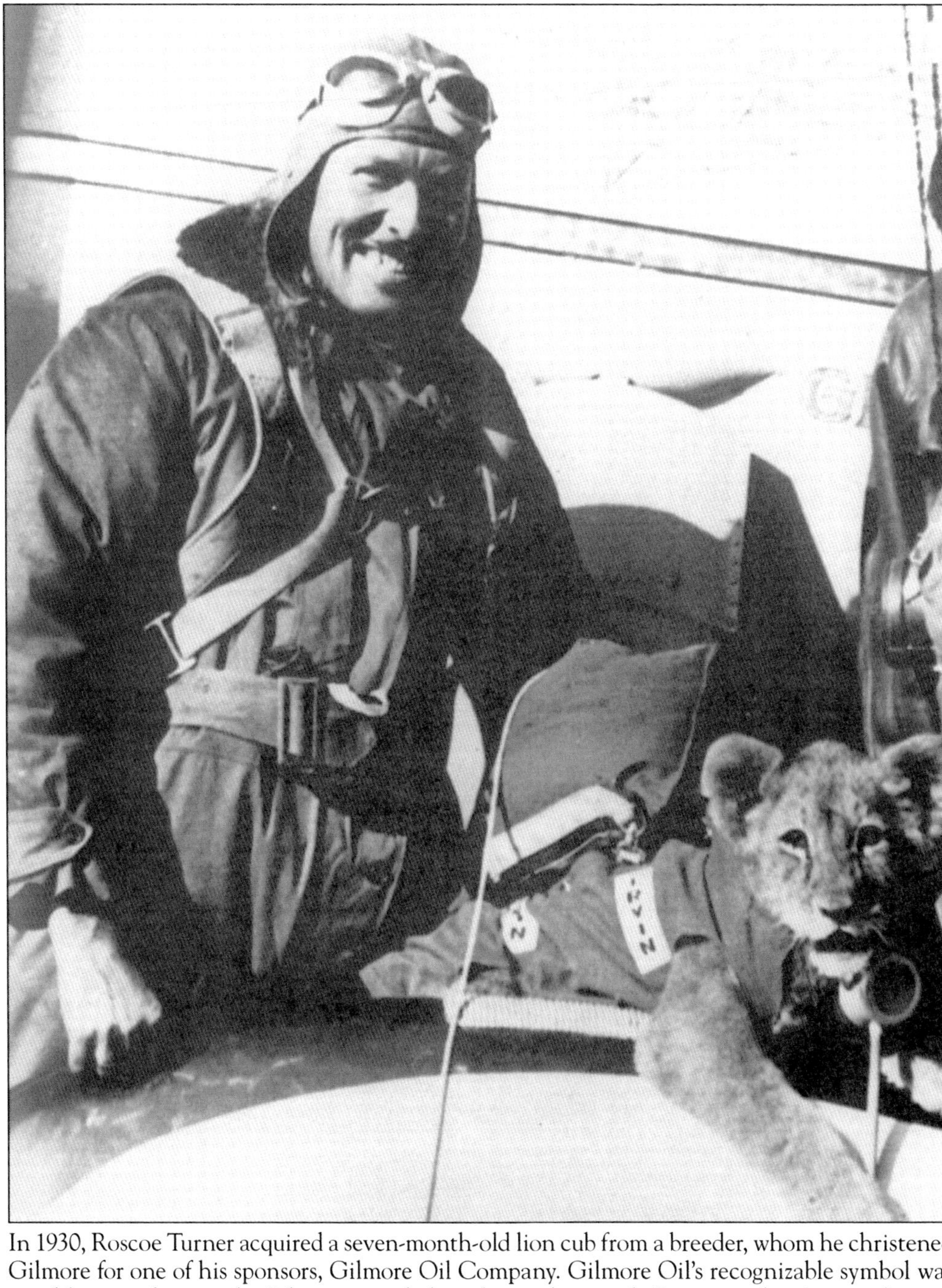

In 1930, Roscoe Turner acquired a seven-month-old lion cub from a breeder, whom he christened Gilmore for one of his sponsors, Gilmore Oil Company. Gilmore Oil's recognizable symbol was a red lion, and as a cub, Gilmore traveled in the cockpit with Roscoe as he shattered speed records all across America. The two high flyers had many adventures together, and Gilmore had his own custom-made parachute and oxygen mask should the need ever arise. By 1932, Gilmore had become too heavy to continue flying, and Roscoe reluctantly retired him to a wildlife refuge outside of Thousand Oaks, California, where he made regular visits to see his beloved mascot. Gilmore lived a long and happy life at the refuge, and when he died in 1950, Roscoe was with his old flying partner holding his paw.

On September 9, 1924, Roscoe Turner wed his first wife, Carline Hunter Stovall, of Kenton, Tennessee, on his 29th birthday. The couple wed while standing in the cockpit of a Curtiss Jenny, albeit one that was parked on the ground with the minister perched precariously on the wing of the plane. The marriage lasted until 1946, when they divorced.

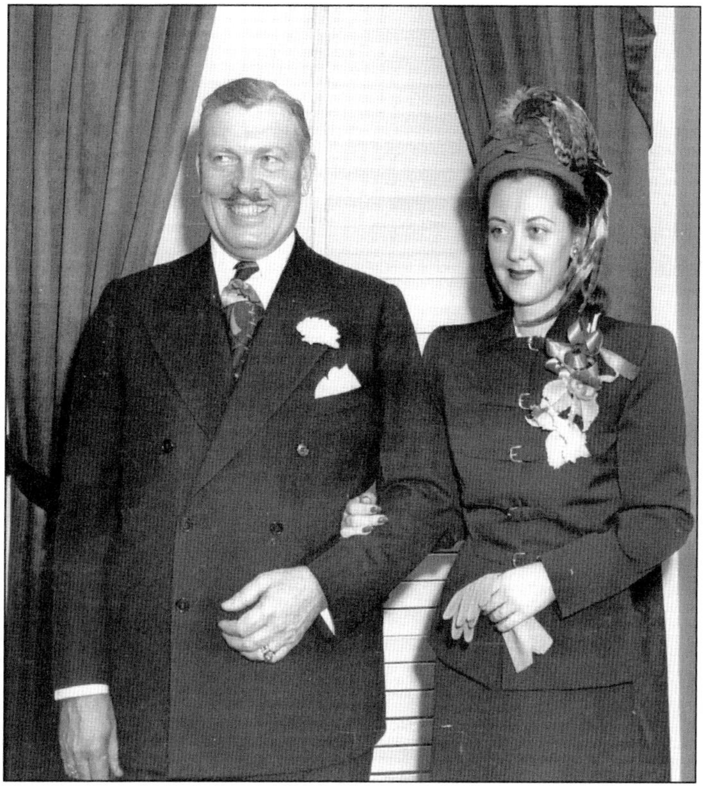

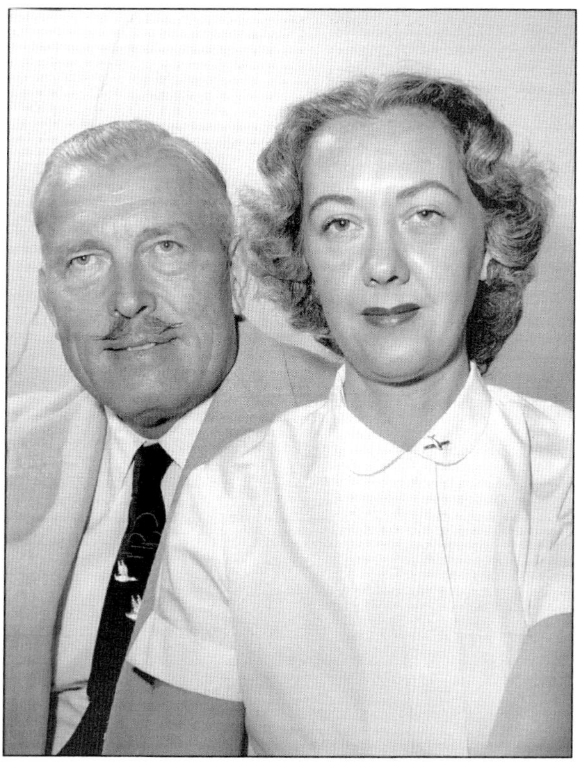

Later that year, Roscoe married Madonna M. Miller of Sheridan, Indiana, in New York City. The ceremony was a small, private affair, attended by a few close friends of the couple, one of whom was popular radio personality Arthur Godfrey. Over time, Madonna assumed much of the running of her husband's business affairs and greatly streamlined the day-to-day efficiency of his office. The couple was happily married for over 20 years until Roscoe's death on June 23, 1970.

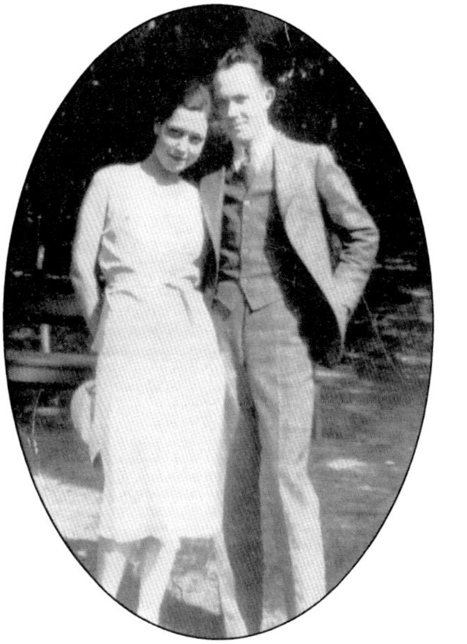

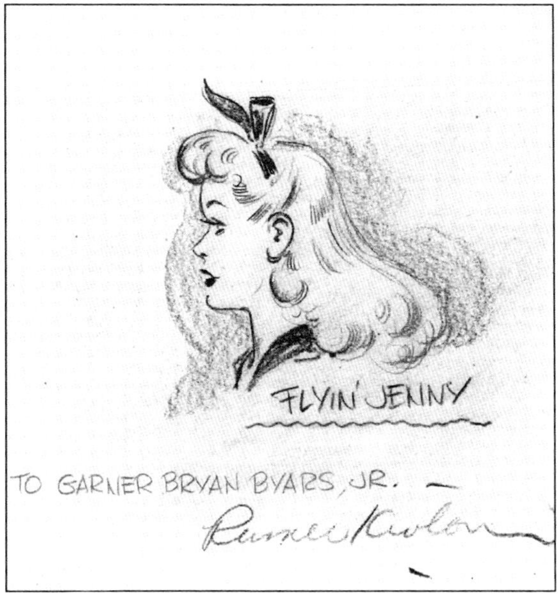


A pilot and flight instructor for the Army Air Corps in World War II, Russell Keaton was known for his work on some of the most popular adventure comic strips of the golden age of comics, including *Buck Rogers*, *Skyroads*, and *Flying Legion*. A Corinth native, he inked his masterpiece *Flyin' Jenny*, which was the only comic strip starring a woman aviator, from 1939 to 1945. Named for and patterned after his wife, Virginia, heroine Jenny Dare was a strong, beautiful, and witty girl fully capable of holding her own with the best of them, whether it was stunt flying, barnstorming, or finding herself up to her wings in adventure, romance, or intrigue. Tragically, Russell Keaton died of cancer at the young age of 35. (Courtesy of Jan Keaton Johnson.)

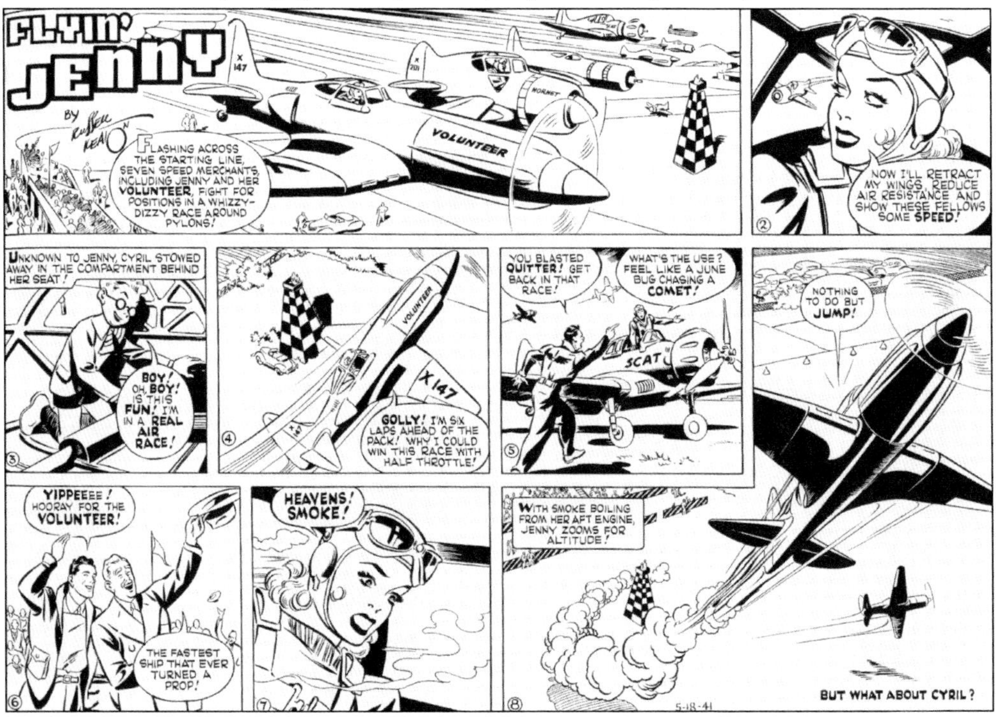

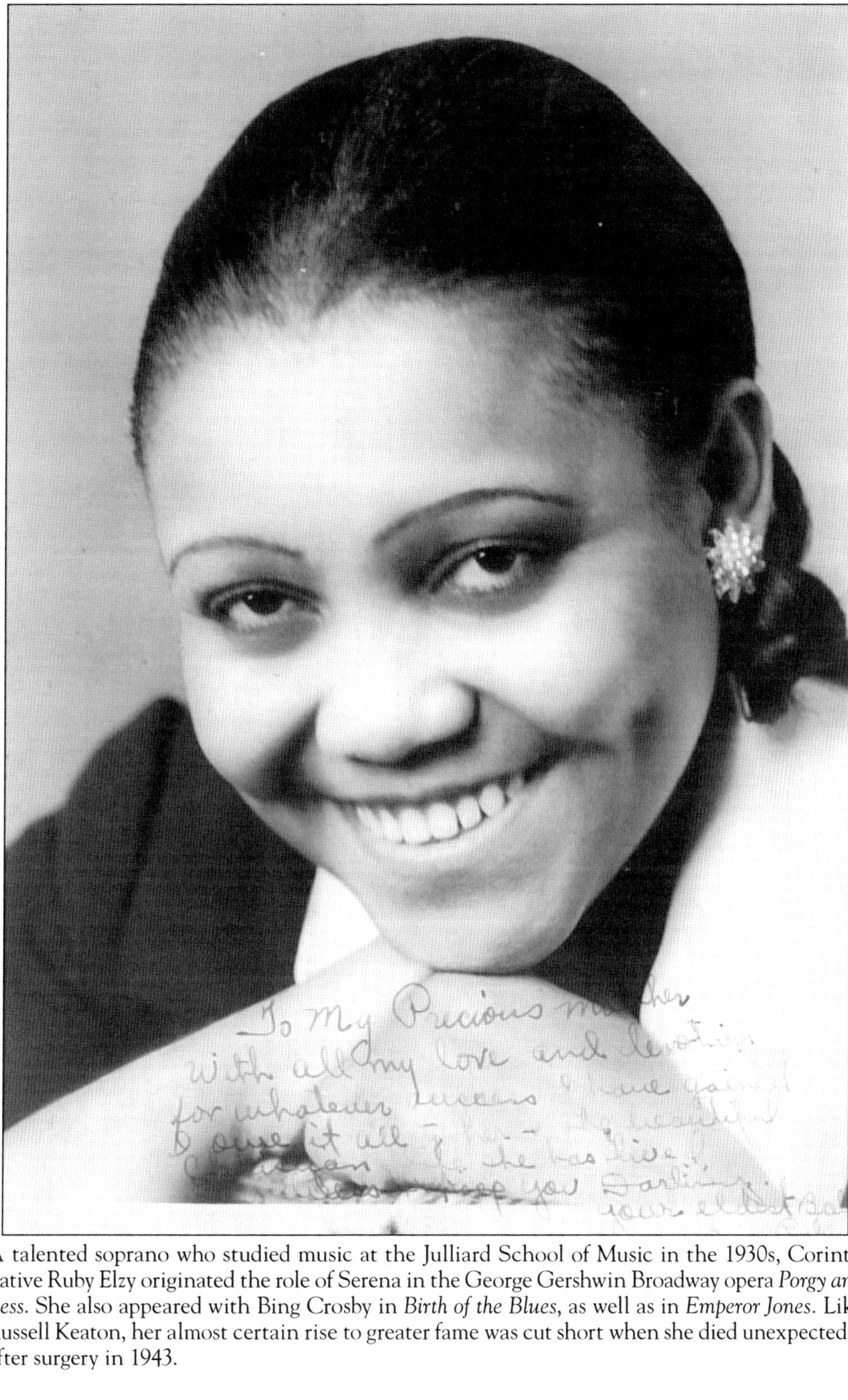


A talented soprano who studied music at the Julliard School of Music in the 1930s, Corinth native Ruby Elzy originated the role of Serena in the George Gershwin Broadway opera *Porgy and Bess*. She also appeared with Bing Crosby in *Birth of the Blues*, as well as in *Emperor Jones*. Like Russell Keaton, her almost certain rise to greater fame was cut short when she died unexpectedly after surgery in 1943.

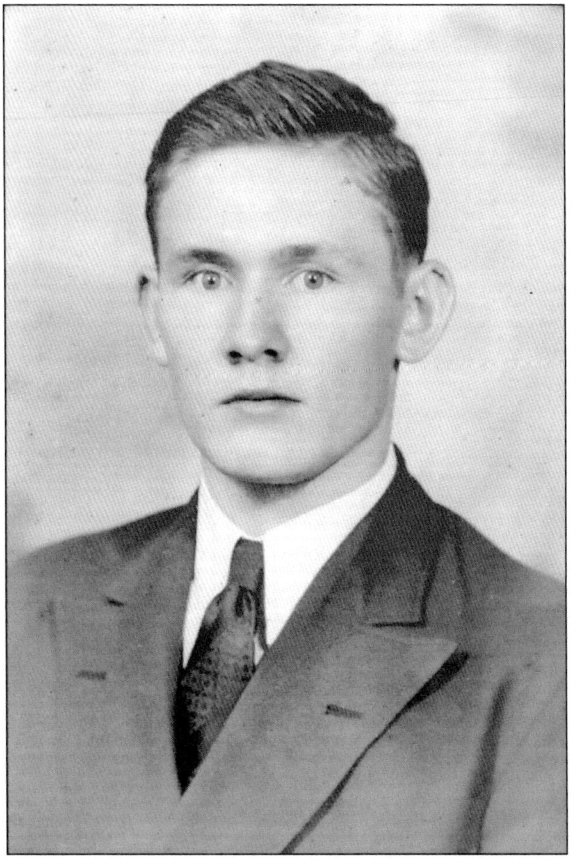

A novelist and screenwriter of the highest caliber, Thomas Hal Phillips's novels include *The Golden Lie*, *Search for a Hero*, *Kangaroo Hollow*, *The Bittersweet Path*, *The Loved and the Unloved*, and *Red Midnight*. As a much sought-after scriptwriter, he penned *Ode to Billy Joe*, *The Autobiography of Miss Jane Pittman*, *Walking Tall II*, *Thieves Like Us*, and the award-winning *Nashville*. Upon retiring, he returned to Corinth, where he died in 2007.

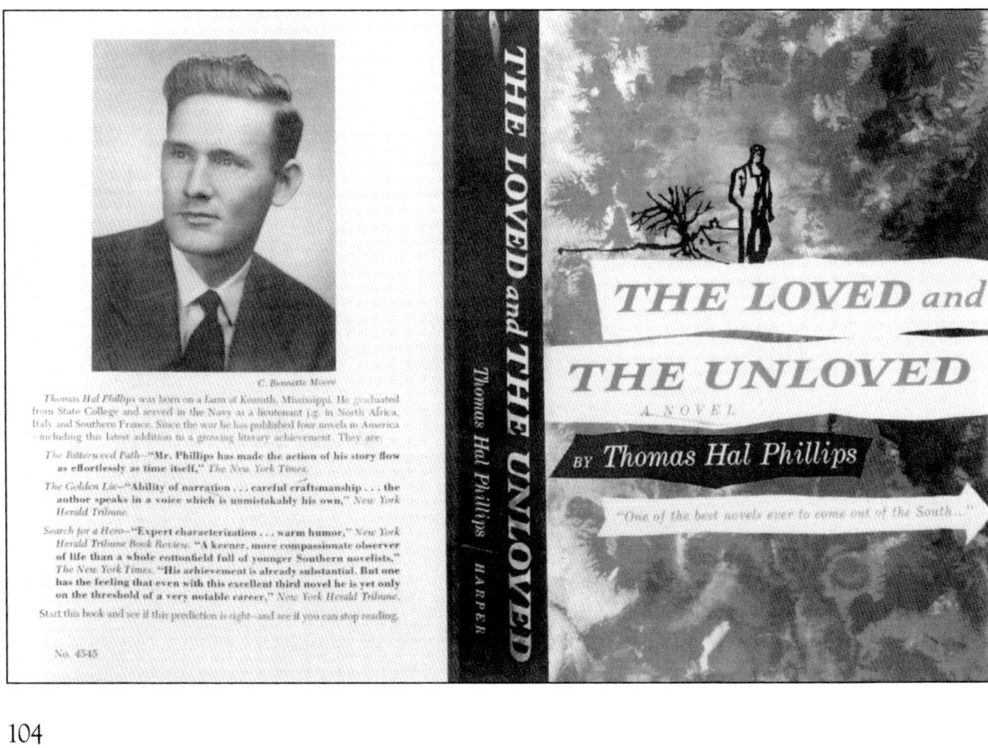

Corinth's own Don Lee Blasingame played 1,444 big-league games spanning 14 years in the major leagues for the St. Louis Cardinals, San Francisco Giants, Cincinnati Reds, Washington Senators, and the Kansas City Athletics. He was elected to the 1955 All-Star Team, placed second in the 1956 National League Rookie of the Year voting, and played for the Reds in the 1961 World Series against the New York Yankees. In 1966, Don began a 14-year career in Japan, serving at various times as player, coach, and manager for three Japanese professional baseball teams until his retirement in 1980. Known as "Blazer" by his adoring fans in the Japan, Don is one of the most illustrious Americans to ever be involved in Japanese professional baseball.

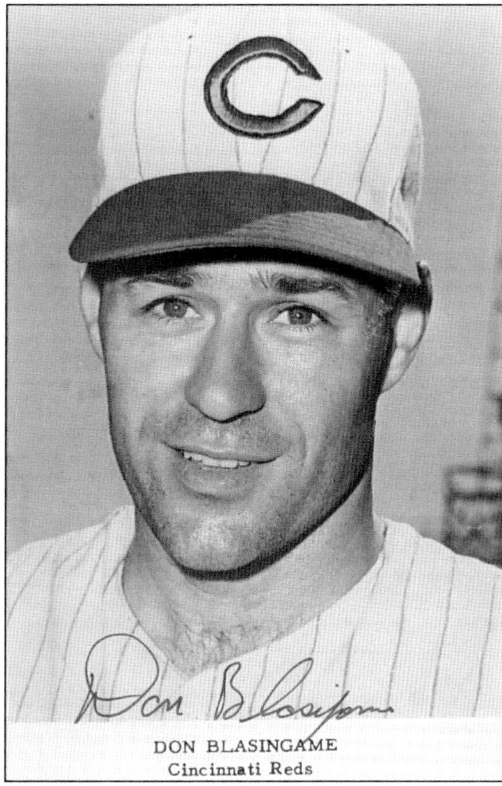


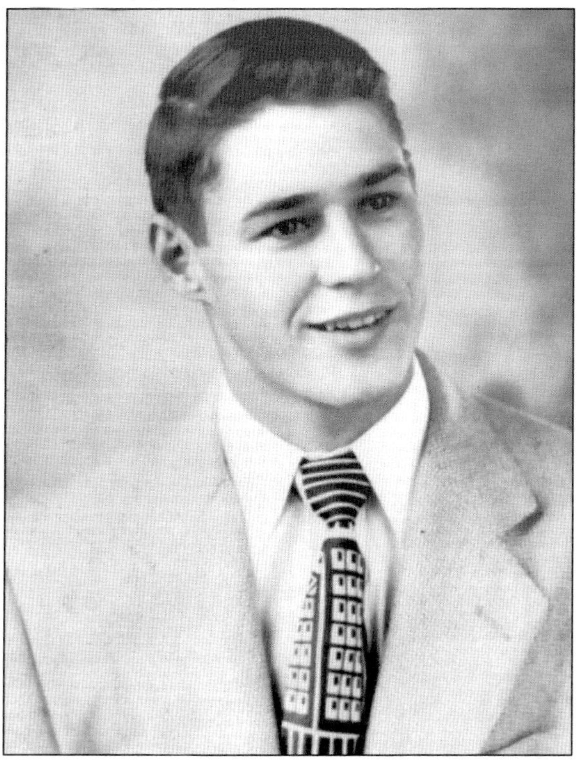

(The Original)

**WHISKEY SPEECH**

*as composed and delivered by*

**N.S. SWEAT, JR.**

MY FRIENDS:

I had not intended to discuss this controversial subject at this particular time. However, I want you to know that I do not shun controversy. On the contrary, I will take a stand on any issue at any time, regardless of how fraught with controversy it might be. You have asked me how I feel about whiskey. All right, here is how I feel about whiskey

If when you say whiskey you mean the Devil's brew, the poison scourge, the bloody monster that defiles innocence, dethrones reason, destroys the home, creates misery and poverty, yea, literally takes the bread from the mouths of little children; if you mean the evil drink that topples the Christian man and woman from the pinnacle of righteous, gracious living into the bottomless pit of degradation, and despair, and shame, and helplessness, and hopelessness, then certainly I am against it.

But,

If when you say whiskey you mean the oil of conversation, the philosophic wine, the ale that is consumed when good fellows get together, that puts a song in their hearts and laughter on their lips, and the warm glow of contentment in their eyes; if you mean Christmas cheer; if you mean the stimulating drink that puts the spring into the old gentleman's step on a frosty, crispy morning; if you mean the drink that enables a man to magnify his joy, and his happiness, and to forget, if only for a little while, life's great tragedies, and heartaches, and sorrows; if you mean that drink the sale of which pours into our treasuries untold millions of dollars, which are used to provide tender care for our little crippled children, our blind, our deaf, our dumb, our pitiful aged and infirm; to build highways and hospitals and schools, then certainly I am for it.

This is my stand. I will not retreat from it. I will not compromise.



Judge Noah S. "Soggy" Sweat was a legislator, district attorney, circuit court judge, and college professor of great note. Most Corinthians agree, though, that the high water mark of his political career was in 1952, when he was asked to deliver an address on his stand on the legalization of alcohol, an issue hotly debated by Mississippi lawmakers at the time. In what "Soggy" himself described as a tour de force, he delivered what became known as "the Whiskey Speech." It was a masterpiece of political doublespeak and Orwellian obfuscation that set a standard rarely exceeded outside of Washington, DC.

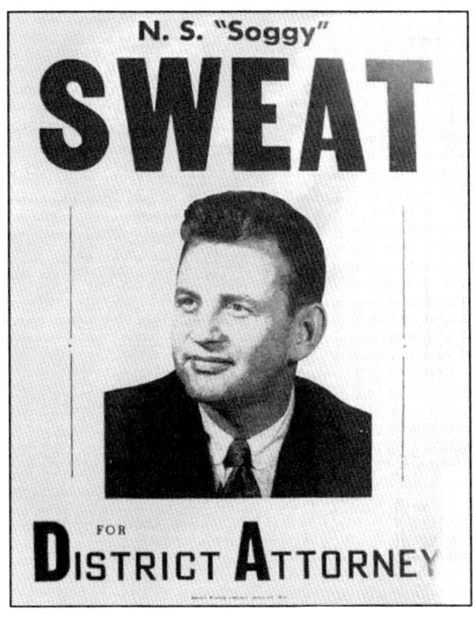

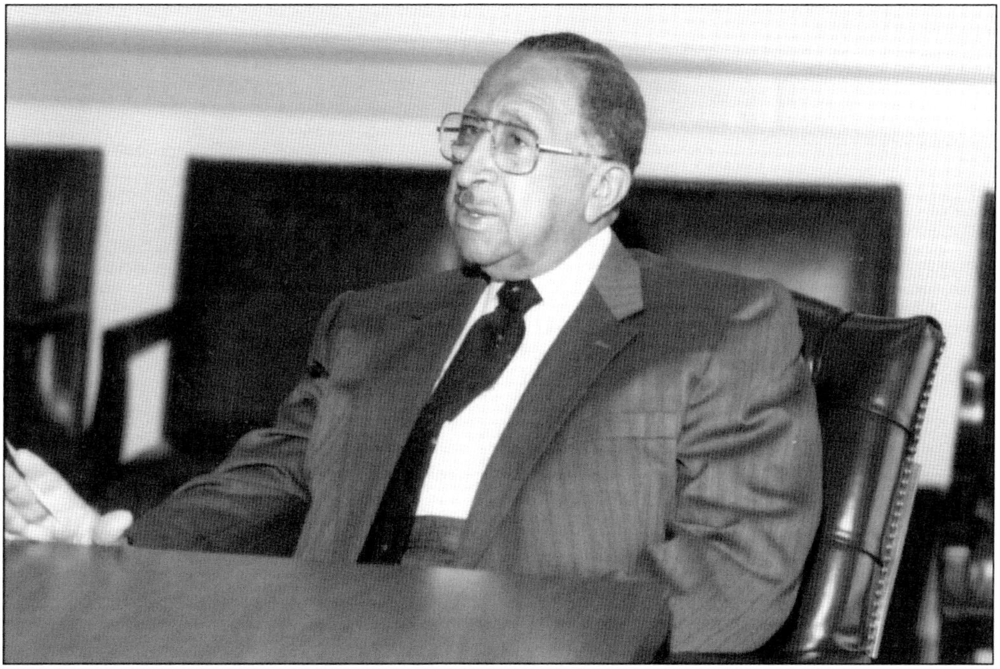

E.S. Bishop came to Corinth in 1935 and assumed the position of principal at the Scale Street Colored School, later renamed Easom High School. His service to the school system spanned 38 years and "The Professor," as all knew him, was credited with helping to usher in an example of peaceful school integration in 1969. He was elected to the board of aldermen in the early 1970s and remained in that position until 1989, when he assumed the duties of mayor when the need arose. Four years later, he ran for and was elected Corinth's mayor in his own right in a city that is 80 percent Caucasian. Upon his retirement from public life, the city dedicated the E.S. Bishop Senior Citizens Center in his honor. (Courtesy of the Corinth Black History Museum.)

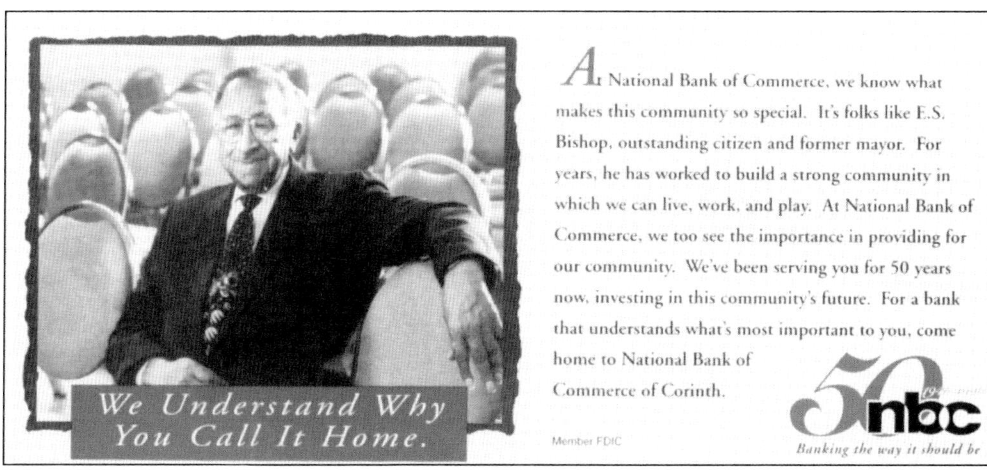

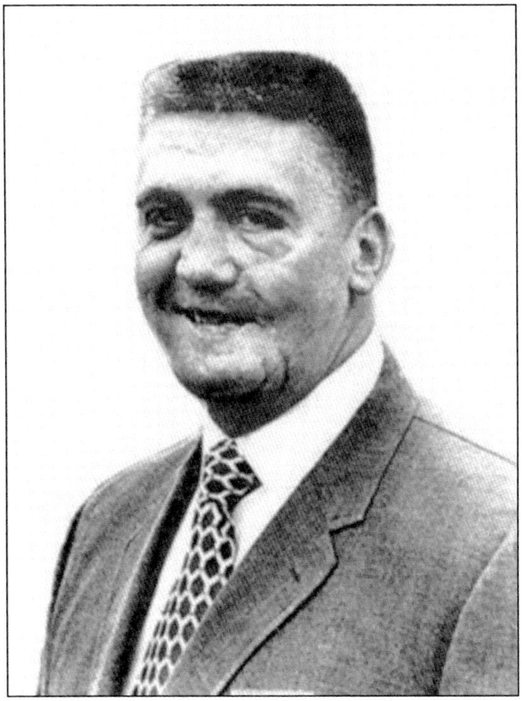

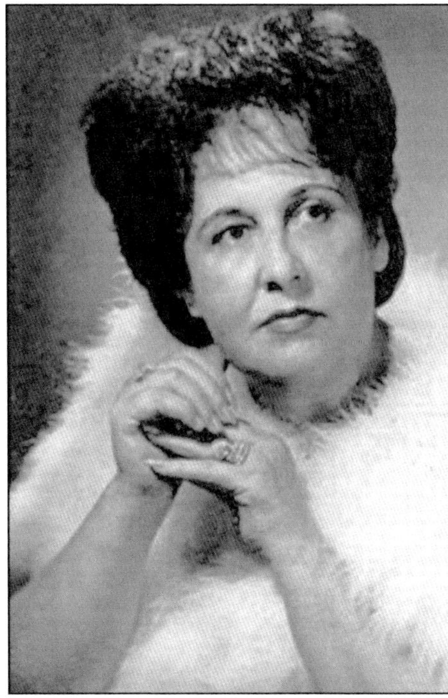

Louise Hathcock was notorious for running state-line clip joints. Prostitution, bootlegging, gambling, rigged dice games, and all sorts of nefarious activities occurred daily. All-out war was waged between Louise (right) and legendary McNairy County sheriff Buford Pusser (left), of *Walking Tall* fame, until he shot her to death in self-defense at her business, the Shamrock Motel, on February 1, 1966.

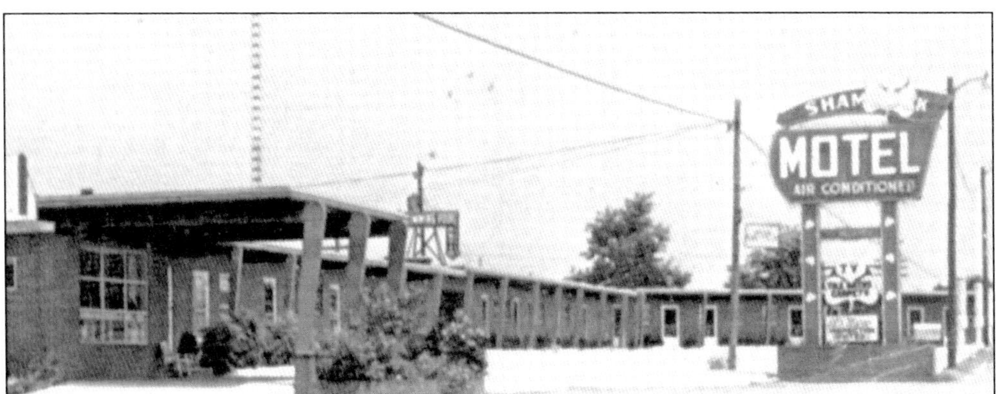


On the flip side of fame, Corinthians had a front-row seat to the infamous and ongoing drama occurring at the Mississippi–Tennessee state line less than five miles away. In his 1990 book *The State Line Mob*, W.R. Morris introduced the world to some characters familiar to many Corinthians from the 1950s through the 1960s.

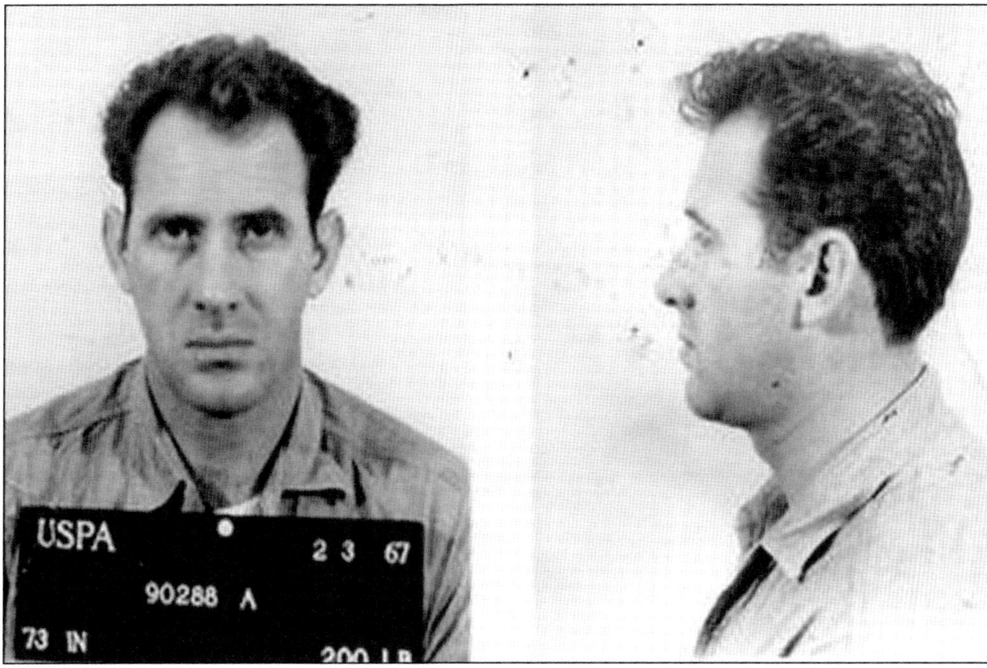


A true disciple of the thug life, Carl Douglas "Towhead" White was one of the most dangerous and feared members of the State Line Mob. Along with his partner Louise Hathcock, White robbed, stole, and bilked hundreds of victims until his own murder by rival outlaw Berry "Junior" Smith at the El-Ray Motel on April 2, 1969.

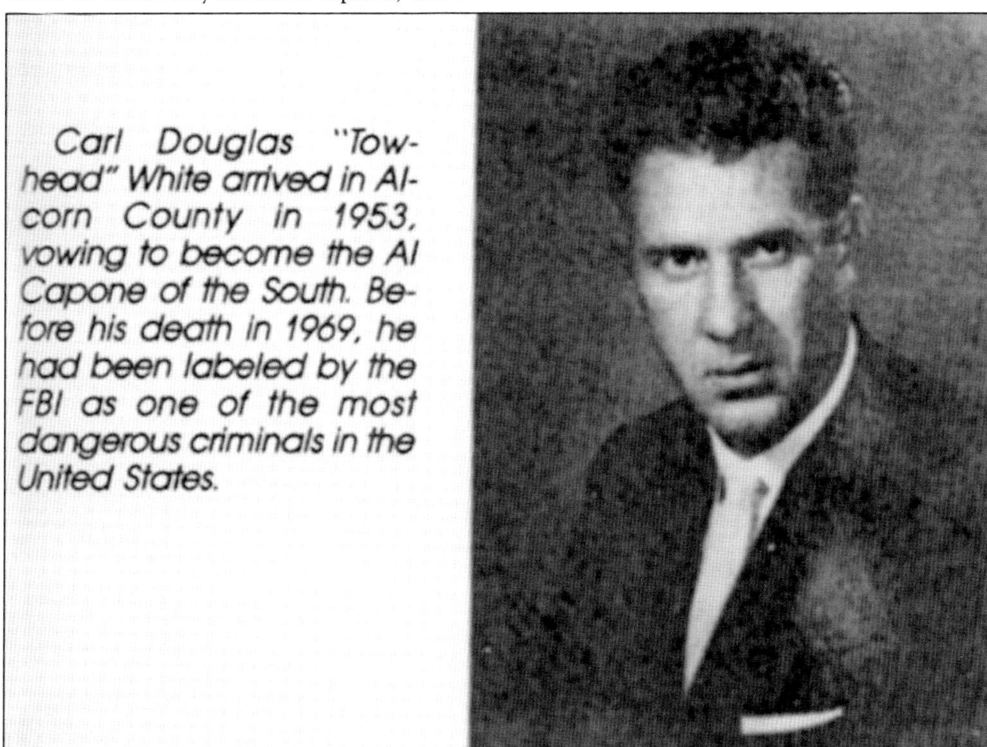

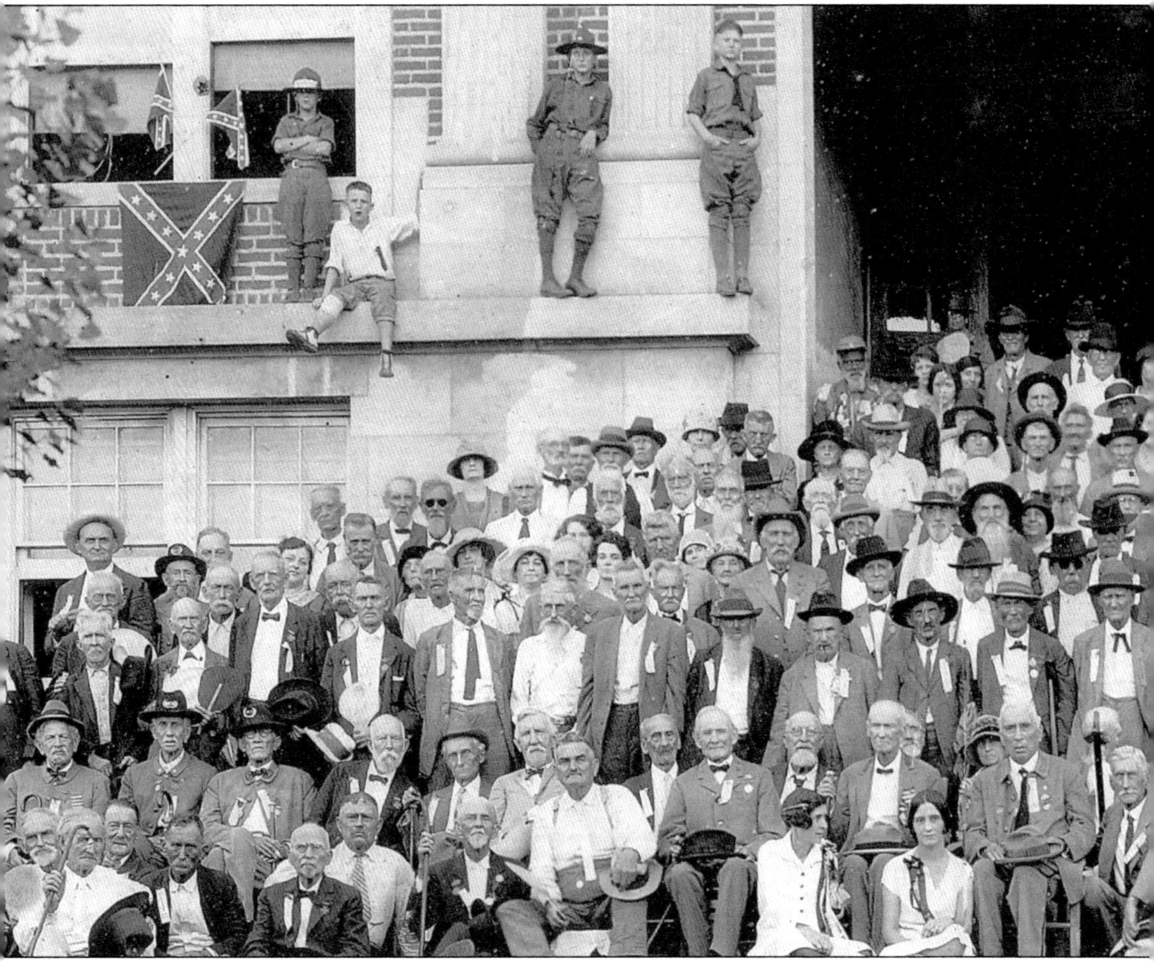

This photograph is entitled: "Thirty-sixth annual reunion Miss. Division U.V.C. Corinth Mississippi September 8th, 9th, and 10th, 1926." It shows Confederate veterans posing with family members as Boy Scouts perch on the window ledges above. In Corinth, as it was across the North and South for Federals and Confederates alike, the old soldiers once again donned their medals and posed for posterity, still proud, still inseparable, and perhaps still dreaming, in the oft quoted words of Pvt. Barry Benson, Army of Northern Virginia in 1880, "In time, even death itself might be abolished; who knows but it may be given to us after this life to meet again in the old quarters,

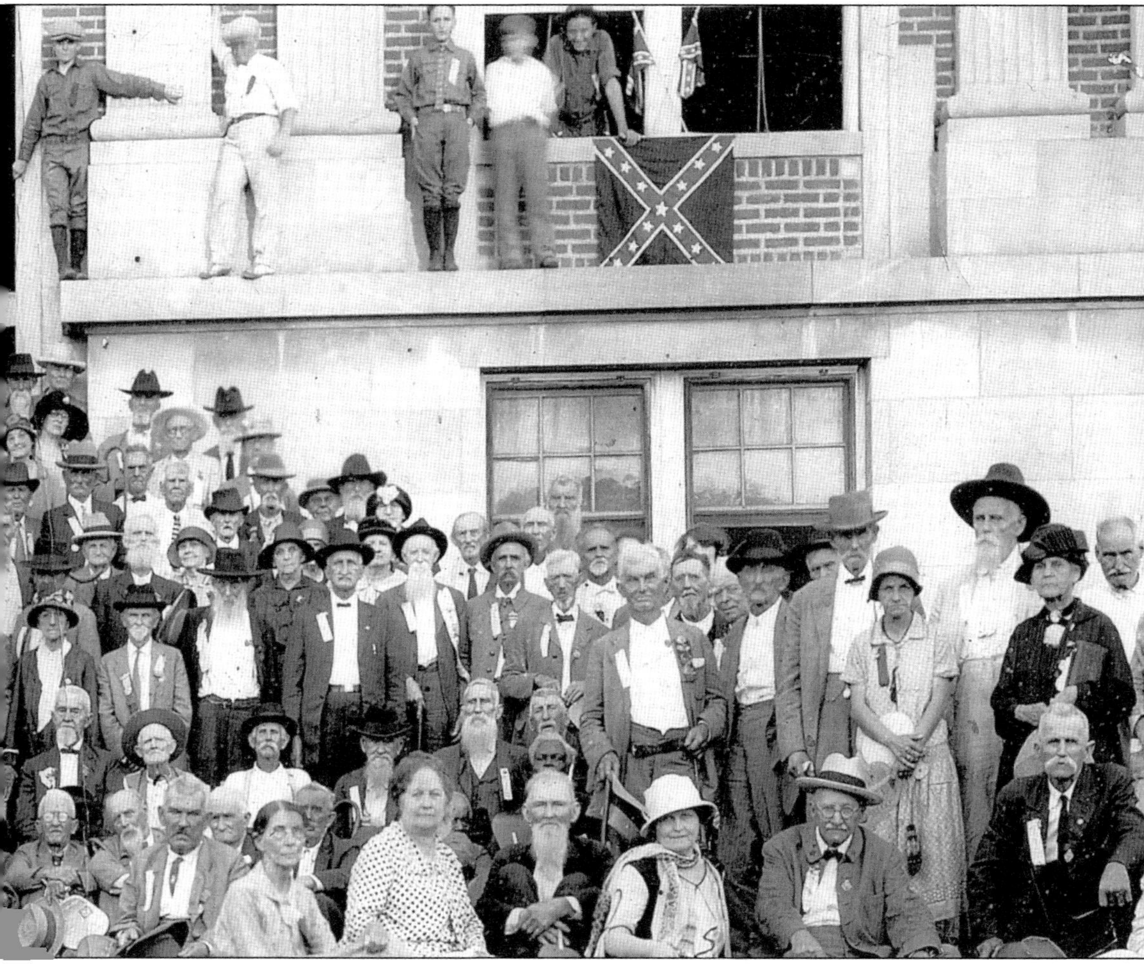

to play chess and draughts, to get up soon to answer the morning roll call, to fall in at the tap of the drum for drill and dress parade, and again hastily don our war gear while the monotonous patter of the long roll summons to battle. Who knows but again the old flags, ragged and torn, snapping in the wind, may face each other and flutter, pursuing and pursued, while the cries of victory fill a summer day? And after the battle, then the slain and wounded will arise, and all will meet together under the two flags, all sound and well, and there will be talking and laughter and cheers, and all will say, did it not seem real? Was it not as in the old days?"

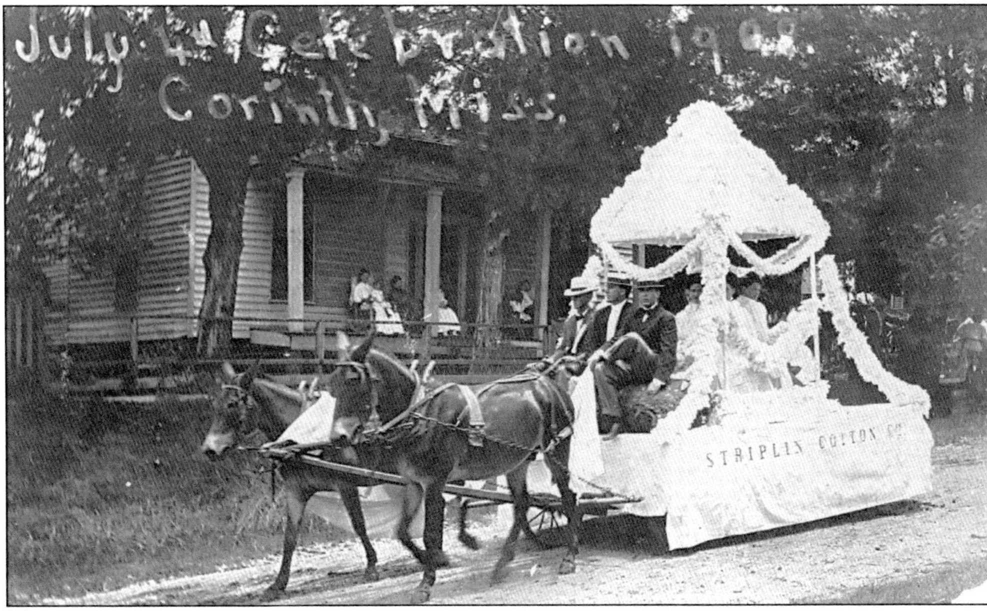


Through the years, the one thing almost every Corinthian can wholeheartedly agree upon is that any excuse to celebrate is a good excuse. For the Fourth of July celebration in 1908, a mule-drawn concoction sponsored by Striplin Cotton Company is pictured cruising down the dirt street as spectators look on from their front porches.

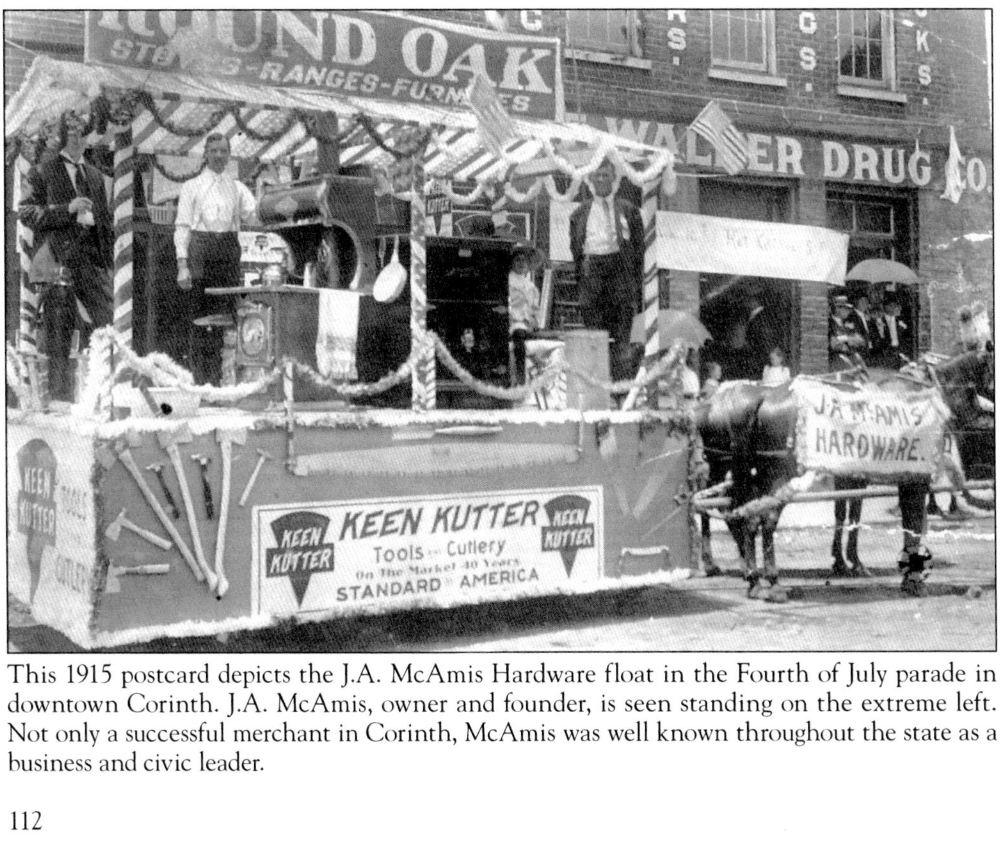


This 1915 postcard depicts the J.A. McAmis Hardware float in the Fourth of July parade in downtown Corinth. J.A. McAmis, owner and founder, is seen standing on the extreme left. Not only a successful merchant in Corinth, McAmis was well known throughout the state as a business and civic leader.

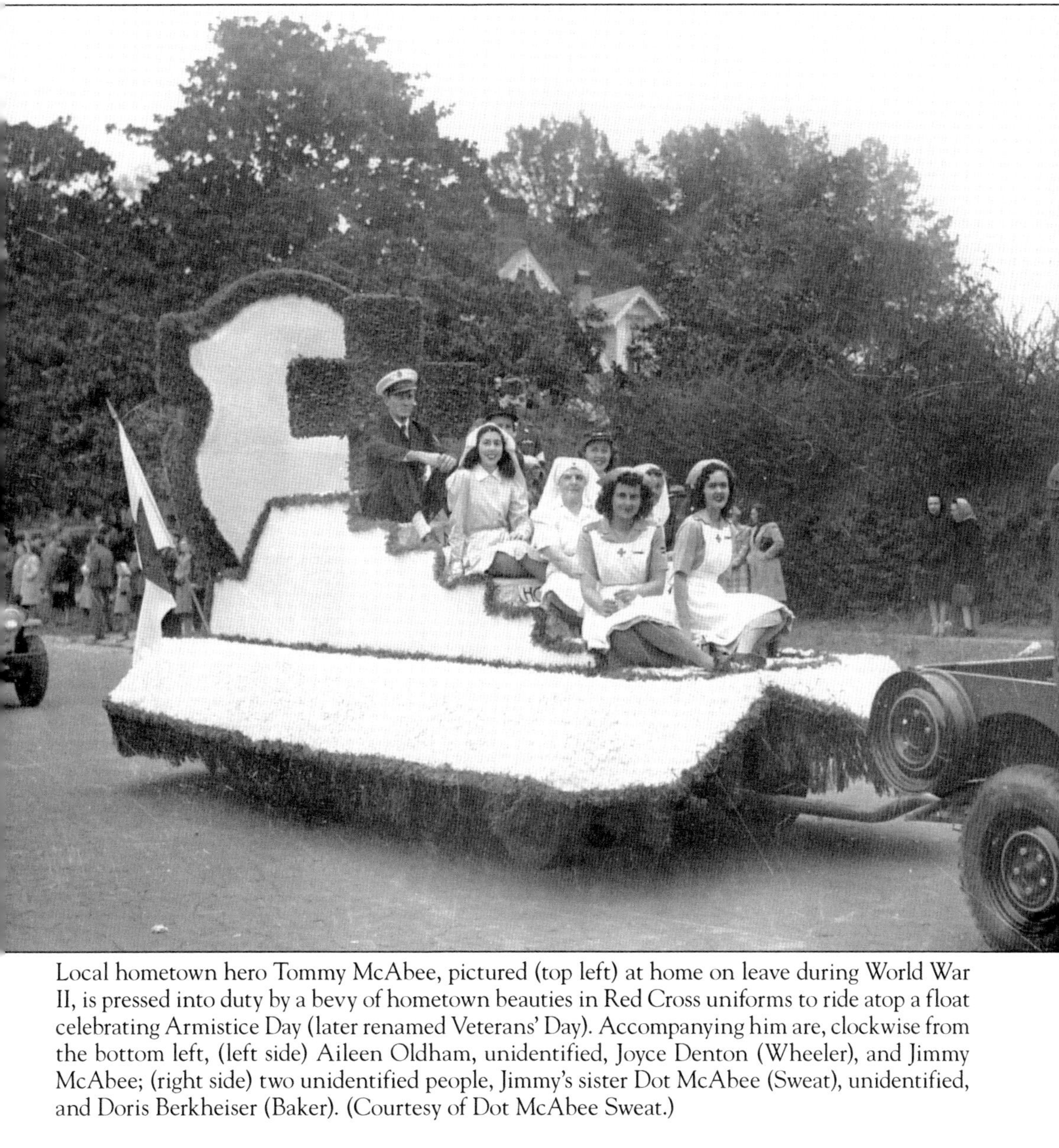

Local hometown hero Tommy McAbee, pictured (top left) at home on leave during World War II, is pressed into duty by a bevy of hometown beauties in Red Cross uniforms to ride atop a float celebrating Armistice Day (later renamed Veterans' Day). Accompanying him are, clockwise from the bottom left, (left side) Aileen Oldham, unidentified, Joyce Denton (Wheeler), and Jimmy McAbee; (right side) two unidentified people, Jimmy's sister Dot McAbee (Sweat), unidentified, and Doris Berkheiser (Baker). (Courtesy of Dot McAbee Sweat.)

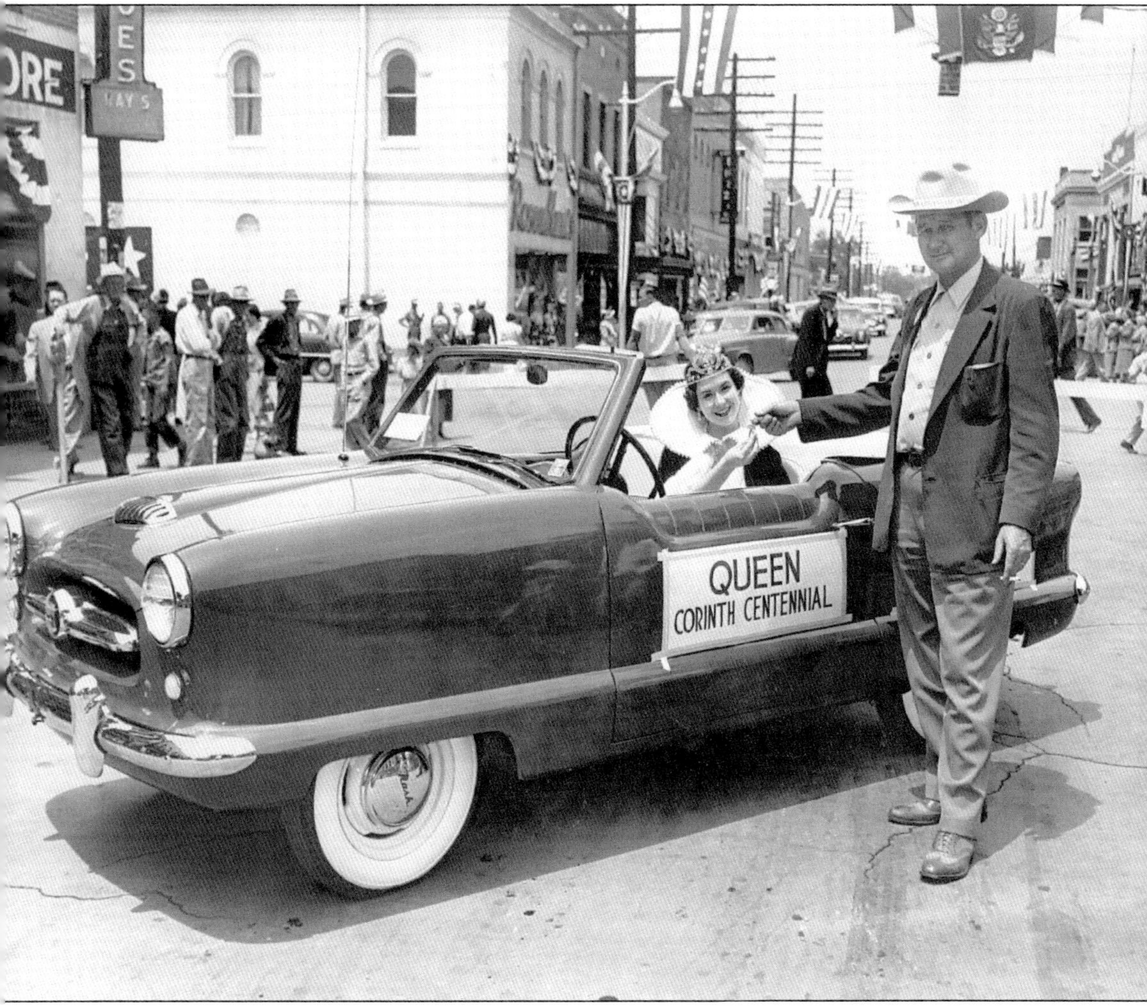


Prominent local car dealer R.C. Johnson proudly drops the keys to a brand-new Nash into the waiting palm of beautiful reigning Centennial Queen Peggy Faires. Downtown Corinth is shown prepared to kick off the centennial celebrations, while the crowd looks on with eager anticipation. Close to 15,000 spectators jammed the parade route on opening day to help celebrate Corinth's 100th birthday.

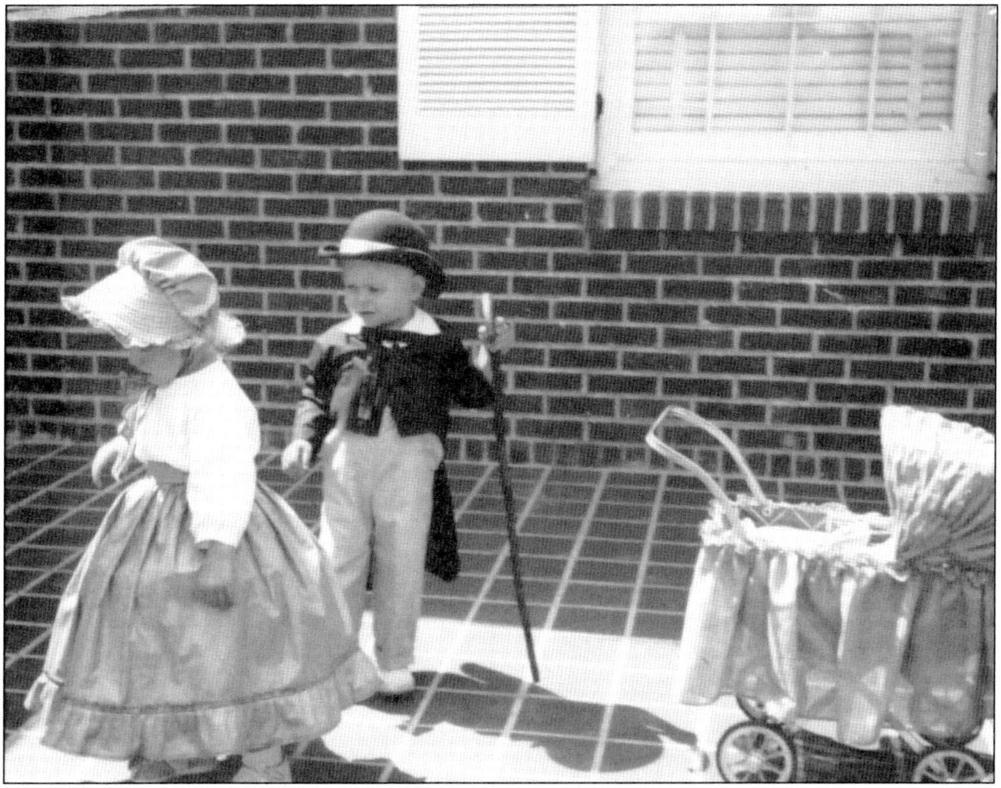

Above, a hoop skirted Virginia (Gingo) Johnson is joined by her first cousin Freddy, who is dapperly decked out as Bat Masterson. They are preparing to march in the celebratory parade for Corinth's 100th birthday. On the right, Freddy Johnson holds the hand of his mother, Emily Dean Johnson, as they parade by the approving crowd in front of the courthouse. (Courtesy of LuAnne Parrish.)

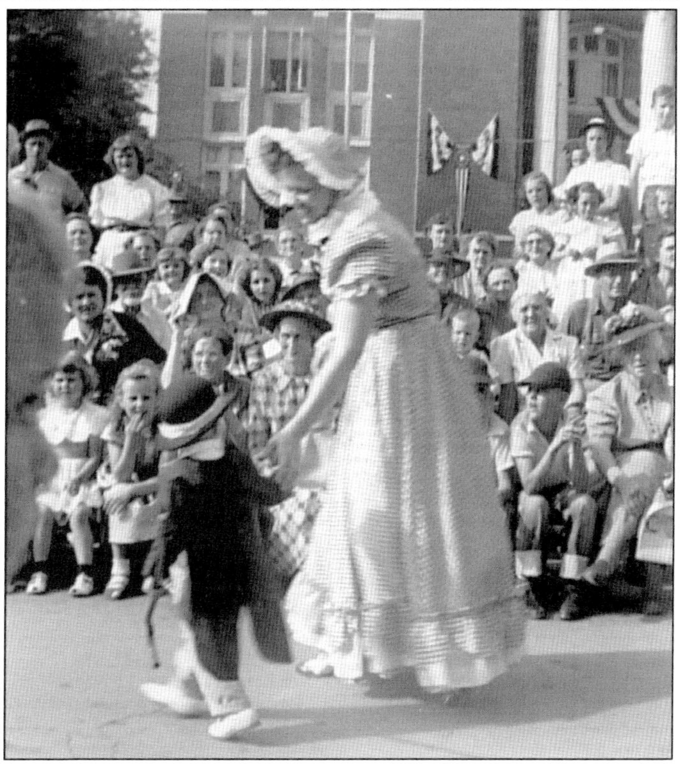

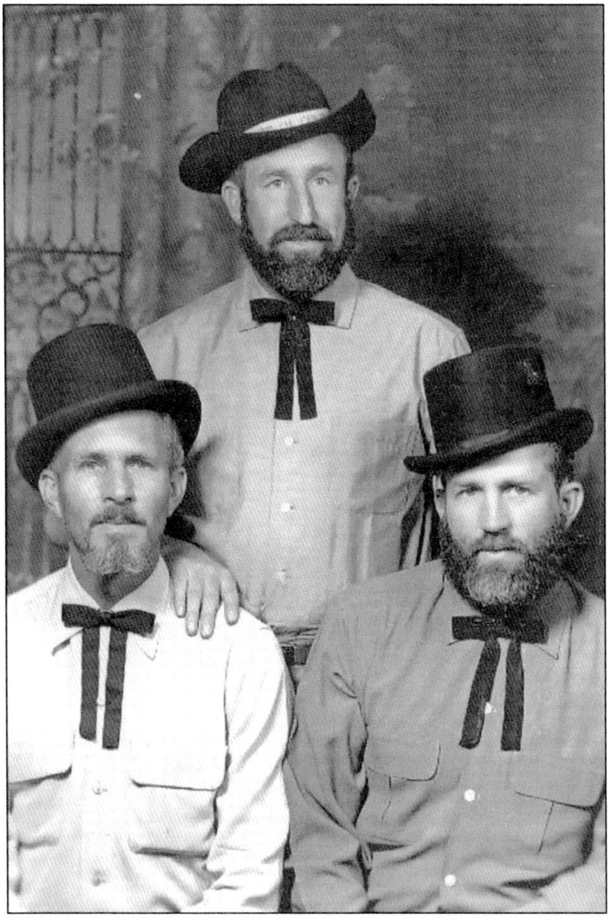

In the months leading up to the 1954 centennial celebrations, hundreds of normally clean-shorn men let their facial hair grow wild in honor of their forefathers—and in hopes of winning the hotly contested "Brothers of the Brush" best beard contest. Among those hirsute competitors "dressed up and decked out" were brothers Frank Worsham (seated left), Leroy Worsham (standing), and Cliff Worsham.

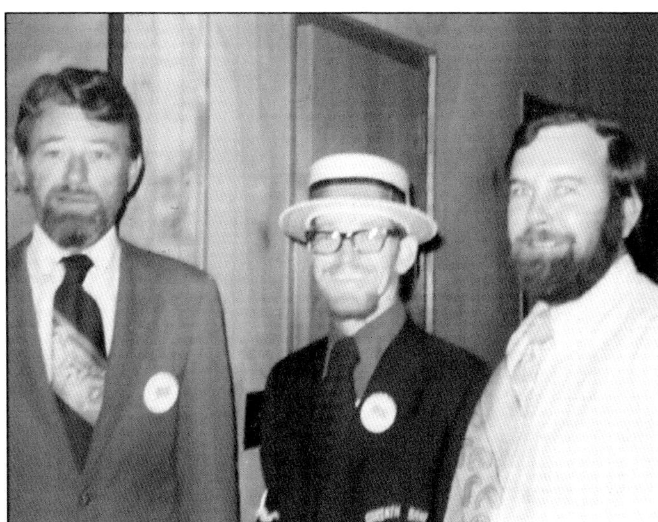

In 1973, 1976, and 1979, Corinth held a Crossroads Jubilee to continue the celebration of its heritage and to keep alive the memories of bygone days. Pictured from left to right are superintendent Eugene Doran, Warrior Band assistant director Ronnie Smith, and Corinth High School principal Harold P. Smith. They are showcasing their own beard-growing abilities, much to the amazement and delight of the CHS student body. (Courtesy of Johanna Smith.)

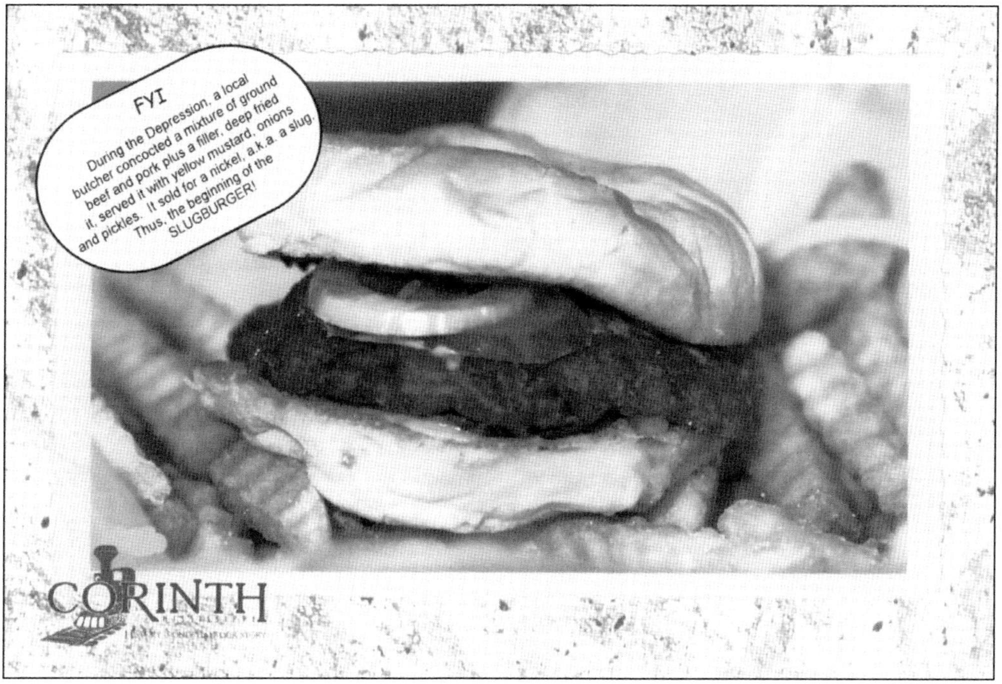


Two of Corinth's annual, not-to-be-missed celebrations have been occurring since the 1980s. The Slugburger Festival is traditionally held in July in celebration of a local delicacy born of ingenuity and desperation. During the hard times of the 1930s Great Depression, the Slugburger was sold for a "slug," which was slang for a nickel.

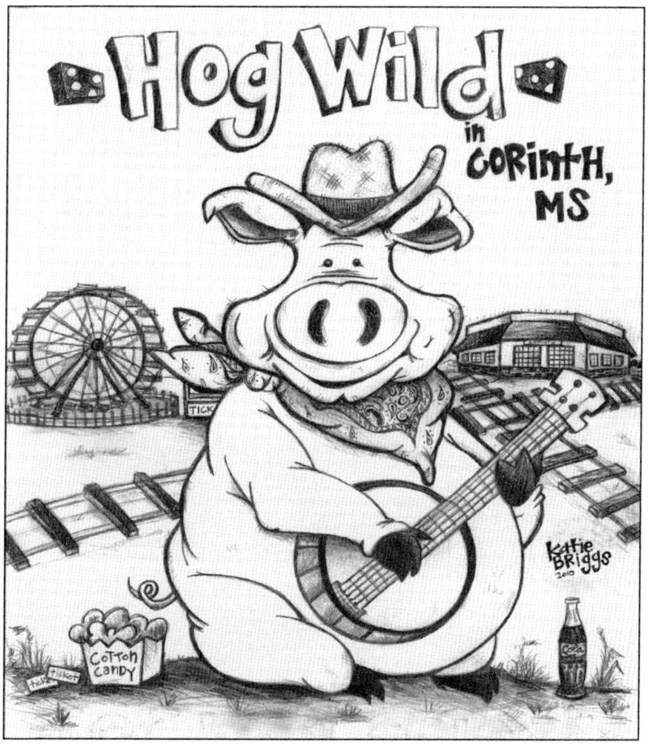


Hog Wild in Corinth, Mississippi, is traditionally held in October and is a sanctioned Kansas City barbeque event, as well as a Memphis in May event, since 1991. Teams with names such as the Hatchie Bottom Smokers, Twist N Snout, Pigs R Us, Bean Bandits, and Pig Medics come from all over the South, aiming to be the winning team covered in glory (and barbeque sauce). (Courtesy of Katie Briggs, artist.)

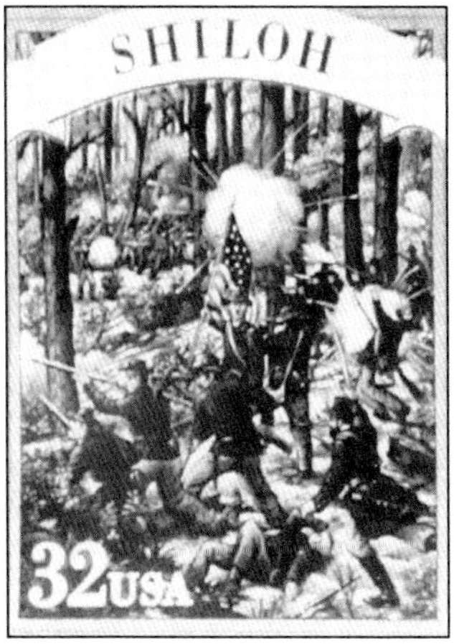


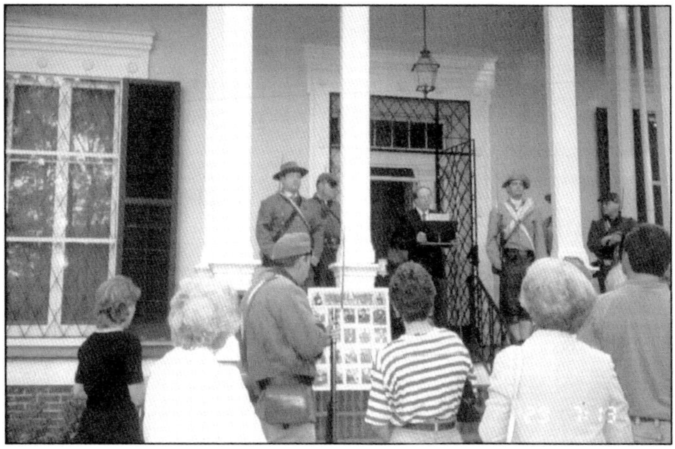

US Postal Service representative Noel Gann, flanked by an honor guard of both Northern and Southern soldiers, presides at the June 29, 1995, dedication of the Civil War commemorative stamps first day of issue on the front porch of Corinth's historic Veranda-Curlee House. The 20-stamp pane featured three stamps of particular interest to citizens of Corinth: Shiloh, Ulysses S. Grant, and William T. Sherman.

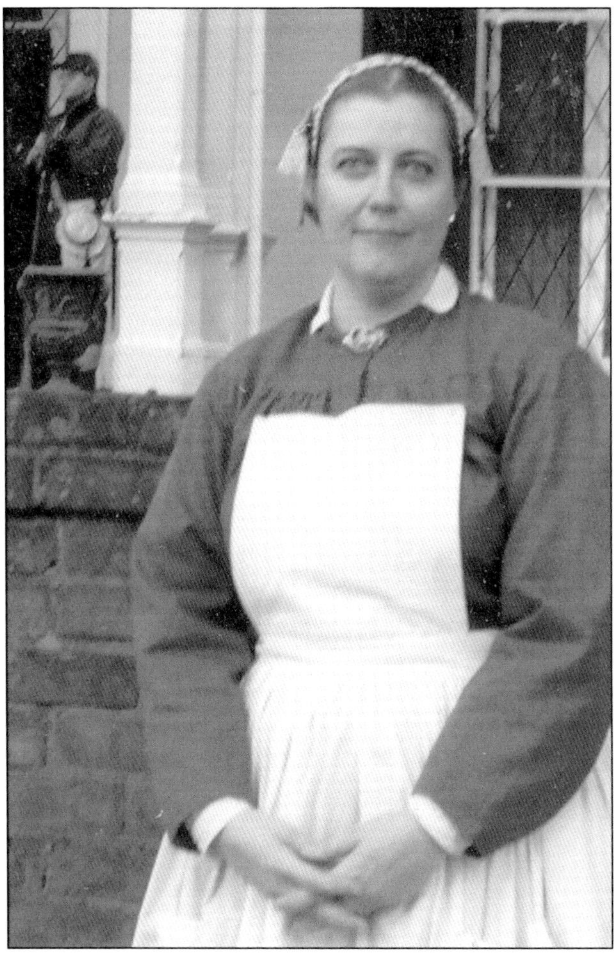

Pictured is the postmistress on the first day of issue of the Civil War commemorative stamps. The author, in her dual roles as a postal clerk and living historian, serves as a reminder to people that women have served as postmasters (more properly referred to as "postmistresses") since the beginning of the US Postal Service in 1775, a proud tradition of over 215 years. (Courtesy of LuAnne Parrish.)

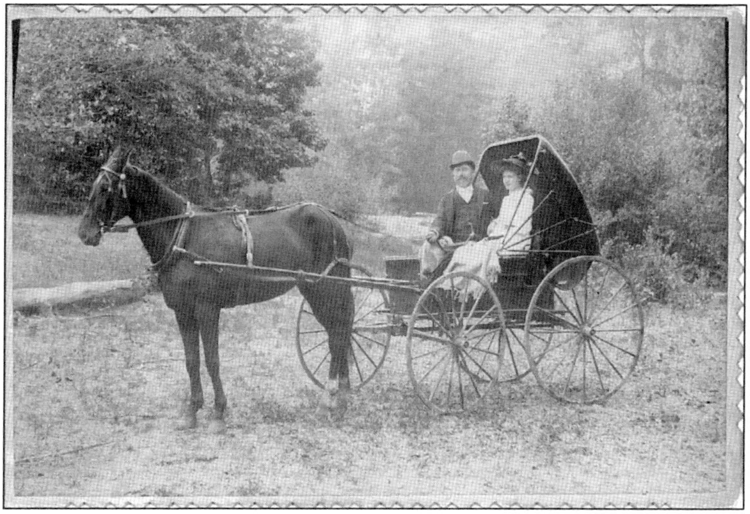

Miss Marie Hammer of Ohio is pictured with Lex Henderson at Morrison's Mills, a favorite picnic and photograph spot in the 1880s. Even in those long-ago horse-and-buggy days, it seems that keeping both hands on the reins was considered good form. Marie Hammer was the piano teacher at Lena Elgin's School for Girls.

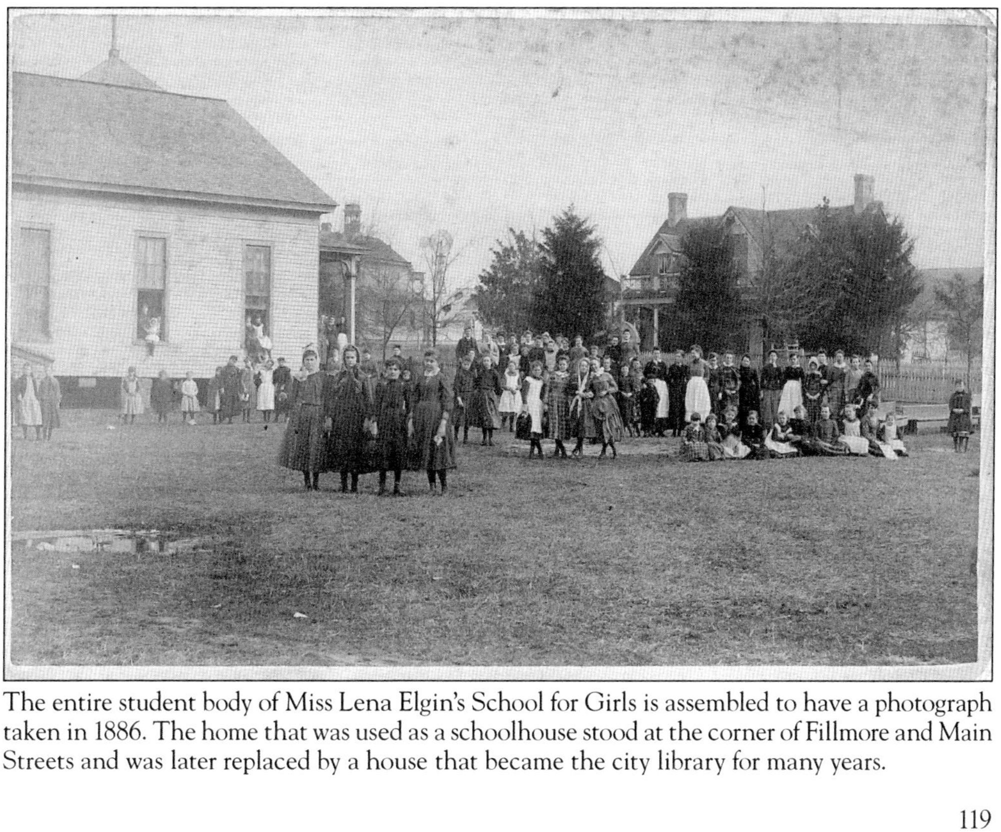

The entire student body of Miss Lena Elgin's School for Girls is assembled to have a photograph taken in 1886. The home that was used as a schoolhouse stood at the corner of Fillmore and Main Streets and was later replaced by a house that became the city library for many years.

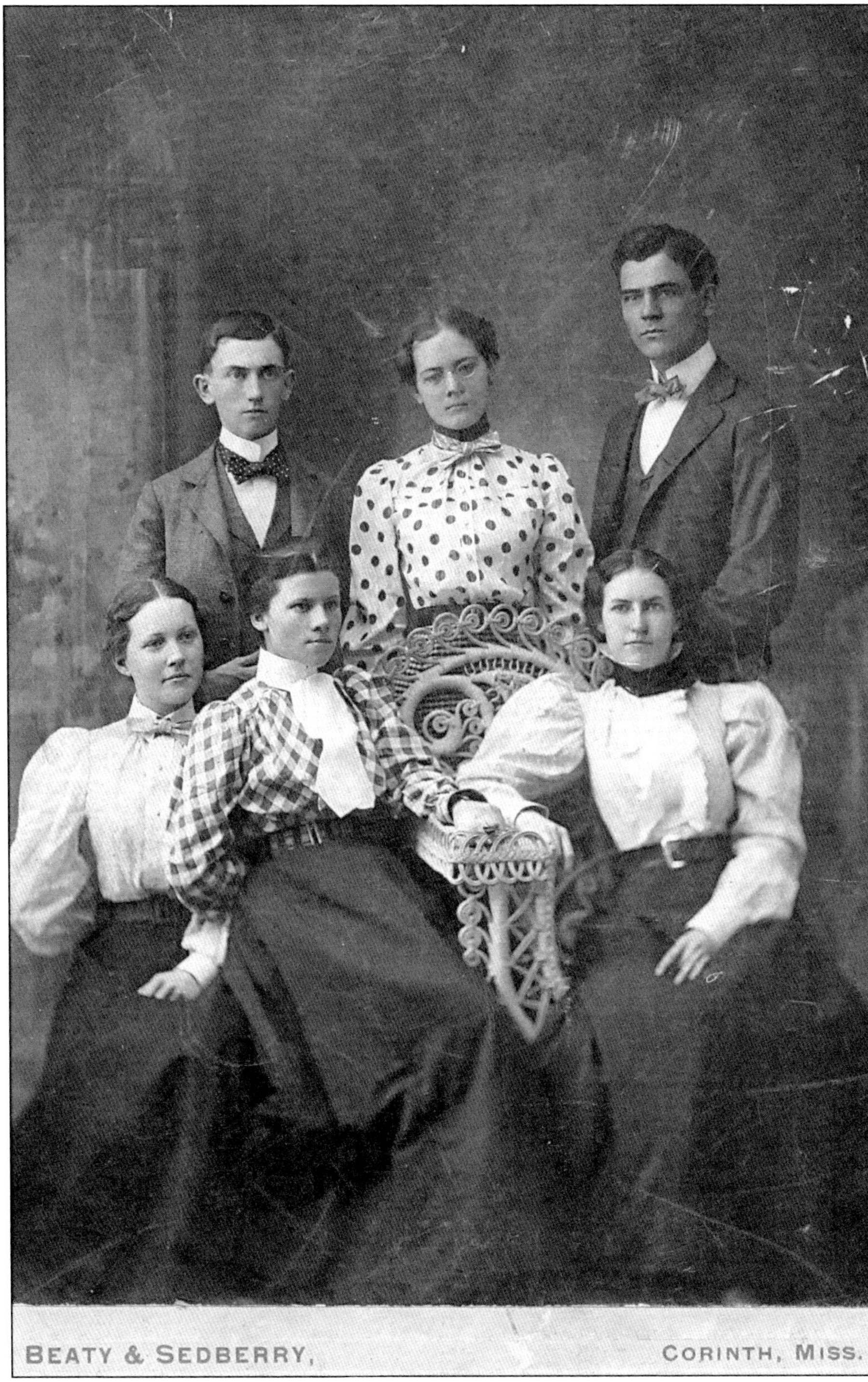



Beaty and Sedberry Photographers took the earliest known photograph of a Corinth, Mississippi, public high school graduating class in 1898. The six-member graduating class was comprised of two boys and four girls. Pictured from left to right are (sitting) Kate Meeks, Toney Stanley, and Blanch Street; (standing) R.B. Warriner, Kate Moore, and Frank Curlee.

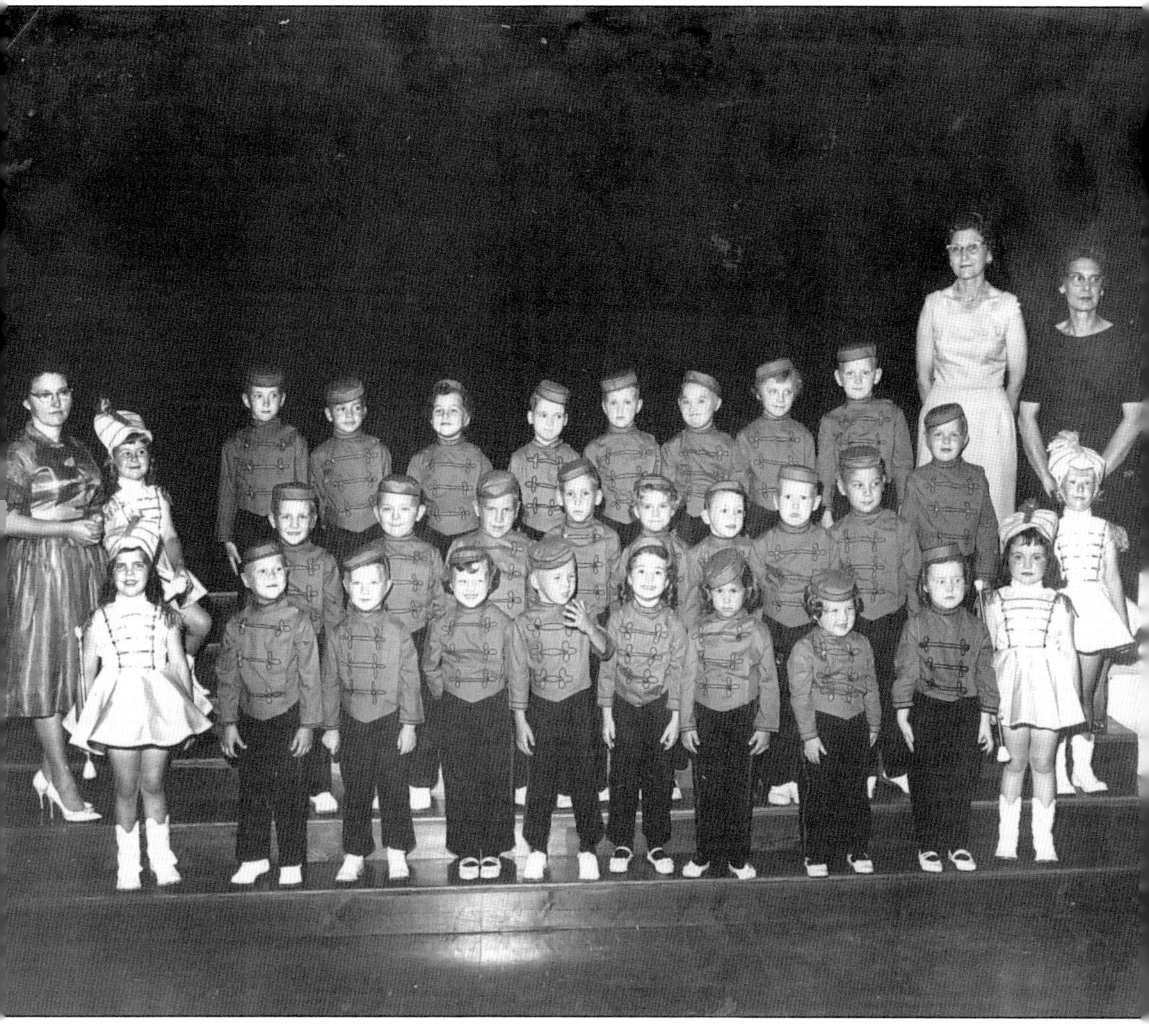

Louise Bennett is pictured around 1960 with her kindergarten class at the *Tom Thumb Band* recital. This event was one of many activities she provided for her students. Subjects included hopscotch, dodgeball, and nap time. Upon commencement, the graduate would have successfully participated in, along with the band recital, a *Tom Thumb Wedding* and a *Tom Thumb Christmas Pageant*. They would also have taken a group trip by passenger train to Iuka's Mineral Springs Park 20 miles away, and a tour the local Coca-Cola Bottling Works, which was capped off with a freshly bottled Coke straight from the line that cost only a penny. Pictured standing in the back row on the far left is Eller Drew Cox, while Louise Bennett is second to the right, and pianist Dorothy Wood is on the far right.

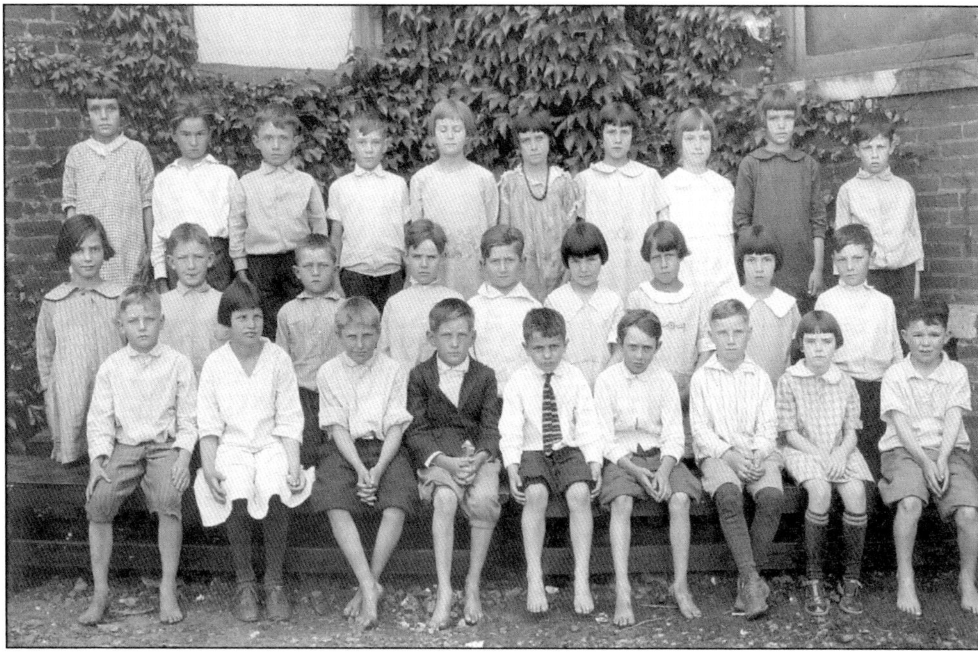

The above image is thought to be a 1922 photograph of the first-grade class at Old Cruise Street Elementary School. The photograph below is of Miss Una Moore's first-grade class in 1962. The school stood at the southwest corner of the block where Cruise and Proper Streets merge. It was torn down in the late 1970s and replaced by the current Corinth School District administration complex.

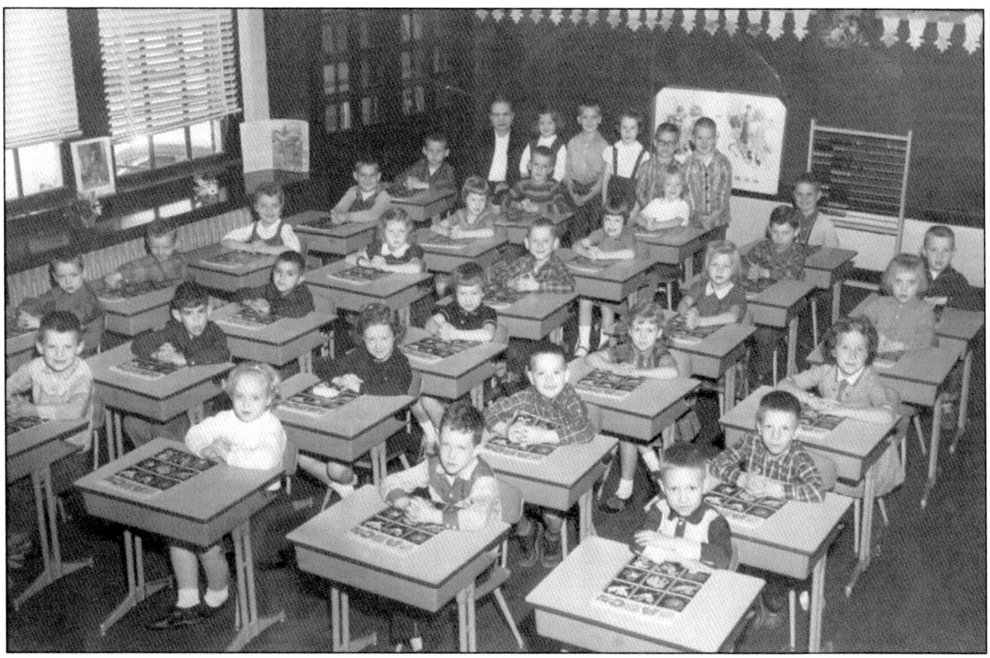

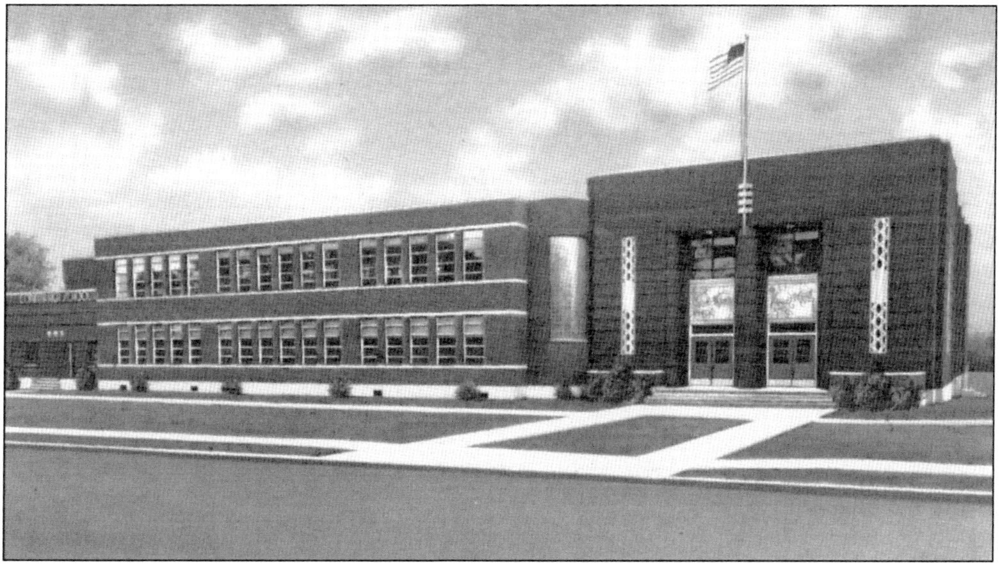

Built in the Art Deco style and opened in 1939, Corinth High School saw generations of Corinth's sons and daughters pass through its halls and classrooms for over 50 years. Each student knew CHS as the home of the Warriors and the Corinth Warrior Band. Everyone would breathlessly await the *Warrior*, a weekly disseminator of all the news that was fit to print (and some that was not if one could sneak it past Mrs. Dalton), and every student strove to break the cryptic code of the gossipy *Tee Pee Talk*. No one could forget the excitement of having classmates sign a copy of the *Corinthian Columns* yearbook, especially senior year.

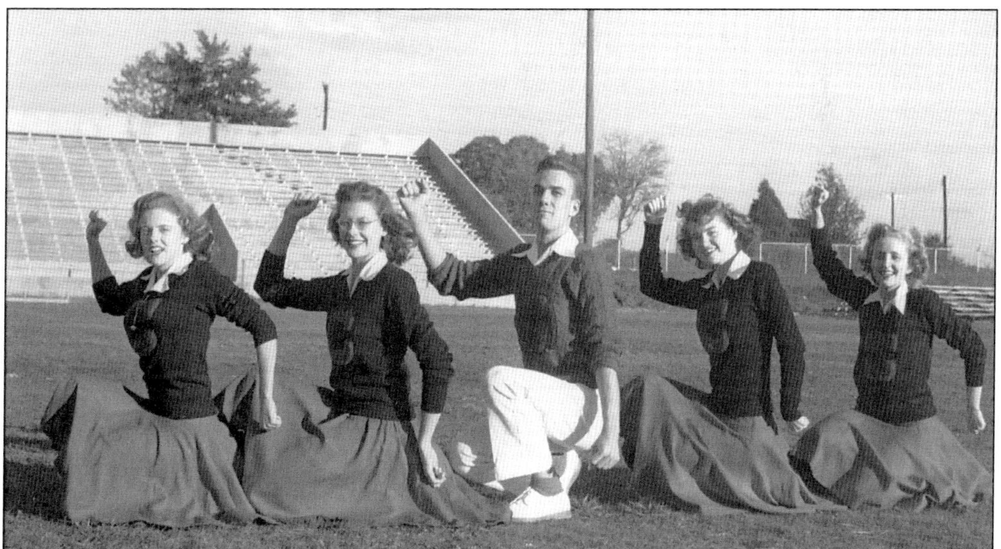

This 1947 photograph shows CHS cheerleaders, from left to right, Martha Houston Reid, Clara Galtney, Howard Moss, Carolyn Cornelius, and Betty Miller. Go Warriors!

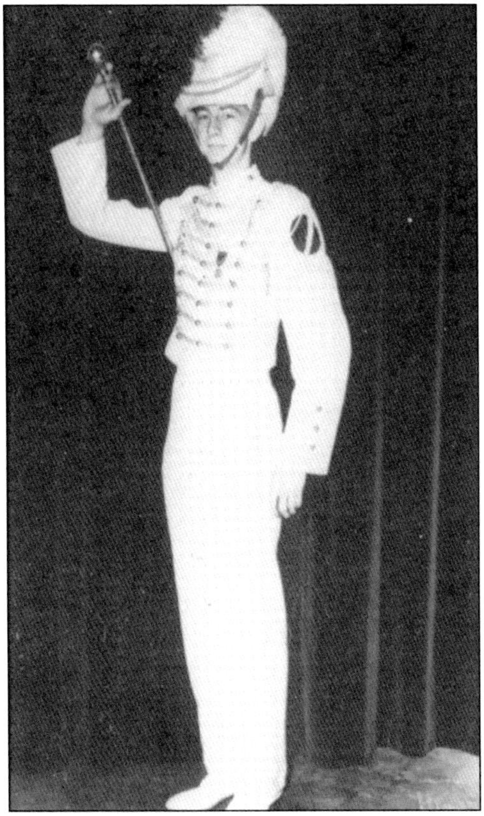

Herbert Beverly Hussey was a member of the Corinth High School class of 1949 and served in the position of drum major for the Corinth High School Marching Warrior Band. Three years later, he was succeeded in the position by his younger brother William C. "Bill" Hussey, part of the CHS class of 1952.

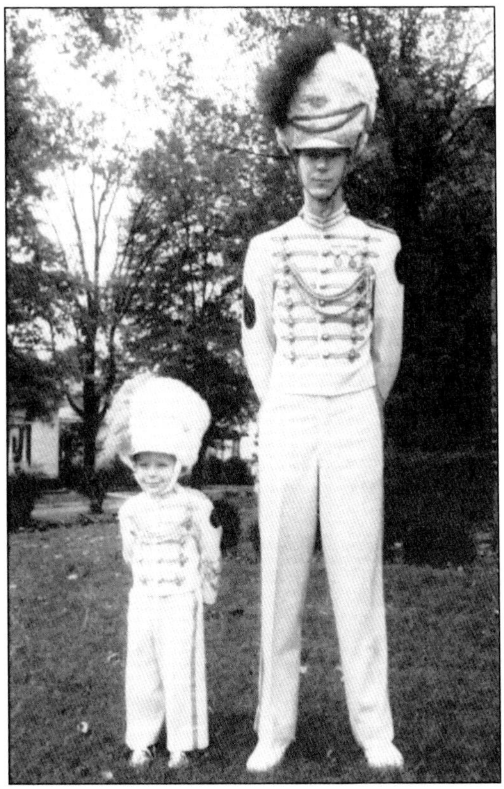

Corinth High School drum major William C. "Bill" Hussey is pictured here with Warrior Band mascot Hull Davis. Hull's uniform is an exact replica of Bill's, right down to the gold-braid trim and matching shakos with plumes. Interestingly enough, both Hull and Bill went on to careers in banking in Corinth: Bill served as president of Security Bank, while Hull became president of National Bank of Commerce and is currently at the helm of Commerce National Bank.

In later years, Bill became a doting father to three beautiful girls—Beth, Sallie, and Kate—each one playing an instrument in the CHS Band. Sallie, part of the CHS class of 1985, was the one chosen to serve as drum major, making her the second generation of the Hussey family to lead the Warrior Marching Band. (Courtesy of Sallie Hussey.)

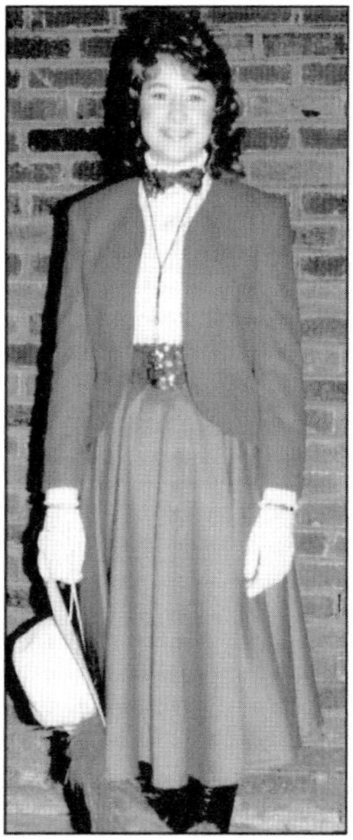

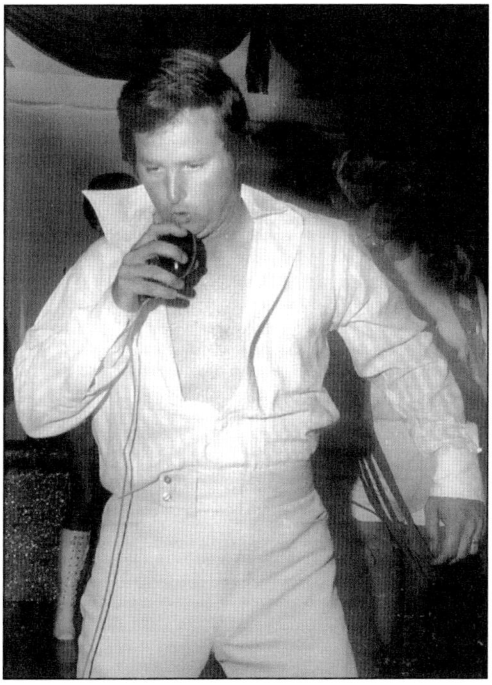

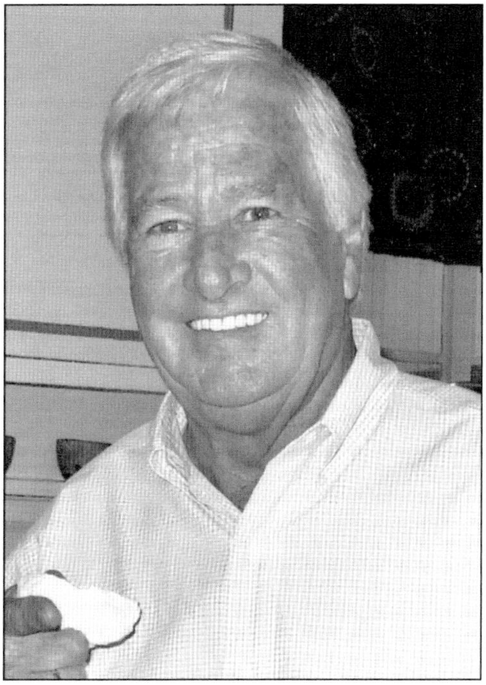

A lifelong ambassador for Corinth, Robert Hayden Worsham (1941–2011) came from a prominent family of engineers, all of whom gave generously their time and talents to the town. Bobby was an especially charismatic personality with a wide range of interests, an outstanding civic leader, and the ultimate CHS booster. Along with his many other achievements, he was acquainted with Elvis, which allowed him the chance to perfect his Elvis impersonation, gladly performed at the mere whisper of a suggestion. Here, he is pictured impersonating the "King" at a local charity event, where he brought joy to everyone who saw the performance and much happiness to all of those who had the privilege of knowing him. Ladies and gentlemen, Bobby has left the building! Rest in peace. (Courtesy of Hayden Worsham.)

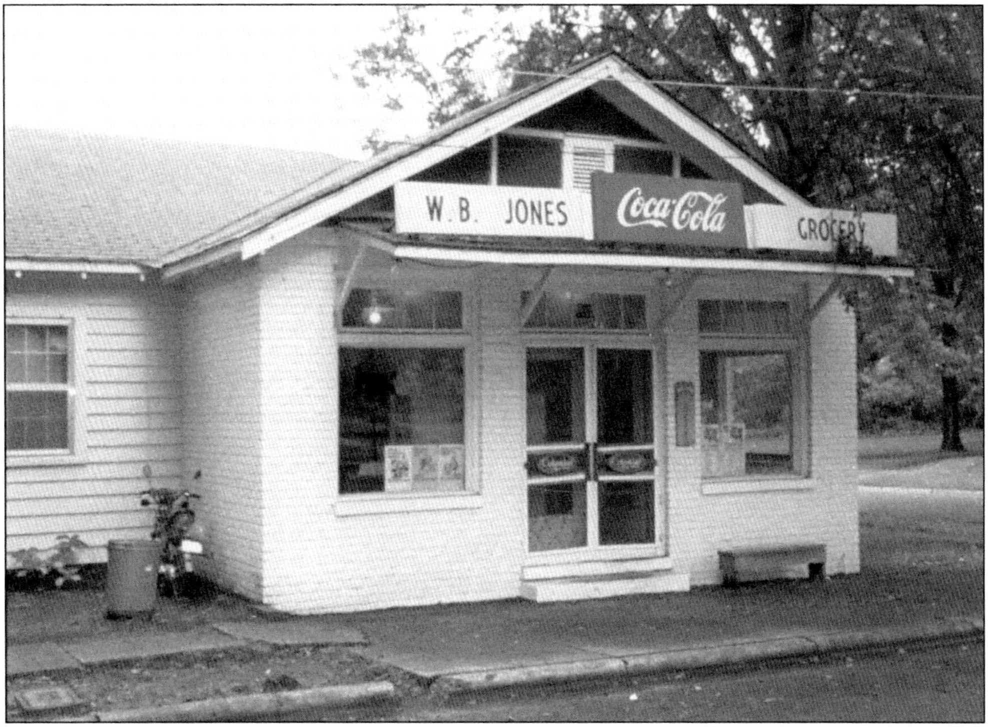


Located one block from Corinth High School and Corinth Junior High School from 1937 until 1989, Bill Reed Jones's Grocery was the place to meet right after school, especially for eighth and ninth graders too young to drive. Whether a student was picking up a snack, trading the latest high school gossip, or watching a couple of boys settle a fight in the yard across the street, for over 50 years, everyone stopped by to see Bill Reed.

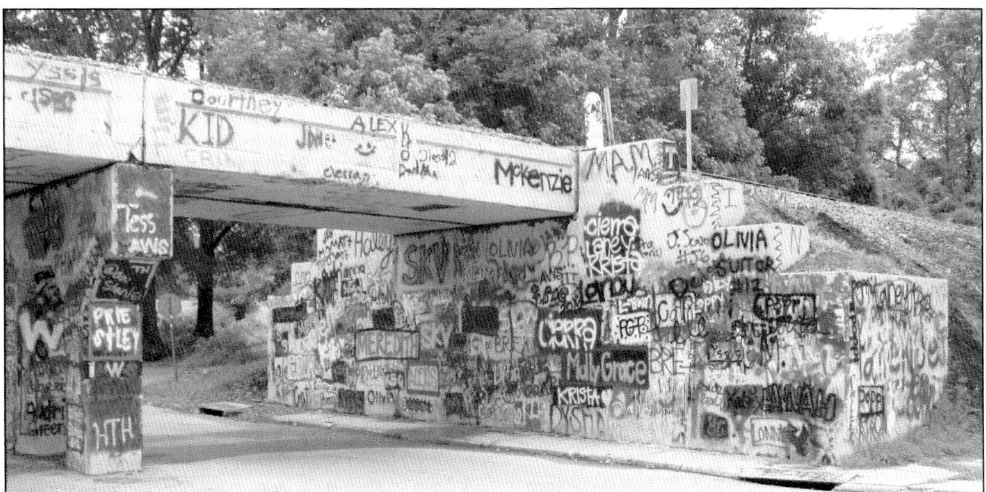


Even though Corinth High School has moved, kids from all over Corinth and Alcorn County still continue the generations-long tradition of painting the Madison Street underpass that is located only a stone's throw from Warrior Circle. In fact, there actually may be a law on the books at city hall stating that as long as the miscreants do not get too explicit, they cannot get into too much trouble, since their moms and dads were doing the same thing when they were at CHS.

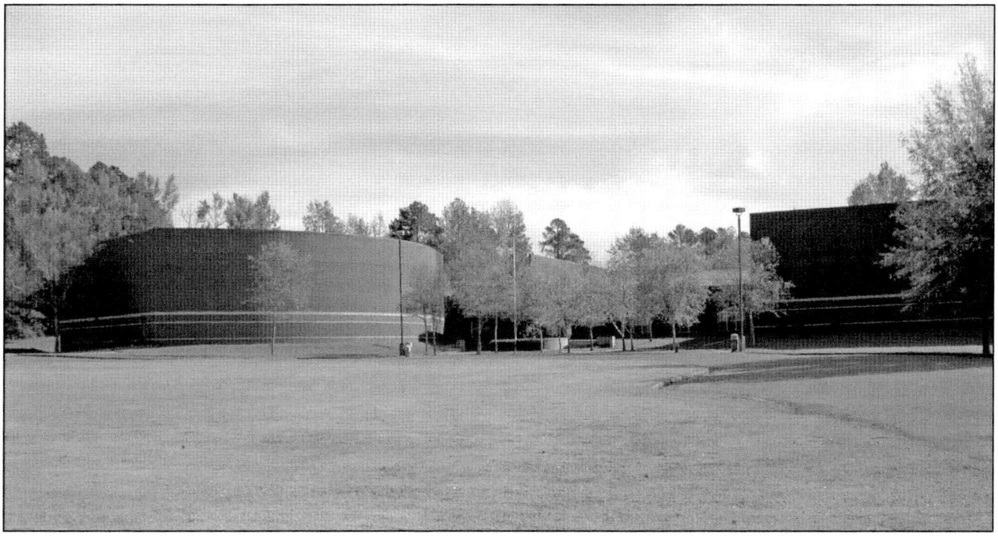

The New Corinth Academic and Performing Arts Center opened during the 1992–1993 school year to continue the tradition and long-upheld standard of excellence begun so many years ago by the teachers and administrators who played such a vital role in helping mold and shape each generation of Corinth students. A state-of-the-art facility, this incarnation of the beloved CHS might very well make it to the 22nd century, as the new generations of Corinthians step up to join the ranks of those who have gone before.

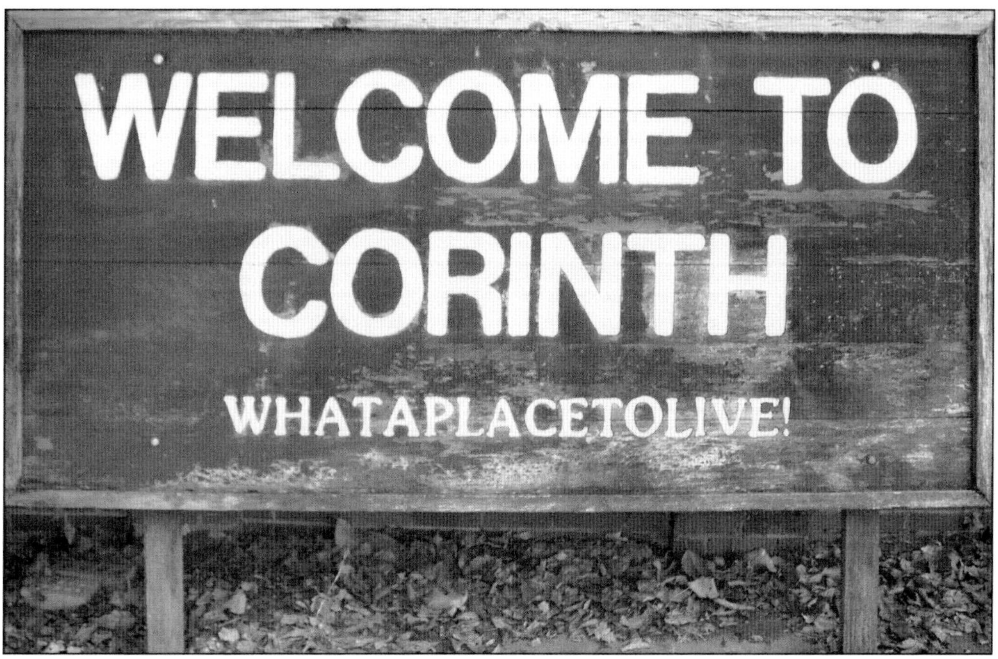


In the early 1970s, the town fathers instituted a new ad campaign touting the wonders and advantages of residing in Corinth, Mississippi. No one can think of a better descriptive phrase to close this "love letter" to Corinth, and there is nothing more to say except, "*Y'all come see us when you can!*"

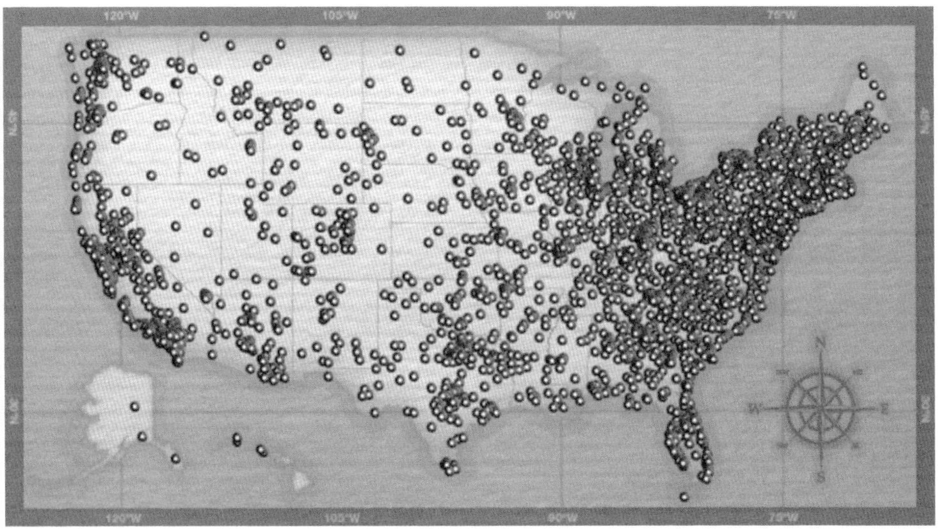